Buying a property
FLORIDA

CADOGANguides

Contents

About the Authors

Christian Moen is a freelance writer based in Washington, DC. He considers Washington his home but spent some of his formative years growing up in Trieste, Rome and Vienna. In 1992 he received a Bachelor of Arts in English from Boston University and received his Master of Arts in Writing from Johns Hopkins University, Baltimore, in 2001. He spent several years as a journalist reporting on issues from federal regulation to healthcare information technology. He has worked as an editor at the headquarters of NASA and most recently he was assistant editor at Smithsonian magazine. He has travelled throughout Europe, the Caribbean and Central America and spent considerable time in the UK. Winter months still find him migrating to southeast Florida to enjoy the tropical climate and exciting nightlife of Miami Beach.

John Howell established John Howell & Co in Sheffield in 1979 and by 1997 it had become one of the largest and most respected law firms in the north of England, employing more than 100 lawyers. On moving to London in 1995, John Howell has gone on to specialize in providing legal advice to clients buying property abroad.

About the Updaters

Christian Williams has been in and out of the USA for the past decade, including spells based in Colorado and New Jersey. He has worked as a travel writer for various publications, including the *Daily Telegraph*, and has written and co-authored several guide books. These have included *The Rough Guide to the Rocky Mountains*, *The Rough Guide to Skiing and Snowboarding*, and Cadogan Guides/*The Sunday Times' Working and Living: USA*. He has also written extensively about Canada, Tenerife and Berlin.

Larry J. Behar, P.A. updated chapters 05 and 06, 'Making the Purchase' and 'Financial Implications'. Thanks also to **Bernie Donth** for some crucial last-minute information.

Author's Acknowledgements

Christian Moen would like to thank those who patiently accepted the few stolen moments he had to offer while he completed this book.

Cadogan Guides
2nd Floor, 233 High Holborn
London WC1V 7DN
info@cadoganguides.co.uk
www.cadoganguides.com

The Globe Pequot Press
246 Goose Lane, PO Box 480, Guilford,
Connecticut 06437–0480

Copyright © Cadogan Guides 2003, 2006
"THE SUNDAY TIMES" is a registered trade mark of Times Newspapers Limited.

Cover photographs: (front) © Patti McConville;
   (back) © Jon Arnold Images
Photo essay photographs © Christian Moen
Maps © Cadogan Guides, drawn by
   XNR Productions Inc.
Cover design: Sarah Rianhard-Gardner
Editor: Linda McQueen
Proofreader: Susannah Wight
Indexing: Isobel McLean

Produced by **Navigator Guides**
www.navigatorguides.com

Printed in Italy by Legoprint
A catalogue record for this book is available from the British Library
ISBN 10: 1-86011-329-X
ISBN 13: 978-1-86011-329-1

Introduction

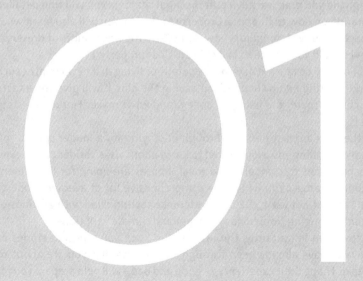

If you spend just a little time in Florida you will quickly find out why so many British, and Americans, of course, have chosen to make it their second home. There is something visitors feel when they arrive that is hard to describe, but which people simply refer to as 'the lifestyle'. Whatever it may be, it makes you feel instantly at home when you get there.

Even before the days of land rushes, when modern developers broke through the panhandle in the north and into the lower peninsula, people have been discovering and rediscovering the Sunshine State. It is a state that offers all the amenities – or simplicity – that one might seek in a home and that still harbours a surprisingly pristine natural beauty.

If you are reading this book, then there is a good chance that you are already thinking of Florida as the place for your second home or retirement. *Buying a Property: Florida* is more about delivering practical information to help guide you through the process of investing in a home abroad than about the reasons why you should buy a property there. If you need a little more convincing, however, our photographic essay will take you on a visual tour of the state and give you a taste of each region.

To help you choose where you might wish to settle, the book breaks down each of the regions to give you a better idea of what is in store. Whether you are drawn to the beautiful white beaches and clear blue waters of the Gulf coast, the laid-back southern charm of the panhandle or the international flavour of the southeast, after exploring the regional breakdown you may discover areas of the state that you never even considered.

But, again, this book is not about showing you the beauty of the state, but about giving you practical advice. In the legal chapters you will find detailed information on how to finance a property in Florida. You will also learn what to expect if you wish to build a new home, and the finer points of preservation law should you decide to invest in an older property.

The book also covers the day-to-day details of living in a new country, such as working, bringing up children and paying the bills. It will give you a taste of the culture there, and help you understand what makes Florida the state that it is.

Whether you are just passing through or staying for a longer period, you will find everything you ever wanted to know about visas, residency and even citizenship. Want to compare how much houses are going for in different metropolitan areas? You will find a comprehensive list of average property values. Last but not least, there is a reference section filled with all kinds of information ranging from holidays to regional climate variations.

Perhaps more importantly, throughout the book you will find stories of people who have already been through the process that you are about to undertake. I hope their experiences – good and bad – will help prepare you for when the time comes to purchase your very own spot in the sun.

First Steps and Reasons for Buying

02

Buying a home is a complicated process no matter where you are investing. When buying overseas, matters naturally become more complex. If you are thinking of buying a home in Florida, this book will help you through the details of making the purchase.

However, before you read any further, you should ask yourself two important questions. First, 'why Florida?' Perhaps there is no one specific reason or perhaps you have a million reasons neatly catalogued. The point is, stop and think through what it is about this particular spot in the world that is driving you to invest time, money and effort in acquiring a piece of it. Then ask yourself, 'why buy?'

Once you have answered these questions – and perhaps you already have even before you bought this book – then you can move on to the second half of this chapter, which provides detailed information about visas, residency and citizenship, so you can spend as little or as much time as you like in your new home.

Why Florida?

Everyone probably has their own variation on the answer to the question 'why Florida?', but it's a safe bet that, in some form or other, the word 'sun' will be in there somewhere. How could it not be? The state boasts 300 days of sunshine a year, an annual average temperature hovering around 21°C (70°F), and a coastline (including all the nooks and crannies) estimated to be somewhere between 1,900 and 2,900km (1,200 and 1,800 miles), 1,600km of which are sandy beaches. You could also guarantee that being close to the water is also somewhere on the list, because it has been said that no place in the state is more than 96km (60 miles) from the coast.

Sunny Days

According to the 2006 Social Trends reports, issued by the Office for National Statistics, the number of UK households owning second homes abroad increased between 2000 and 2004 by 45 per cent. Now over a quarter of a million people – out of a total 1.1 million UK households that own a second home – own property abroad. Sunny climates top the list of preferred locations, indicating that you are not alone if sun is what you are seeking in a second home.

Let's start by comparing Florida with popular European locations for second homes (for example, Spain and France, where the British already own 1.2 million properties). These countries offer sunshine, just like Florida, but do they offer it year-round? If you are going to invest in a second home, wouldn't it be nice if you could head there at almost any point in the year for a bit of sunshine? If you are not keen on learning another language, the fact that English is spoken in Florida may just tip the balance in its favour.

So, whether you are planning an extended holiday or permanent retirement, there's a good chance that Florida did not come to mind just because of its abundance of fresh seafood. However, the fact that there is no shortage of places where you can eat the freshest seafood while looking out over the Atlantic Ocean, the Gulf of Mexico or the Caribbean should count for something on your list.

Friendly People

Regional variations in the USA are not limited to climate: the people are different, too. While Florida is technically in the south, it actually has a split personality. Its northern half tends to be more 'southern' and relaxed in temperament, while its lower half tends to be more 'northern'. Both halves share a sense of hospitality, and you may be surprised at how friendly its residents can be. Perhaps it is the proximity to the open sea and the abundance of sun that relaxes people to a point where they almost invariably seem to talk to everyone they meet, stranger and acquaintance alike. After a few days, you will also find yourself greeting people at random as you amble down the streets of Pensacola or St Augustine.

Mickey Mouse and the New Urbanism

There's more to the Sunshine State than just sun and friendly English-speakers. There is, of course, Walt Disney World®. Whether or not the 'Magic Kingdom' is an actual incentive for you to buy a home in Florida, it is among the top holiday destinations in the world, and it would be hard to discuss Florida without mentioning the Mouse who devoured central Florida. Because of – or despite, depending on who you talk to – its proximity to so many attractions, Orlando is one of the hottest housing markets in Florida. For a number of years, the British community in the area has been growing steadily. Many people have invested in homes for business reasons, but there are plenty of others who live there. The landscape of central Florida changed forever when Walt Disney decided to build his theme park there in the early 1970s. Not only did it spawn more parks by Disney and his followers, but it created a whole industry surrounding them. The suburbs of Orlando have become an overwhelming tribute to fun, with theme parks, water parks and every other kind of park and attraction you can imagine.

More recently, Disney built a home town called Celebration, not far from the park that started it all. Celebration is almost a suburb of Orlando and is based on the concept of new urbanism, which brings back the notion of a town square and which has become increasingly popular over the last couple of decades in the USA. New urbanism provides some respite from the 'cookie-cutter' developments that you can see in every suburb across the country.

In addition to Disney's Celebration, Florida is home to one of the true pioneers of new urbanism. Seaside is a charming town hidden along the panhandle's Gulf coast. Built only 20 or so years ago, the little town and its vibrant streets have brought accolades to its creators. The design ensures that everyone has equal access – visual and actual – to the snow-white beaches and clear blue waters of the Gulf. Although it is basically a modern housing development, nevertheless it is a surprisingly worthwhile place to visit.

History

Despite its attempts to mask modern construction under traditional façades, by British standards the USA is a young nation. Florida gives the impression that it is somehow even younger than the rest of the country. Perhaps this is because some of the things that it is most well known for – NASA and Disney World®, for example – are quite modern concepts. But do not be fooled: Florida has its share of history.

The presence of early native American (Indian) tribes and their descendants, the Seminole Indians, goes back hundreds of years before Juan Ponce de Leon, supposedly in search of the fountain of youth, 'discovered' the peninsula in 1513 and claimed the entire continent for Spain. The busy little town of St Augustine, to this day still guarded over by the Castillo de San Marcos (begun in 1672), became the first permanent European settlement anywhere in continental USA. Throughout the state, in cities like Tampa and especially way down into the Keys, you will find the visible remains of a long history of fishing and shipping.

Natural Beauty

Ernest Hemingway described the Gulf Stream in his book, *In a Season of Fishing*: 'You will see it oily flat as the becalmed galleons saw it while they drifted to the westward; white-capped with a fresh breeze as they saw it running with the trades; and in high, rolling blue hills, the tops blowing off them like snow as they were punished by it.' The days when Hemingway placed the Gulf Stream among 'the last wild country there is left' are long gone, but the legacy of fishing remains evident in the many chartered fishing trips that take tourists out in search of big fish.

In many ways, tourism is an important part of what keeps Florida alive today, but, thankfully, the natural beauty of the state survives despite the aggressive development that has raced along its coasts. Florida is home to 26 national refuges. More importantly, it is home to the very first one. One hundred years ago, President Theodore Roosevelt created the Pelican Island Reservation, the first federal bird preserve and the first piece in a large patchwork of sanctuaries that would become known as the National Wildlife Refuge System. Legend has it that the president created the reserve after hearing that Palm Beach yachtsmen were shooting brown pelicans for sport as the birds flew to their nests on a small island in the Indian River Lagoon, not far from Melbourne. Today, the state counts some of the premier birding areas among its many refuges.

In addition to its refuges, the state is also home to 11 national parks, which include memorials, preserves and recreational areas.

Why Buy?

By now you should have answered the question 'why Florida?', or at least you have given it some serious thought. Now you must ask yourself a far more complicated question: 'why buy?' Your first instinct may be to regard the purchase as an investment: as house prices continue to soar in the UK at rates not seen since the peak of the 1980s housing boom, buying overseas may seem all the more attractive.

Mortgage-lenders seem eager to emphasize this point. As one of the spokes-people from the One Account puts it, 'More and more people are looking to buy property abroad rather than in the UK, as not only do they get better value for money but it acts as a sound investment for the future.'

However, buying a second home is not quite the same as buying your first property, although part of the reason for doing so is really no different: why throw away money when you can be putting it towards owning a property, especially when you are travelling to the same place each year? Of course, if you are only using the property for a few weeks a year and letting it out for the remainder, then you should take into consideration the work and expense that is involved with owning and managing an overseas property.

The decision to buy, rather than to rent a place for a few weeks and then be able to walk away from all the burdens that an owner must carry year-round, is one that will ultimately depend on how you feel about an area and at what level you wish to invest in it. Of course, there is always a good argument to be made for renting initially, especially if you are not familiar with an area. Nevertheless, it is important to see a place in all its different aspects.

A Second Home

Many of us aspire to the idea of an overseas holiday home. The cost of owning a property where you spend a few weeks or months of the year could probably be offset by letting the place for the remainder of the year.

The good thing about Florida is that its year-round good weather means that finding tenants should not be too difficult, and there are businesses dedicated to facilitating such short-term arrangements. Of course – and it cannot be stressed enough – there are no guarantees when it comes to rental income. Be wary of any seller who tells you otherwise.

The one thing you can count on when you own your own place is that it is there when you want it – assuming, of course, that you let it on a short-term lease. You also have the freedom to add to it, or improve it as your needs arise. From a purely sentimental perspective, having your own second home means that all the things that accumulate when a family returns to the same place each year will have a home as well.

Investment

We are used to property appreciating in the UK and there is generally a sense that it is important to buy now or else we might lose the opportunity in the future. We fear that a property we can afford this year will be financially beyond our reach next year. This is no different when buying overseas. The fact that the property (real estate) market in Florida is currently extremely hot underlines this feeling. This also means that buying will require a significant amount of work. It can be a seller's market, and a property you see for sale one day may not be available a few weeks later.

If you are not looking to invest in sentimentality but are more concerned with the 'bottom line', then you could do a lot worse than invest in Florida. Given a strong pound, your money will go further in the USA than in the UK; and with 11 of the USA's top 20 highest-appreciating house price areas (according to the government Office of Federal Housing Oversight, December 2005) in Florida, buying in the state also promises to be a great investment.

Experts warn, however, that it is important to enter into such an investment with your eyes open. Do not look for an immediate return. Buying a house is a good way to make money in terms of capital appreciation, but is not so good in terms of letting. While homes in Florida do appreciate, you must bear in mind that this is a business. If you use your home 8–10 weeks a year and let it out for the remainder, the property will probably pay for itself. Despite what some real estate agents might tell you, it is unlikely to make you a fortune.

Another thing to be aware of is that, although we speak the same language, the whole process of buying a home in the USA is entirely foreign to us. For example, the completion (closing) costs are far higher in the USA than in the UK and you should therefore take such things into account when drawing up your budget.

Living in Florida

Starting a Business

If you scan the *Union Jack*, America's national British monthly newspaper, you will see that there is a concentration of businesses in Florida that cater specifically for a British clientele. The paper is filled with ads for mortgage-lenders, seaside pubs and various shops offering everything from sausages and pork pies to teapots and clotted cream.

Clearly, many British who have moved to Florida have gone for more than just sun. Whether it is a lifelong dream or a business opportunity that has suddenly appeared, starting a business or taking over an existing one can be a satisfying way of integrating into a new society.

As with any business – or a home for that matter – you must know what you are getting into. Avoid jumping into anything without doing all the necessary research first. Many have lost their life's savings by buying into something that was not all that it seemed.

Self-employment

The idea of self-employment fits well with Americans' concept of themselves: be your own boss; answer to no one; do it yourself. Certainly, if you are looking to escape the confines of a traditional office, and set up shop wherever you like, Florida offers a number of choice settings with unbeatable views.

More importantly, in addition to scenery, the state – actually the USA as a whole – offers a large amount of help to those who want to go out on their own. Government agencies such as the Small Business Administration offer invaluable advice on business loans and business plans. In addition, there are associations, such as the National Association for the Self-Employed, that give their members all sorts of benefits, including discounted health insurance.

In short, if you want to go it alone, you won't really be alone.

Educating and Raising Children

For the very reasons that Florida may be attractive to you as a holiday destination, it may also be an attractive place to raise children. The abundance of good weather offers plenty of opportunities for outdoor recreation, ensuring that your children lead a healthy, active lifestyle. In addition, as already mentioned, there is Disney World®. When it comes to education, however, Florida is no different from the rest of the USA, where public education can be somewhat uneven. Regular promises of increased funding for public education and of 'leaving no child behind' seem to fade away once the political campaigns come to an end. But, as with many things, there are very good state (public) schools and there are not so good ones – quality can vary even within a state – and only research will tell you which kind is available in your particular region.

Of course, if you are a non-resident owner of a home in Florida, your children will not even qualify for any public schooling, and your only option then is private school, so the quality of the American public education system will be of little interest to you. Otherwise, anyone wanting to put their children into the public schooling system would have to produce evidence of residency which would at least include some form of working visa.

Retirement

In the USA, 'moving to Florida' is practically synonymous with retirement. The so-called 'snowbirds', or older people from the north who head south for the winter or for good, are not an elusive rare species, but rather a part of the land-scape of many Floridian communities. If Ponce de Leon came to Florida today looking for the fountain of youth and landed at Naples Pier, he might turn his ship around, thinking that the state was home to something quite different from the legendary fountain.

Catering to the foreign and domestic retirement community is big business in the state, and the local powers seem to pride themselves on this fact. Perhaps the most obvious example of this pride is in their choice of 'The Swanee River' as a state song, subtitled 'Old Folks at Home'.

If you are hoping to settle into a nice warm retirement in Florida, the good news is that you can take your UK pension with you. If you qualify for a pension in the UK, it can be sent to you no matter where you are and, again, with the pound currently holding its own against the dollar your money should go a bit further in Florida. Unlike in some countries, such as Canada, Australia and New Zealand, if you retire to the USA your UK pension will not be 'frozen', but rather will increase over time, as it would if you were still living in Britain.

The bad news is that, once you are in the USA, you may need that extra buying power for health insurance. Nearly all health insurance in the USA is private. There are a few government programmes, such as Medicare (for the elderly), Medicaid (for those below a certain income level or disabled) and SCHIP (for children who cannot otherwise get insurance), but unless you are at least a permanent resident you will not qualify for any of these.

You will therefore need to provide your own medical insurance coverage, which can be purchased through a private American insurer, or else through travel and personal possessions insurance from a UK provider prior to each journey. In the case of medical coverage this would, typically, run into millions of dollars' worth of cover for emergency, hospital or doctor's expenses. It would also, almost certainly, provide for repatriation by air ambulance back to the UK if treatment back home was less expensive than treatment in the USA.

Visas and Permits

Visa-processing, like many other things in the USA, has changed to some degree since the terrorist attacks of 11 September 2001. The first change is that the office you may have known as the Immigration and Naturalization Services (INS) no longer exists – or at least not as the INS. It is now known as the **US Bureau of Citizenship and Immigration Services (USCIS; www.uscis.gov)**, a department of the Office of Homeland Security, a cabinet created by President George W. Bush in response to heightened concerns over terrorist threats.

Visa applications, in some instances, take longer to process and therefore the US government recommends that you apply for visas well in advance of your proposed date of travel and that you do not finalize your travel plans until the visa has been issued. In short, do not purchase non-refundable tickets until a visa has been issued.

For more detailed visa information, visit the website for the US Embassy in London at **www.usembassy.org.uk**.

Visa Waiver Program

Much has happened since President Clinton signed into law the Visa Waiver Permanent Program Act on 30 October 2000. The Visa Waiver Program (VWP) makes it possible for the citizens of 27 countries, including the UK, to enter the USA without a visa provided they do not plan to study, work or stay more than 90 days.

As the Bush administration focuses more on homeland security, however, there has been some talk that the 90-day period may be reduced to 30 days at some point in the future. For the time being this is simply speculation, and there are many forces that are strongly opposed to such change. Foreigners buying holiday homes are big business, especially in Florida, and estate agents (realtors) are well aware of the huge amount of money that would be lost if these potential investors were discouraged in any way. In the USA, money has a very persuasive voice.

So for the time being the situation is this: as a British citizen (or a citizen of Andorra, Australia, Austria, Belgium, Brunei, Denmark, Finland, France, Germany, Iceland, Ireland, Italy, Japan, Liechtenstein, Luxembourg, Monaco, the Netherlands, New Zealand, Norway, Portugal, San Marino, Singapore, Slovenia, Spain, Sweden or Switzerland) you may travel visa-free to the USA for business, pleasure or transit, and stay for three months. If you are travelling under the Visa Waiver Program, your passport must be valid for at least 90 days from the date on which you enter the USA, otherwise you will be admitted only until the expiry date on the passport. You should also carry with you evidence of, for example, strong social and economic ties to your place of permanent residence, which will indicate your intention to depart the USA at the end of your visit. Finally, since 2003 all children entering the USA under the Visa Waiver Program must have their own passport. Families affected should apply for a separate passport for their children from the UK Passport Service (**t** 0870 521 0410, **www.ukpa.gov.uk**), which costs £35.

Transit

If you qualify for visa-free travel under the Visa Waiver Program, you are also eligible to transit the USA. You apply for entry on the arrival/departure form I-94W, which the airline or shipping company should provide.

If you are transiting the USA to a destination in Canada, Mexico or the adjacent islands, you may re-enter the USA on the return journey using any mode of transport, as long as the total visit, including both periods of time spent in transit and in Canada, Mexico or the adjacent islands, does not exceed 90 days.

If you are transiting to a destination outside Canada, Mexico or the adjacent islands, your return journey must be on a participating carrier, but does not have to be within 90 days, as you will be required to make a new application for admission.

Where to Apply

The first place to inform yourself of the application procedure for your specific visa is **www.usembassy.org.uk**, where many of the initial application forms are available to print out. If the website doesn't answer your questions you will need to contact the embassy using its prohibitively expensive operator-assisted visa information line (**t** 09042 450 100) that operates Monday to Friday 8am–8pm, Saturdays 9am–4pm. The cost is £1.20 per minute from BT landlines and it is available only in the UK. Once your procedure is clear and your postal application has been accepted you will be required to attend an interview at either the US Embassy in London; or at the Belfast consulate for Northern Ireland residents:

American Embassy
24 Grosvenor Square
London W1A 1AE
United Kingdom
t [44] (0)20 7499 9000
Open Mon–Fri 8.30am–5.30pm.

US Consulate General
Queen's House
14 Queen Street
Belfast BT1 6EQ
Northern Ireland
t [44] (0)28 9032 8239
f [44] (0)28 9024 8482
Open Mon–Fri 8.30am–5pm.

Neither embassy nor consulate is open for walk-in enquiries and both are closed on Saturdays, Sundays and for American and British holidays. The Belfast office is also closed for Northern Irish holidays.

Types of Visas

Non-immigrant Visas

If you are planning to stay in the USA longer than 90 days, or you wish to work or study for a temporary period, then you will need a visa.

The first step up from the visa-waiver scheme, and necessary if you if you are a British citizen staying for more than 90 days, are the B visas. You will need to prove that a stay of more than 90 days really is necessary to be granted this visa. The **B-1** is the business visitor visa, **B-2** the tourist visa.

In most cases, your spouse and/or children may qualify for derivative visas based on the visa that you will be travelling on. Consult the American embassy (**www.usembassy.org.uk**) or consulate for more detailed and, crucially, the most up-to-date information about the limitations of such derivative visas.

The following is a list of the different non-immigrant visas that the USA grants for specific travel purposes. If your activity does not fit the description below, then you may need to obtain an exchange visitor (J-1) or temporary work (H-1) visa.

Academics and Researchers

• **Exchange Student:** If you wish to study at an academic institution in the USA, you will require a student (F-1) visa. However, if you are a student on a full course of study at an academic institution outside the USA and are required to study at a US academic institution for a term or academic year as part of your curriculum, you may require an exchange visitor (J-1) visa.

• **Professor/Lecturer/Speaker:** If you are a member of the academic profession and are coming to the USA to engage in usual academic activities such as lecturing, you may travel on a B-1 visa provided there is no remuneration from a US source other than expenses incidental to the visit.

• **Medical Elective:** If you are undertaking a period of training that involves practical experience and instruction in the various disciplines of medicine under the supervision and direction of faculty physicians at the US medical school's hospital, you may do so on a B-1 visa, as long as the post is an approved part of your school's education and no remuneration will be received from the hospital. You will need a letter from the US medical school outlining the nature and duration of the visa, and the source of remuneration, if any, should accompany your application.

Athletes, Artists and Entertainers

If you are an athlete, artist or entertainer planning to travel to the USA, your sponsor must file an application, form I-129 O or P, on your behalf with USCIS. The following is a list of the types of visas that might be granted in this case, but your sponsor or employer should contact the USCIS for further information.

- **O-1 Visa:** If you have exceptional ability in the sciences, arts, education, business or athletics, or extraordinary achievement in motion picture and television production, you and your essential support personnel may be able to enter the USA on an O visa. Only individuals qualify for the O-1 visa category and the visa is granted for a specific event, such as a tour, lecture series or project.

- **O-2 Visa:** If you are an integral part of an athlete's or entertainer's performance and have skills and experience that are not available in the US location of the event, you may be able to apply for an O-2 visa to accompany an O-1 visa holder.

- **P-1 Visa:** Certain athletes, entertainers and artists, and essential support personnel, may be able to enter the USA on a P-1 visa. Individual members of the entertainment industry are not eligible for the P-1 visa classification, but individual athletes are. For members of the entertainment industry, the visa will be issued for a specific event only. However, individual athletes may be admitted for five years and a team for a period of six months.

- **P-2 Visa:** If you are an artist or entertainer, either an individual or group, involved in a reciprocal exchange programme between an organization or organizations in the USA and one or more foreign countries that provides for the temporary exchange of artists and entertainers, you may be able to enter the USA on a P-2 visa.

- **P-3 Visa:** If you are an artist or entertainer, either an individual or group, who wants to perform, teach or coach under a programme that is culturally unique, you may be able to enter the USA on a P-3 visa.

Cultural Exchange

If you are participating in an international cultural exchange programme designed to provide practical training, employment and sharing of your native culture, you will require a classification **Q visa**. The activity must be approved in advance by the USCIS in the USA on the basis of an application, form I-129 Q, filed by your US sponsor. A new application must be filed each time a qualified employer wants to bring additional persons into the USA on Q status.

A Q visa application is approved for the length of the programme, or for 15 months, whichever is shorter. If you hold a Q visa and have spent 15 months in the USA, you may not be issued a visa or be readmitted under the Q visa classification unless you have resided and been physically present outside the USA for one year.

Before an application may be filed, the following criteria must be met:

• The culture-sharing must take place in a school, museum, business or other establishment where the public is exposed to aspects of a foreign culture as part of a structured programme.

• The cultural component must be an essential and integral part of the participant's employment and training, and must be designed to exhibit the attitude, customs, history, heritage, philosophy and/or tradition of the alien's country of nationality.

• The alien's employment and training may not be independent of the cultural component.

• The organization must demonstrate that it has the ability to conduct a responsible international cultural exchange programme and has the financial ability to remunerate the participant and offer him/her wages and working conditions comparable to those accorded local domestic workers similarly employed.

• The applicant must be at least 18 years of age, be qualified to perform the stated service or labour or receive the specified type of training, and have the ability to communicate effectively about his or her culture.

Diplomats and Government Officials

With the exception of a head of state or government, who qualifies for an A-1 visa regardless of the purpose of his or her visit to the USA, the type of visa required by a diplomat or other government official depends on his or her reason for entering the USA.

To qualify for an **A-1** or **A-2 visa**, you must be travelling to the USA on behalf of your national government to engage solely in official activities for that government. The fact that there may be government interest or control in a given organization is not in itself the defining factor in determining whether or not you qualify for an A visa; the particular duties or services to be performed must also be of an inherently governmental nature.

Local government officials representing their state, province, borough or other local political entity do not qualify for A visa status; they require **B-1/B-2 visas**. Government officials travelling to the USA to perform non-governmental functions of a commercial nature or travelling as tourists require the appropriate H, L or B visa, or, if qualified, travel visa-free; they do not qualify for diplomatic visas.

Qualified A visa applicants travelling to the USA for assignments of less than 90 days will be issued visas annotated 'TDY' (temporary duty).

Foreign officials who intend travelling to the USA on official business must obtain an A visa prior to their entry. They cannot travel on tourist visas or visa-free under the Visa Waiver Program.

Employees of International Organizations and NATO

International organizations: To qualify for a G visa, you must be entering the USA on official duties. Members of a permanent mission of a recognized government to an international organization are eligible for **G-1 visas**; representatives of a recognized government travelling to the USA temporarily to attend meetings of a designated international organization are eligible for **G-2 visas**; and representatives of non-recognized or non-member governments are eligible for **G-3 visas**. **G-4 visas** are issued to personnel who are proceeding to the USA to take up an appointment at a designated international organization, including the United Nations.

NATO: You will be classified under the symbol **NATO-1**, **NATO-2**, **NATO-3**, **NATO-4** or **NATO-5** if you are seeking admission to the USA under the applicable provision of the Agreement on the Status of the North Atlantic Treaty Organization, national representatives and international staff, or are a member of the immediate family of an alien classified NATO-1 through NATO-5.

However, many armed forces personnel are exempt from passport and visa requirements if they are either attached to NATO allied headquarters in the USA and are travelling on official business, or are entering the USA under NATO Status of Forces Agreement. In the case of the latter, they must carry official military ID cards and NATO travel orders.

Exchange Visitors

If you wish to take up prearranged employment, training or research in the USA under an officially approved programme sponsored by an educational or other non-profit institution, you will require an exchange visitor (**J-1**) visa. Those covered by these programmes include postgraduate students, medical students coming to the USA as residents or interns, foreign scholars sponsored by universities as temporary faculty, and some business trainees. To perform services as a member of the medical profession or to receive graduate medical education in the USA, you may be required to pass the National Board of Medical Examiners (NBME) Parts I and II, or an examination that is determined to be equivalent.

With a J-1 visa, you may enter the USA up to 30 days before the designated start date on the DS-2019 and you may remain for up to 30 days following the completion of the programme.

Holiday Visitors

If you are travelling to the USA on holiday, you will require valid **B-2 visas** unless you are eligible to travel visa-free under the Visa Waiver Program (*see* pp.15–16), or are a national of a country that has an agreement with the USA allowing their citizens to travel to the USA without B-2 visas. Otherwise, you will be required to apply for a visa before travelling. While nationals of certain countries are required to pay a B visa issuance fee, British passport-holders will not be charged.

All B-2 visa applicants are required to:

• Complete the visa application form DS-156. To obtain a form, either:

  • download the DS-156 from the US Embassy's website, www.usembassy.org.uk.

  • contact the Operator Assisted Visa Information Service (t 09042 450 100; calls cost £1.20 per minute).

• Pay a visa application fee. Every visa applicant is required to pay a visa application fee of US$100.

• Present a passport or other travel document valid for at least six months beyond the holder's period of stay in the USA with at least one blank page (the six-month requirement does not apply to UK passports).

• Provide one colour passport photograph which meets State Department regulations.

• Present:

  • evidence of sufficient funds to cover all expenses while in the USA.

  • proof that the applicant has a residence abroad to which he/she intends to return at the end of the stay in the USA. This is generally established by evidence of family, professional, property, employment or other ties and commitments to some country other than the USA sufficient to cause the applicant to return there at the conclusion of his/her stay.

Media

If you are a representative of the foreign media travelling to the USA on assignment, you may be eligible for classification under the I visa category. Representatives of the foreign media include, but are not limited to, members of the press, radio or film whose activities are essential to the foreign media function, such as reporters, film crews, editors and persons in similar occupations. Only those who are actually involved in the news-gathering process are eligible.

The Immigration and Nationality Act is very specific about the qualification requirements for the I visa category. I visas may only be granted to members of the media and freelance journalists and employees of independent production companies under contract to media organizations. Members of the media engaged in the production or distribution of film will only qualify for I visas if the material being filmed will be used to disseminate information or news and the primary source of funding and point of distribution is outside the USA.

Individuals and/or companies commissioned to work on film projects of a commercial or entertainment value require the appropriate work visas (O, P or H), which will involve obtaining employment authorization from the office of the USCIS before applying for a visa at the embassy or consulate.

I visas are also appropriate for foreign journalists working for an overseas branch office or subsidiary of a US network, newspaper or other media outlet if the journalist is going to the USA to report on US events solely for a foreign audience. If the journalist will replace or augment American journalists reporting on US events for an American audience, either an H or O visa will be required.

Religious Workers

If you are a religious minister or worker, you may qualify for the religious worker classification **R visa** if, for the two years immediately preceding the time of application, you have been a member of a religious denomination that has a bona fide non-profit religious organization in the USA.

The initial admission period for ministers and religious workers entering the USA in R status is limited to three years. Employers must file an I-129 application with the USCIS to request an extension. Extensions may be granted for a total stay of not more than five years.

When applying for entry into the USA as a voluntary worker with a visa or under the Visa Waiver Program, you should provide a letter from your US sponsor containing a detailed explanation of the nature of your trip, as well as the following information:

- **Your name and date and place of birth.**
- **Your foreign permanent residence address.**
- **The name and address of initial destination in the USA.**
- **The anticipated duration of your assignment.**

The following is a list of religious activities that may be undertaken on a B-1 visa:

- **Missionary Work**: If you are carrying out missionary work on behalf of a religious denomination you may be eligible for a B-1 visa, provided you will receive no salary or remuneration from the USA other than an allowance or other reimbursement for expenses incidental to your stay, and the work which you are to perform in the USA will not involve the selling of articles or the solicitation or acceptance of donations.

- **Evangelical Tour**: If you are to engage in an evangelical tour and do not plan to take an appointment with any one church you may be eligible for a B-1 visa, provided you will receive no remuneration from a US source other than the offerings contributed at each evangelical meeting.

- **Preaching**: If you will be preaching in the USA for a temporary period, or will be exchanging pulpits with your US counterpart, you may be eligible for a B-1 visa, provided you will continue to be reimbursed by your church in the UK and you will receive no salary from the host church in the USA.

- **Voluntary Service Programme**: If you are participating in a voluntary service programme that benefits a US local community, and you establish that you are a member of, and have a commitment to, a particular recognized religious or non-profit charitable organization, you may be eligible for a B-1 visa if the work to be performed is traditionally done by volunteer charity workers; you will receive no salary or remuneration from a US source, other than an allowance or other reimbursement for expenses incidental to your stay; and you will not engage in the selling of articles and/or the solicitation and acceptance of donations.

Students

If you are a student planning to attend a university or other academic institution in the USA, you will require a student (**F-1**) visa; if you plan to attend a vocational or non-academic institution, you will require an **M-1** visa. Holders of visitor (B-2) visas and those who have entered the USA visa-free under the Visa Waiver Program are prohibited from entering into full-time study. Contact the Fulbright Commission Educational Advisory Service (**www.fulbright.co.uk**) for information about studying at colleges and universities in the USA.

• **Academic (F-1) Visa**: If you plan to attend a university or other academic institution in the USA, including primary and secondary schools, or a language training programme, you will require an F-1 visa. Section 214(l) of the Immigration and Nationality Act (INA), prohibits the issuance of F-1 visas to students who are going to the USA to attend public elementary schools (grades K-8, approximately ages 5–14) and publicly funded adult education programmes, such as foreign language classes. Students applying for F-1 visas to attend public secondary schools (grades 9–12, approximately ages 14–18) are limited to a maximum of 12 months of public high school in F-1 status and must show proof that payment has been made for the full, unsubsidized cost of the education before a visa can be processed. Students attending private elementary and secondary schools are not affected by this ruling.

• **Non-academic (M-1) Visa**: If you plan to pursue a course of study that is not principally academic in nature at an established vocational or other recognized non-academic institution such as a post-secondary vocational or business school, you will require an M-1 visa.

Immigrant Visas

It is considerably harder to obtain an immigrant visa than a non-immigrant one, and the process is quite different. If you plan to reside in the USA permanently, US immigration law provides for immigrant visas to be issued in four general categories: immediate relatives, family-based, employment-based and the Diversity Immigrant Visa Program, more commonly known as the 'green card' lottery. Unfortunately because the lottery is aimed at countries with low rates of immigration to the USA, natives of the UK are no longer eligible.

Immediate Relatives

Immediate relatives of US citizens are eligible to qualify for immigration in the immediate relative category. Grandparents, aunts, uncles, in-laws and cousins cannot sponsor a relative for immigration.

- **Spouse or minor child of a US citizen**: An immigrant visa may only be processed for a child if he or she has no claim to US citizenship.
- **Parent of a US citizen**: The US citizen must be 21 or over.
- **Step-parent or child of a US citizen**: The step-parent/step-child relationship must occur before the child's 18th birthday.
- **Spouse of a deceased US citizen**: The application must be filed within two years of the death of the US citizen.

Family-based Immigration

Persons seeking to immigrate in one of the family-based preference categories will qualify for immigrant status only if they have the necessary relationship to a US citizen or lawful permanent resident as described below. Grandparents, aunts, uncles, in-laws and cousins cannot sponsor a relative.

- Unmarried son or daughter over the age of 21 of a US citizen.
- Spouse or unmarried son or daughter of a lawful permanent resident.
- Married son or daughter of a US citizen.
- Brother or sister of a US citizen – US citizen must be 21 or over.

Employment-based Immigration

In general, a specific offer of employment from a US-based employer is required to qualify for immigration in the employment-based categories.

- **Priority workers**: Persons of exceptional ability in the sciences, education, arts, business or athletics; outstanding professors and researchers and certain multinational executives and managers.
- **Members of 'the professions'**: Persons with exceptional ability in the sciences, or in arts and business – defined as a member of the professions holding an advanced degree or equivalent, or baccalaureate degree plus at least five years of progressive experience in the speciality, and persons of exceptional ability in the sciences, arts and business.
- **Professionals**: A person who holds a baccalaureate degree and who is a member of the professions.
- **Skilled and unskilled workers**: Skilled workers with at least two years' training or experience and unskilled workers whose skills are in short supply in the USA. The embassy does not keep a list of these professions.
- **Special immigrants**: Certain religious workers and ministers of religion, certain international organization employees and their immediate family

members, qualified and recommended current and former employees of the US government and returning residents.

• **Investors**: Persons who will create employment for at least 10 unrelated persons by investing a minimum of $1 million in a new commercial enterprise in the USA.

Administrative Departments in Florida

The Bureau of Citizenship and Immigration Services has a local (field) office in Miami that serves the immigration needs of the entire state. However, there is a satellite office in West Palm Beach, as well as sub-offices in Jacksonville, Orlando and Tampa that serve specific counties.

For more detailed information about field offices, visit **www.uscis.gov/graphics/fieldoffices/alphaa.htm**.

Miami

Miami District Office
7880 Biscayne Boulevard
Miami, Florida 33138

The information office (at the rear of the building) is open Monday–Friday 7am–3.30pm, and the cashier 7am–2.30pm. Appointments are arranged 8am–2.30pm. Original copies of supporting documents (birth certificates, passports) are required at the time of interview. To speak to an immigration information officer, you have to make an appointment via the Internet at **www.infopass.uscis.gov**. If you do not have Internet access, you may use a kiosk at the Miami District Office to schedule an appointment. Immigration forms are available next to the front main entrance Monday– Friday 7am–2.30pm.

The Naturalization Office, where scheduled naturalization interviews are conducted, is separate from the main District Office:

Naturalization Office
77 SE 5th Street, 2nd Floor
Miami, Florida 33131
t (305) 415 6500

West Palm Beach

West Palm Beach Satellite Office
326 Fern St
Suite 200
West Palm Beach, Florida 33401

The West Palm Beach satellite office serves the following counties: Glades, Hendry, Highland, Indian River, Martin, Okeechobee, Palm Beach and St Lucie. The office is open to the public 7am–3pm. Information services are by appointment only. Appointments may be made via the Internet at **www. infopass.uscis.gov**. To obtain forms by post, call **t** 1-800 870 3676.

Jacksonville

Jacksonville Sub-Office
4121 Southpoint Boulevard
Jacksonville, Florida 32216

The Jacksonville sub-office serves the following counties: Alachua, Baker, Bay, Bradford, Calhoun, Clay, Columbia, Dixie, Duval, Escambia, Franklin, Gadsden, Gilchrist, Gulf, Hamilton, Holmes, Jackson, Jefferson, Lafayette, Leon, Levy, Liberty, Madison, Nassau, Okaloosa, Putnum, Santa Rosa, St Johns, Suwanee, Taylor, Union, Wakulla, Walton and Washington.

The Jacksonville sub-office is open to the public Monday–Friday 9am–noon. The office is closed on Saturday, Sunday and federal holidays. To talk to an immigration information officer, you may must an appointment via the Internet at **www.infopass.uscis.gov**. Walk in visits are reserved for emergencies.

Tampa

Tampa Sub-Office
5524 West Cypress Street
Tampa, Florida 33607-1708

The Tampa sub-office serves the counties of Charlotte, Citrus, De Soto, Hardee, Hernando, Hillsborough, Lee, Manatee, Pasco, Pinellas, Polk and Sarasota. The office is open to the public Monday–Friday 7.30am–4pm, but only sees people by appointment made at **www.infopass.uscis.gov**.

Orlando

Orlando Sub-Office
9403 Tradeport Drive
Orlando, Florida 32827

The Orlando sub-office serves the counties of Brevard, Flagler, Lake, Marion, Orange, Osceola, Seminole, Sumter and Volusia. The Orlando District Office is open to the public Monday–Friday 8am–4pm for interviews; for information 8am–noon. The office is closed on Saturday, Sunday and federal holidays. To talk to an immigration officer, you must book online at **www.infopass.uscis.gov**, though walk-ins are possible in emergencies.

Permanent Residency

Eligibility

Once you are in the USA on an immigrant visa, you may apply for **legal permanent resident (LPR)** status.

The best source for detailed immigration information is the USCIS website **www.uscis.gov/graphics/howdoi/lpreligibility.htm**.

You may be eligible to apply if one or more of the following categories apply to you.

- **Family Member:**

  - You are the spouse, parent, unmarried child under 21, unmarried son or daughter over age 21, married son or daughter, or the brother or sister of a US citizen and have a visa application approved on your behalf.

  - You are the spouse or unmarried son or daughter of any age of a lawful permanent resident and you have a family-based visa application approved on your behalf.

- **Employment**: You are an alien who has an approved visa application filed on your behalf by a US employer.

Note: If you are a family- or employment-based applicant, you must have an **immigrant visa number** available from the State Department unless you are in a category that is exempt from numerical limitations. Immediate relatives of US citizens are exempt from this requirement. Immediate relatives of US citizens are parents, spouses and unmarried children under 21. (For instance, you can apply to adjust to permanent resident status at the same time that your US citizen daughter files an application for you to become an immigrant.) Other immigrant categories that are exempt from numerical limitations and do not need a visa number include special immigrant juvenile and special immigrant military applications. USCIS form I-360 provides more information on special immigrant juvenile and special immigrant military applications. For the unmarried son or daughter (over 21 years of age) of a US citizen, brother or sister of a US citizen, or the spouse or children of lawful permanent residents, visa numbers are limited by law every year. This means that even if the USCIS approves an immigrant visa application for you, you may not get an immigrant visa number immediately. In some cases, several years could pass between the time USCIS approves your immigrant visa application and when the State Department gives you an immigrant visa number.

- **Fiancé(e)**: You were a fiancé(e) who was admitted to the USA on a K-1 visa and then married the US citizen who applied for the K-1 visa for you. (If you married the US citizen but not within the 90-day time limit, your spouse also must now file USCIS form I-130, Petition for Alien Relative.) Your unmarried, minor children are also eligible for adjustment of status. If you did not marry the US citizen who filed the K-1 application on your behalf, or if you married another US citizen or lawful permanent resident, you are not eligible to adjust status in the USA.

• **Asylee**: You are an asylee or refugee who has been in the USA for at least a year after being given asylum or refugee status and still qualify for asylum or refugee status.

• **Diversity Visa**: You received notice from the Department of State that you have won a visa in the Diversity Visa Lottery.

• **Cuban Citizen**: You are a Cuban citizen or native who has been in the USA for at least a year after being inspected, admitted or paroled into the USA. Your spouse and children who are residing with you in the USA may also be eligible for adjustment of status.

• **US Resident Since Before 1 January 1972**: You have been a continuous resident of the USA since before 1 January 1972.

• **Parent's LPR Status**: Your parent became a lawful permanent resident after you were born. You may be eligible to receive following-to-join benefits if you are the unmarried child under 21 of the lawful permanent resident. In these cases, you may apply to adjust to permanent resident status at the same time that your parent applies for following-to-join benefits for you.

• **Spouse's LPR Status**: Your spouse became a lawful permanent resident after you were married. You may be eligible to receive following-to-join benefits. In these cases, you may apply to adjust to permanent resident status at the same time that your spouse applies for following-to-join benefits for you.

Filing for Permanent Residency

In order to become a lawful permanent resident in the USA, you must file the following items with the USCIS:

• Form I-485: Application to Register Permanent Residence or Adjust Status.

• Form G-325: A Biographic Data Sheet (between the ages of 14 and 79).

• Form I-693: Medical Examination Sheet (not required if you are applying based on continuous residence since before 1972, or if you have had a medical exam based on a fiancé(e) visa).

• Two colour photographs taken within the last 30 days (*see* USCIS form I-485 for more information on photographs).

• Form I-864: Affidavit of Support (completed by the sponsor). (This requirement may not apply if you are adjusting to permanent resident status based on an employment application.)

• Form I-765: Authorization for Employment (if seeking employment while case is processed).

In addition:

• If you have already been approved for an immigrant application, you must submit a copy of the approval notice sent to you by the USCIS.

• If someone else is filing or has filed an application for you that, if approved, will make an immigrant number immediately available to you, you must submit a copy of the completed application that is being filed for you. Such applications include only immediate relative, special immigrant juvenile or special immigrant military applications.

• If you were admitted into the USA as a fiancé(e) of a US citizen and married that citizen within the required 90 days, you must submit a copy of the fiancé(e) application approval notice and a copy of your marriage certificate.

• If you are an asylee or refugee, you must submit a copy of the letter or form I-94 (arrival–departure record) that shows the date you were granted asylum or refuge in the United States. You also must submit USCIS form I-643 (health and human services statistical data).

• If you are a Cuban citizen or native, you must use USCIS form I-485 (application to register permanent residence or adjust status) and submit evidence of your citizenship or nationality.

• If you have been a continuous resident of the USA since before 1 January 1972, you must submit evidence showing that you entered the USA prior to 1 January 1972 and that you have lived in the USA continuously since your entry into the country.

• If your parent became a lawful permanent resident after you were born, you must submit evidence that your parent has been or will be granted permanent residence. You must also submit a copy of your birth certificate and proof of your relationship to your parent.

• If your spouse became a lawful permanent resident after you were married, you must submit evidence that your spouse has been granted permanent residence. You must also submit a copy of your marriage certificate and proof that any previous marriages entered into by you or your spouse were legally terminated.

US Citizenship

While the USA does not officially recognize dual citizenship, it appears to turn a blind eye to it in most cases, since it is not uncommon for Americans to have passports from other countries as well.

Generally speaking, once you have become a permanent resident you are eligible to apply for American citizenship through the naturalization process. In addition to the naturalization process, the USA recognizes the US citizenship of individuals according to two fundamental principles: *jus soli*, or right of birthplace, and *jus sanguinis*, or right of blood. In other words, if you were born in the USA or in a US jurisdiction – with some exceptions – you are guaranteed citizenship (*jus soli*). If one of your parents is a US citizen – with some exceptions – no matter where you were born, you are guaranteed citizenship (*jus sanguinis*). To become a citizen, the following requirements apply:

- You must be at least 18 years old.
- You must have been lawfully admitted to the USA for permanent residence.
- You must have resided continuously as a lawful permanent resident in the USA for at least five years prior to filing, with absences from the USA totalling no more than one year.
- You must have been physically present in the USA for at least 30 months out of the previous five years (absences of more than six months but less than one year break the continuity of residence unless you can establish that you did not abandon your residence during such period).
- You must have resided within a state or district for at least three months.
- Generally, you must show that you have been a person of good moral character for the statutory period (typically five years or three years if married to a US citizen or one year for armed forces expedite) prior to filing for naturalization. You will not be considered to be a person of good moral character if during the last five years you:
  - have committed and been convicted of one or more crimes involving moral turpitude.
  - have committed and been convicted of two or more offences for which the total sentence imposed was five years or more.
  - have committed and been convicted of any controlled substance law, except for a single offence of simple possession of 30 grams or less of marijuana.
  - have been confined to a penal institution during the statutory period, as a result of a conviction, for an aggregate period of 180 days or more,
  - have committed and been convicted of two or more gambling offences.
  - have earned your principal income from illegal gambling.
  - are or have been involved in prostitution or commercialized vice.
  - are or have been involved in smuggling illegal aliens into the USA.
  - are or have been a habitual drunkard.
  - have practised polygamy.

- have wilfully failed or refused to support dependants.

- have given false testimony, under oath, in order to receive a benefit under the Immigration and Nationality Act.

• You must show that you are attached to the principles of the Constitution of the USA.

• You must be able to read, write, speak and understand words in ordinary usage in the English language, unless you:

- have been residing in the USA subsequent to a lawful admission for permanent residence for at least 15 years and are over 55 years of age.

- have been residing in the USA subsequent to a lawful admission for permanent residence for at least 20 years and are over 50 years of age.

- have a medically determinable physical or mental impairment, where the impairment affects the applicant's ability to learn English.

• You must demonstrate a knowledge and understanding of the fundamentals of the history and of the principles and form of government of the USA, unless you have a medically determinable physical or mental impairment, where the impairment affects your ability to learn US history and government. If you have been residing in the USA subsequent to a lawful admission for permanent residence for at least 20 years and are over the age of 65, you will be afforded special consideration in satisfying this requirement.

The final step in becoming a citizen is reciting the oath of allegiance. But if swearing to support the Constitution and obey the laws of the USA, and renouncing any foreign allegiance and/or foreign title, is a little more than you are looking for in a holiday, and all you really want to do is to relax in the sun under a palm tree for a few weeks each year, then that's fine, too. You can still buy your piece of paradise without swearing to bear arms for the United States of America. Read on.

Social Security Number

Once you arrive, you may want to find out how to get a social security number. It is not absolutely necessary and you could easily get by without one. The longer you plan to stay in Florida, however, the more you may find you need one. At the very least, you will need it to open a bank account, but you may also need it if you plan to work. It may also make the process of getting a driver's licence a bit easier, even though you do not actually need a social security number to do so.

The Social Security Administration (SSA) will grant numbers to non-citizens who are not otherwise eligible for them for the following non-work purposes:

- A federal statute or regulation requires that the alien provide his or her SSN to get the particular benefit or service.

- A state or local law requires the alien to provide his or her SSN to get general assistance benefits to which the alien has established entitlement.

- A state or local law requires the non-citizen to provide his SSN to get a driver's licence.

Your application for a social security number must be accompanied by documentation from the appropriate government entity explaining the need for it. It should be enough to bring a letter from the branch manager of your prospective bank. The letter should be dated and be on headed stationery. It must specifically identify you, as well as the non-work reason why the number is necessary, along with the relevant statute or regulation. The letter should also include the name and telephone number of an official who can verify the information. You can download an application form to apply for a number at the Social Security Administration's website (**www.ssa.gov/online/ss-5.html**).

If for some reason you do not qualify for a social security number but must report income for tax purposes, then you may have to apply for an Individual Taxpayer Identification Number (ITIN).

To apply, contact the Internal Revenue Service (IRS) and ask for form W-7 (Application for IRS Individual Taxpayer Identification Number). The agency can be contacted by:

- **Telephoning the IRS toll-free number, t 800 829 1040.**

- **Accessing the IRS website at www.irs.gov.**

- **Telephoning or visiting any local IRS office.**

Where in Florida: Profiles of the Regions

03

Making the decision to buy a home in Florida is the easy part. Now you must decide where to buy. There is a surprising amount of regional climatic variation along the peninsula, ranging from light snowfalls in the north to year-round warm temperatures in the south. It is in your own interest to get to know all the regions as well as you can and to take your time deciding which is the right place for you. Use this as an opportunity to savour the pine-shaded regions of the north, the snowy white beaches of the Gulf Coast and the abundance of wildlife at every turn. Then decide which area feels most like a second home. The state is made up of 67 counties, which readily divide into 11 regions. You may not be able to visit every region, but in this chapter you will find a small taste of each just to get you started. You may discover that the breakdown of the regions might vary slightly depending on whom you ask, but for property (real estate) purposes the state is broken down as in this chapter.

Geographically, Florida is clearly in the 'south' of the USA. North and south are delineations of considerable historical importance in America, although the Civil War is long over. For the most part the division today is quite amicable, but it is a division nonetheless. Florida, however, seems to stand apart in its own category. It is a retirement and vacation destination to many, while to those from the Caribbean and South America it is their first taste of America – but to which part of America does it belong?

This brings up an interesting paradox. Because of its proximity to the regional 'south', namely Alabama and Georgia, the northern part of the state tends to have a more 'southern' feel and temperament to it. Whether it is the

The Flat State?

If you are serious about mountain-climbing, you had better plan on spending some time outside Florida. The state is flat. There's really no other way of putting it. Its highest point is Britton Hill, located in the panhandle not far from the Alabama border. At 345ft, it is the lowest highest point of any American state. As if being the lowest is not low enough, the state could end up with an even lower highest point if a central Florida organization gets its way. In a display of panhandle–peninsula rivalry, a small band of residents outside Orlando recently organized a protest against Britton Hill's designation, claiming that the peak does not truly represent the state because of its proximity to Alabama. The group is demanding that a 312ft mountain called Sugarloaf be given the honour of being the highest point.

A few dedicated climbers have scoured the state (**www.southeastclimbing. com/climbing_areas/florida/gen_florida.htm**) in search of rocks to climb and met with moderate success. However, most of the members of any Florida climbing groups you are likely to meet do much of their climbing on rock walls at private gyms.

slow pace, the plantation homes tucked away in the overgrown suburbs or the hospitality with a hint of a drawn-out accent, this part of the state just feels 'southern'. The southern part of the state, on the other hand, with its noticeably transient or transplanted population of people from colder climates, and more cosmopolitan feel, is noticeably 'northern' in temperament. Of course, like the north and south generally, this distinction has blurred over the years as more and more of the state is discovered – or rediscovered – by an increasing number of people, resulting in the mingling of populations and the gradual fading away of regional differences.

The North

The northern part of Florida is made up of three regions: Northwest, North Central and Northeast, where you can find an unusual mix of gorgeous beaches, city life and quiet country roads. The area includes a relatively thin sliver of land known as the panhandle, and extends from the Alabama border in the west along the Gulf Coast and across to Jacksonville on the Atlantic. Although the winter is generally mild, with high temperatures in the 60s Fahrenheit, this part of the state does experience four distinct seasons, probably more so than anywhere south of Orlando. At times the temperature in some parts may be a full 20 degrees lower than in Miami, but freezing temperatures and snowfall are irregular and short-lived and during the summer the long sunny days rarely hit 90°F (32°C). When temperatures heat up in the south, you will be thankful for those few extra degrees of coolness.

Northwest

The Northwest region of Florida is a quiet, relatively rural area made up of farms and woodlands in the state's panhandle. It consists of 12 counties: Bay, Calhoun, Escambia, Franklin, Gulf, Holmes, Jackson, Liberty, Okaloosa, Santa Rosa, Walton and Washington. It is bordered on the east and north by Alabama and extends some 300km (180 miles) to the border of Georgia. The influence of the region's northern neighbour is evident in the fact that some locals along the border have dubbed a stretch of it 'Lower Alabama'. Even though it is home to some of the most beautiful beaches the state has to offer, as a whole it is an area that does not feature prominently in most people's minds when compared with the more popular destinations in Florida. So far, this has been a good thing, in that for the most part it has kept housing prices reasonable and development has been restricted.

The most populated county by far in the region is Escambia, the primary focus of which is the port town of **Pensacola**. The town is next to Eglin Air Force Base, a military base so large that it spans three counties and accounts for a considerable portion of the area's population and employment. For a relatively small city, Pensacola has a considerable amount of history. It has been nicknamed the 'City of Five Flags' because it has been under the control of five different nations since the Spanish first landed in Pensacola Bay in 1559. After the Spanish came the French, the British, then the United States and finally the Confederate States of America, answering in part the question whether this part of the world belongs to the 'south'. A lot of the city's history is visible and well marked in exposed archaeological digs, as well as an antique section of town that has been restored to the clean perfection of a movie set. Decorative wrought-iron balconies extending over pavements (sidewalks) offer a glimpse of Spanish influence.

However, it is the beaches that are the real jewels of the Northwest. The Gulf Coast, with its brilliant sand and blue waters, is an amazing sight to first-timers, and the sunset is tinged with magic. You will find some of the highest-rated beaches in the world here, from Perdido Key, which straddles the Alabama–Florida border, to Cape San Blas. Of course, there is always the well-known and developed **Panama City**, which is a popular destination with young people and families alike. Panama City's 43km (27 miles) of world-famous snow-white sand is actually made up of quartz crystals that were washed down from the Appalachian Mountains centuries ago into the Gulf of Mexico, where they were bleached, ground, smoothed and polished, until the waves deposited the powder-fine white grains on the shore.

No place in the Northwest makes better use of the beaches than the utopian town of **Seaside**, a 20-year-old planned community that launched a new way of thinking in housing development in the USA (*see* box, opposite). The small town, about two-thirds of the way between Pensacola and Panama City on the Gulf coast, is picture-perfect, but, unlike Pensacola, it actually *was* a movie set, at least for a brief period. Say what you like about Hollywood, but they know there what looks good on film. Several years ago, when location scouts discovered Seaside, they knew it would be the perfect idyllic backdrop to a movie about small-town life that is too good to be true. Soon aftewardsr, cast and crew descended on the small town to film *The Truman Show* starring Jim Carrey.

The limited availability of property in Seaside means that the town is probably one of the pricier places you could find to buy a home in this region. A small cottage a block off the beach can cost just under a million dollars, but the majority of properties are well over the million-dollar mark.

The area around Pensacola is considerably more modest, and you can easily find a number of good-sized, modern three- or four-bedroom homes for under $250,000, some even closer to $150,000. In fact, the Pensacola area is one of the most inexpensive housing markets in the state. At the beginning of 2006, according to the Florida Association of Realtors (FAR), the average (median) price for an existing single-family home in Pensacola was $158,100. Of course,

Picture-perfect Seaside

Noted urban designer Leon Krier once illustrated with a diagram how 80 acres is the area encompassed within a quarter-mile radius; a quarter-mile, he explained, was the distance a person would comfortably walk each day to go to work, to shop or to go out to eat. Robert Davis, a recognized builder and developer in Miami during the 1970s, happened to have access to 80 undeveloped acres near Seagrove Beach in Northwest Florida that his grandfather had bought in 1946.

Clearly a nostalgic man, Davis conceived of developing a place that would serve as a tribute to his countless memories of family vacations spent in breeze-filled cottages along the Gulf Coast of his youth. Since the cottages he remembered suddenly seemed scarce, he also envisaged reviving the area's tradition of building idyllic but sturdy wood-frame homes with deep roof overhangs, ample windows and cross-ventilation in all the rooms.

He called upon Miami architects Andres Duany and Elizabeth Plater-Zyberk to help with the revival. The team explored small towns throughout the American south and Florida in order to understand the origin of the buildings that Davis had in mind. The group soon came to realize that they had to think in terms of the whole town, not just the individual home.

Duany and Plater-Zyberk were followers of Krier, who had designed the English model village of Poundbury near Dorchester for the Prince of Wales, and who was an ardent proponent of the human-centred traditional urbanism. Krier's theories evolved into what came to be known as 'new urbanism' in America, and the town that Davis and his architects ended up building in the early 1980s was the movement's first child.

The town of Seaside is the embodiment of the ideal that being able to walk to get a pint of milk is not about convenience, but rather about removing people from the isolation of their cars (automobiles). Liberating man from his machine comes at a price, however. The town's founders imposed a series of strict building codes meant to ensure that their creation would allow for originality while still maintaining its strong sense of place.

Seaside met with remarkable success early on, and is now home to over 300 cottages. More importantly, there are newer housing developments all over the USA that owe some part of themselves to Davis's childhood memories.

the closer you get to Pensacola Beach, the higher the price – especially if you are looking for waterfront property.

However, not far away, things start to change drastically. According to FAR, the median sales price for an existing single-family home in Panama City sits at $223,300 at the beginning of 2006, placing the area among the higher-priced communities in the state. Even though Panama City has been a popular exception among the lesser-known communities of the panhandle, for some time it has shared the region's modest housing prices. Clearly, this is changing. In fact, some experts predict that Panama City may head the housing appreciation for the entire state over the coming decade.

North Central

This region, which runs along the border of Georgia, stopping a couple of counties short of hitting the Atlantic, includes one last bit of the panhandle before it dips down into the main peninsula. The region is home to 16 counties: Alachua, Bradford, Columbia, Dixie, Gadsden, Gilchrist, Hamilton, Jefferson, Lafayette, Leon, Levy, Madison, Suwanee, Taylor, Union and Wakulla. Despite being populated by more counties than any other, and despite being home to the capital Tallahassee, this region is probably the most rural in the whole state and includes large sections of open land dotted with only a few small towns.

Tallahassee, with its broad streets canopied by towering, ancient oak trees which lead to old plantation homes, feels very like the 'old south'. The Old Capitol building – open to visitors, but no longer used for official purposes – feels part of another era, despite the modern towers of the New Capitol looming just behind it. The city's inland location also helps to separate it from the sun and beach lifestyle of the rest of the state.

This region includes a good-sized portion of Gulf Coast but, surprisingly, not a single significantly recognizable beach town. In fact, the coastline is dotted with barely a handful of tiny towns. Look on a map and you will see a distinct lack of towns and villages along this part of the coast when compared with other parts of the state. Substantial development has passed this area by and nature clearly reigns over commerce, resulting in the area's straightforward nickname of the 'Nature Coast'.

One of the few towns you will encounter is **Cedar Key**, a quaint island village that once served as a strategic port to the Confederate States of America and today is a commercial fishing centre. Cedar Key marks the southern tip of the North Central region. The island, located where the Suwannee River dramatically enters the Gulf of Mexico, is also a very good example of the triumph of natural attractions over man-made ones. Even for Florida, the village appears to be at the centre of a remarkable concentration of wildly beautiful parks and refuges. Off the coast from Cedar Key is **Cedar Keys National Wildlife Refuge**, a group of barrier islands accessible only by boat. The **Lower Suwannee National Wildlife Refuge**, with its 52,000 acres of unspoiled habitat, is a stone's throw from the island; **Manatee Springs State Park** comes down to the shores of the Suwannee River; and finally there's **Cedar Key Scrub State Reserve**.

Inland, the region maintains its openness and does not hold too much more in the way of major commercial development west of I-75, the interstate highway that roughly separates the North Central region from the Northeast region and terminates in Tampa. In this central part of the region there are only a few small towns punctuating the gently rolling hills and vast green pastures. Two of the larger towns are **Gainesville** and **Ocala**, both of which seem to exist for specific purposes: the first is home to the University of Florida and therefore primarily a college town, and the second is the centre of Florida horse country, concentrating primarily on thoroughbred breeding and training. Ocala has been developing a name for itself in the breeding world over the years and a number of Arab stud farms have made their home recently in the pastoral countryside surrounding the town, with new ones following all the time.

Perhaps because of its prominence as the seat of state government, Tallahassee does not run the risk of being 'discovered' and therefore is a relatively stable housing market. The city's inland location also guarantees that pioneers will not be descending on its quaint streets in search of the next new coast. In terms of housing prices, Tallahassee has maintained modest but steady growth and, according to FAR, at the beginning of 2006, the median price for an existing single-family home was $175,500.

Gainesville's real estate fortunes, on the other hand, seem to rise and fall with the academic year, but it has witnessed some remarkable increases in prices, and at times its housing prices approach those of Tallahassee. At the beginning of 2006, however, the median price in Gainesville was $223,100, a considerable increase from the end of the previous year when prices hit $140,400. Ocala, with a median price of $166,200 at the start of 2006, remains among the lowest-priced markets in Florida, despite its 39 per cent increase in median prices over the previous year.

Northeast

After travelling across the pleasantly open expanse of northern Florida, by the time you hit the Northeast region and its seven counties – Baker, Clay, Duval, Flagler, Nassau, Putnam and St Johns – you may be lulled into thinking that the whole northern half of the state is nothing but quaint towns, beautiful beaches and endless pristine wilderness. Then you enter **Jacksonville**. Jacksonville is the first city that you will encounter in the north that actually feels like a major city. It is. In terms of population, it is larger than Pensacola and Tallahassee put together but, most surprisingly, in terms of geographic size it is larger than New York City. In fact, it is the largest city in the contiguous USA (only Anchorage in Alaska is bigger).

Like the rest of the north, Jacksonville proudly shows off its abundant 'old south' charm, which is mainly to be seen in the smaller residential neighbourhoods. Unlike the rest of the region, however, it is also home to an equal, or perhaps greater, density of industry. The city is the leading commercial centre for the region, has a sizeable centre (downtown) and a distinct skyline. Unlike New York City, however, the sun and sky still make their presence felt throughout Jacksonville. The city's considerable size is primarily horizontal, with the city spreading outwards for some 1,968 square km (760 square miles).

The downtown area is modest and welcoming and hardly seems fitting for a city of this size. Not far from the downtown, you can also still find plenty of quiet, leafy neighbourhoods filled with grand old homes. In addition, the city has made an effort in recent years to clean up its waterfronts, and several major development projects have livened up the areas along the wide St John's river, where ferries and pleasure boats regularly cruise the waters. The city hugs the river on both sides, extending a good way north, south and east, following it all the way until it reaches the Atlantic.

Not far from the urban environment of Jacksonville is the **Timucuan Ecological and Historic Preserve**, which brings together some of the best assets of the entire state: nature and history. The preserve is located between the Lower St Johns and Nassau rivers and consists of 46,000 acres of estuarine natural resources and historic and prehistoric sites. There are four important areas to the preserve: Fort Caroline National Memorial (commemorating an attempt by the French to establish a colony here in 1564), Kingsley Plantation (home to the oldest remaining plantation house in Florida), the Theodore Roosevelt Area (preserving a maritime hammock forest and salt marsh and evidence of the Timucuan people who once inhabited the area) and Cedar Point (an undeveloped area filled with informal hiking trails).

Although Jacksonville is recognized as the capital of the 'First Coast,' as the Northeast region is known, the origin of the nickname has more to do with the city of **St Augustine**. In 1565, the Spanish established St Augustine as a settlement to protect Spain's claim in the New World. The city has been occupied ever

The Versatile Coquina

The Castillo de San Marcos, the imposing Spanish fortress in St Augustine, was built out of *coquina*, a stone formed from the compressed shells of a creature of the same name. The stone was the Spaniards' favourite building material in the area, and at one time the land around the town would have been filled with *coquina* pits. In old St Augustine you may still find buildings that once served to house the numerous *coquina* quarriers brought over to do the heavy lifting. The workmen in 1670 would have been paid one *real* a day (20 cents), plus a corn ration, to haul *coquina* blocks so that they could be mortared into the rising fortress on the city's waterfront.

However, the *coquina* apparently produces more than just a durable building material. According to a local recipe, the tiny clams are the main ingredient in a delicate broth as well. During summer months, the *coquina* burrows into the sand as the tide washes them ashore. Simply scoop them from the sand, rinse them and place them in a pot with enough water to cover. Cook for about five minutes over medium heat until the shells pop open. Strain the broth and discard the shells. Add a little butter and light cream to taste. Garnish with chopped parsley or chives to add colour.

Case Study: There's No Place Like Home

Kathy Brimicombe arrived in Florida for the first time in May 1987. She was on holiday visiting her sister who was living just outside Miami with her American husband and son. It turned out to be the best holiday of Kathy's life. She felt at home and immediately knew she wanted to live in the Sunshine State. That same year, her sister and brother-in-law agreed to sponsor her so that she could apply for permanent residency in the USA. Kathy's daughter, Lucinda, was five years old at the time. By the time her mother received her green card in 2000, Lucinda was at the University of London.

'For those interim 13 years I put my life on hold while I waited for permission to move,' Kathy says. 'I devoured everything I could find on Florida: books, TV programmes, videos, anything and everything. I was obsessed with it. Each time I came over for a holiday I would go back with newspapers, magazines and brochures and study them at home.'

In December 2000, she moved to Florida from Felixstowe in Suffolk, one month after receiving her residency. Her daughter had decided to finish her education in the UK, so Kathy, whose sister had by then moved to Seattle, arrived in Florida on her own.

'I landed with $7,000, two suitcases, a hire car for three weeks and a rented villa for three weeks,' she says. 'My goal was to find somewhere to live, a car and a job in that time. It took a month to find a car but three weeks to move into an apartment and to start a job. I was very proud of myself.' She moved into the apartment with no furniture and waited for her personal possessions to arrive two months later.

The housing situation in Florida turned out to be much more complicated than Kathy had anticipated. She moved around a lot, and occasionally tried living with Americans, which never seemed to work out. During the worst periods, she found herself desperately wanting to return to the UK.

'When my health started to suffer I knew it was time to take matters into my own hands,' she recalls. 'Something prompted me to try and buy my own home so I applied for a mortgage.' With the salary from her office job, she was only able to secure a low mortgage. She put her dream of a beautiful villa with a pool on hold, and after a bit of searching found a decent home in Winter Springs, northeast of Orlando. She moved in February 2003.

'I have been so much happier since living in my own place. My health is getting back to normal and I feel much more relaxed and happy with my life. The downside is that I am a long way from my British friends in Kissimmee. But I can still see them at weekends.'

since. The most prominent feature of St Augustine is the Castillo de San Marcos National Monument, a stunning example of Spanish colonial fortification built between 1672 and 1695. In a country as young as the USA, any building that pre-dates the Civil War is especially impressive, and the Castillo definitely stands out. Not too far away, through the old City Gate, is the Spanish quarter, lined with restored 18th-century buildings which confirm that architecturally you cannot go much further back in time in America than in St Augustine.

There are still opportunities to buy some historic properties in downtown St Augustine, some of which may even be officially registered as such, but buying in historic districts often brings with it a lot of regulatory headaches, along with high prices. If you do choose to buy a home in this or any other area that is in any way designated as a historic district of some kind, be sure to research all the regulations and restrictions that accompany such a designation. Otherwise, you could end up with severe restrictions on what you can do on and to your own property or face huge bills trying to comply with historic building codes.

Outside downtown St Augustine, a number of family homes can be found in the $150,000 range. The median housing price in the area of St Augustine is probably not far from that of Jacksonville, which is the closest city listed in the periodic survey of housing prices by the FAR. At the beginning of 2006, the median price for an existing single-family home in Jacksonville was an affordable $197,900, a 17 per cent increase over the previous year.

The Centre

The centre of the state, like the north, is broken up into three regions: Central West, Central and Central East. This area of Florida is truly the state's heart, geographically and economically, especially if by 'heart' you mean the machine that pumps the life-blood, also known as tourist dollars, into the rest of the state. Even if only a small percentage of the millions of tourists who come to Florida to see the sprawling Walt Disney World® and other attractions decide to visit other areas of the state, it would still be a very noticeable contribution.

Nowhere is central Florida's prominence more evident than on a road map, where it is clear that all roads really do lead to Orlando, more so than the capital Tallahassee or even the international capital of Miami. This was not always the case. The population of the whole state has been expanding at a rate that has been called alarming by some, but the boom witnessed by the centre over the last three decades is in a category all by itself.

Clearly, for many, vacationing in Florida is about entertainment, and the growing number of people who continue to choose the Orlando area as their part-time home bodes well for the continued growth. However, the Central region, with its long periods of temperate weather (and few, usually short, periods of relative winter cold), has more to offer than just copyright-protected magic: there are internationally renowned car races, space shuttle launches, and a stunning variety of wildlife, including the rotund and docile manatee.

Legendary Mermaids

After what must have seemed a very, very long time at sea, Christopher Columbus and his crew spotted West Indian manatees in Caribbean waters and immediately assumed that they had come upon the legendary mermaids reportedly seen by earlier sailors. Or so one legend goes. Some legends do not mention Columbus, but from close up it is hard to believe that anyone – especially a seasoned traveller like Columbus – would confuse these marine mammals with even half of a woman, no matter how wishful their thinking.

The Florida manatee is actually a subspecies of the West Indian species, but it still sports a similar large girth and the decidedly unfeminine whiskered snout. It bears a similarity to an oversized toothless walrus but is actually a distant relative of the elephant.

The Florida manatee is an incredibly docile creature that feasts primarily on seagrass and other vegetation and, although it is mostly a solitary animal, it occasionally huddles together with others of its kind in its constant search for warm waters. Its gentle nature, slow movements and vegetarian diet make it easy to understand the manatee's other name: sea cow. But, according to some, the name actually comes from the fact that the animal tastes like beef.

Today in Florida it would be inconceivable even to suggest eating this endangered species, but in fact hunting is what put the animal on the endangered species list in the first place. Relatives of the Florida manatee are still hunted for meat off the coasts of Africa, but the ones found in warm waters all over the Sunshine State have very few natural predators now that they are protected. Unfortunately, because they are drawn to the same warm waters that attract people, recreational sailors have become their biggest enemy, for they are vulnerable to dangerous and sometimes deadly engine propellers.

Central West

The Central West region, with its several hundred miles of white sand coastline, where the shallow waters of the Gulf of Mexico are swimmable even in winter, is made up of eight counties: Citrus, De Soto, Hernando, Hillsborough, Manatee, Pasco, Pinellas and Sarasota. The urban area all around Tampa, St Petersburg and south to Sarasota has developed more slowly than other areas but has seen accelerated growth over the last few years. Today it is home to a couple of million people, ranging from retired or semi-retired families to young professionals.

When compared with the Atlantic coast, it is surprising that the area's charms have remained undiscovered for so long, especially when you realize that the bay was discovered by Spain in 1539 and was the launching point for the first large-scale European expedition into the interior southern USA. On the south shore of Tampa Bay, a national memorial to the expedition's leader, Hernando de Soto, commemorates this historic event.

Today, the city of **Tampa** is the business and commercial centre of the west coast, and has the skyscrapers and motorway (freeways) – and rush hour – to prove it. It also has the requisite museums and other cultural attractions that make it an important urban centre for the entire region. The city is an active international port and hosts several major cruise companies, which bring in important tourism business as well as everything else that goes along with docking vessels often the size of small cities. The presence of an international port has also had the side-effect of injecting a varied and interesting ethnic mix into the Tampa area; Greek, Scottish and Cuban enclaves, among several others, are interspersed throughout the area.

Ybor City is recognized today as a Cuban neighbourhood just on the edge of Tampa, but a walk through its quaint streets reveals a slightly more mixed past, including Italian and Portuguese roots commemorated in signs and plaques all over the neighbourhood. More recently, Ybor City has developed into a trendy area and signs of an active nightlife abound, with exciting restaurants, bars and clubs tucked underneath the wrought-iron balconies. The turnaround of the neighbourhood has brought with it larger-scale commercial development, including shops and cinema complexes.

Just across the bay, St Petersburg serves as an idyllic counterpart to the more urban Tampa. The city boasts a beautiful waterfront area and surprising cultural offerings, including the most comprehensive collection of original work by Salvador Dalí. The 95 oil paintings in the Salvador Dalí Museum were collected over a 45-year period by A. Reynolds Morse and Eleanor Morse, and have become a mecca for fans of the Spanish surrealist and art lovers in general.

The southernmost county in the Central West region is Sarasota, and within its boundaries is a well-established resort town also called Sarasota. In addition to being known as an artists' retreat, the town of **Sarasota** has an unexpected association with the circus; John Ringling, the circus tycoon, chose the town to be a vacation home for his performers when they were not on the road performing (*see* box opposite). He also built a small palace for himself on Sarasota Bay, which today is open to the public along with his art museum and a museum dedicated to circus memorabilia.

Ringling may have brought laughter and wonder to the masses, but he defi-nitely did not live among them; Sarasota is one of the most expensive housing markets in the state. According to FAR, at the beginning of 2006 the average price for an existing single-family home was $353,500. The Tampa–St Petersburg area is a relative bargain in comparison, with an average price of $219,700 for the same period. But, while the housing prices may hover just below the state average, the Tampa–St Petersburg area leads the way in terms of number of homes sold. With over 2,749 sold in the first month of 2006, the city is clearly home to a disproportionately large and active housing market. The combined population of Tampa and St Petersburg is still less than Miami's, but the number of homes sold is almost five times the size.

The Ringling Museum of the American Circus

In 1927, when John Ringling moved the winter quarters of the Ringling Bros and Barnum & Bailey Circus from Bridgeport, Connecticut to Sarasota, the west Florida town suddenly became inseparably associated with the magical world of the circus.

The winter quarters opened its doors to visitors on Christmas Day 1927, and it quickly became the number one tourist attraction in the state. Granted, back then it did not have too much competition, but it did draw hundreds of thousands of people who came to find out what circus people did when they were not actually performing. The mix of clowns, exotic animals and flexible performers must have made an interesting addition to the sleepy town.

The Ringling Museum of the American Circus was established in 1948, ostensibly as a way of keeping alive the memory of the man who brought the circus to Sarasota permanently. The museum documents, preserves and exhibits the history of the circus in America, which began in 1793 in Philadelphia.

The collection includes rare handbills, art prints, circus paper, business records, wardrobe and performing props, as well as all types of circus equipment, including beautifully carved parade wagons, tent poles and massive bail rings. A large collection of circus history and literature includes newspaper clippings dating as far back as 1816. Not surprisingly, the sizeable number of circus people still living in the immediate area of Sarasota helped the museum's collection to expand quickly.

Central

Three decades ago, few people outside Florida had heard of Orlando or Kissimmee. Some people recall the area back then as a natural magic kingdom of emerald lakes, citrus groves and dirt roads, where farming communities lived side by side with communities of alligators and egrets. Where a few select people might have come for fishing or birdwatching in the 1960s, today millions travel each year to visit cartoon characters, defy gravity, and watch animals do tricks on command, or roam in fake freedom.

As an official central Florida attraction, the recently closed Cypress Gardens predated the 1971 opening of **Walt Disney World®** by over 30 years, but it is undisputed that Disney's transformation of 28,000 acres of farmland into a family playground is what put **Orlando** on the map. Other companies soon followed, banking on the hope that some of that Disney magic would rub off. Clearly, it did. The success of Disney World® is even more impressive if you stop and think that its creators chose not to capitalize on the state's most bankable asset – its abundance of beautiful coastline – and chose instead to build inland. However, this does not mean that the Orlando area is dry; in fact, it has one of the highest concentration of lakes anywhere in the continental USA, and is by all accounts a boating paradise.

Gone in the Wind

Say the names Wilma, Katrina, Jeanne, Frances, Charley to most Floridians and they'll know you're not going through a party guest list but reciting the names of the major hurricanes that spun out of control, causing violent winds, incredible waves, torrential rains, floods, devastation and death, in Florida in 2004 and 2005 alone. Over the last hundred years Florida has had around 60 major hurricanes – about a third of all those hitting the USA. Since 1979 a rotating list of Atlantic storm names has been used. These alternate between male and female names and provide a handy form of reference for locating, warning and making insurance claims; and to reduce confusion when several storms occur simultaneously. The names of the most destructive hurricanes are usually retired.

A hurricane is the most violent form of a tropical cyclone – the term for a low-pressure system that typically forms in the tropics, producing strong thunderstorms, well-defined surface circulation and sustained winds of 74mph upwards. The hurricane season runs from early June to late November, with each rated between 1 and 5 on Saffir-Simpson Scale according to wind strength. Yet, though Category 5 hurricanes have the strongest winds, they won't necessarily inflict the most damage. This depends more on their location and what associated hazards they bring, particularly in terms of floods.

As much of Florida still remembers, the costliest hurricane ever was Hurricane Andrew, which devastated the Homestead and southern Miami-Dade areas in 1992 with winds of up to 177mph. After predicting for days that the storm would pass just north of them, most people in Miami and Homestead were

Even after factoring in prices for the rather exclusive and frighteningly charming (the downtown has its own musical soundtrack, piped in through small, ground-level speakers) town of **Celebration** – Disney's interpretation of Seaside – the median price for an existing single-family home in the area remains reasonable and a good $10,000 below the state average, according to FAR. Prices may not stay that way for long. At the beginning of 2006, the average price in the Orlando area was $254,100, a significant jump from $187,800 the year before. In addition, like the Tampa–St Petersburg area to the west, Orlando's housing market is an active one. The population of the Orlando area is not even a million, yet it comes in a very close second in terms of numbers of houses sold.

Central East

The 'Thunder Coast', as the Central East region is sometimes known, is home to five counties – Brevard, Indian River, Okeechobee, St Lucie and Volusia – a couple of which are responsible for the area's nickname. If you are interested in investing in this area for its beaches, do not be put off by the nickname, because unprepared for the change in path. In the event 23 lives were lost and the estimated damage was $26.5 billion. In the wake of the hurricane came new construction standards stipulating various improvements including storm shutters. However, Florida's fiercest and deadliest hurricane on record struck the Florida Keys over the Labor Day weekend in 1935. With record-setting low barometric pressure of 892mb, winds are thought to have reached almost 200mph. Thankfully in those days the Keys were not very heavily populated, yet all the same 390 people died as roads, buildings, viaducts, bridges and the railroad were annihalated and the tiny island of Islamorada taken clean off the map.

High winds that destroy poorly constructed buildings are clearly one of the major hazards of a hurricane as signs and roofing materials turn into flying missiles, and sometimes hurricanes give birth to tornadoes. Yet the effects of the associated floods are every bit as destructive, causing more than half the deaths associated with hurricanes. Seawater pushed shorewards by winds produces an advancing surge, which can combine with the normal tides to form a hurricane storm tide, often increasing the water level by more than 15 feet.

As a homeowner it is vital that you investigate your home's vulnerability to storm surges, flooding and wind; the checklist of the National Hurricane Center (**www.nhc.noaa.gov**) can help organize your thoughts. Also check your insurance coverage, since flood damage is not usually covered by homeowners' insurance. The National Flood Insurance Program (**www.floodsmart.gov**) exists to give you the heads-up on this.

it has nothing to do with the weather. The 'thunder' comes from the world-famous Daytona Speedway, which fills the air around Daytona Beach with the roar of racing cars, and also from the rocket blasts that propel one of NASA's shuttles into space at Cape Canaveral, occasionally shattering the silence of the Merritt Island National Wildlife Refuge.

The presence of NASA's **John F. Kennedy Space Centre** is responsible for the area's more-recognized nickname – the 'Space Coast' – but it also helped create the longest stretch of preserved coastline on the east coast of Florida. The presence of the agency in the area required a buffer from any kind of development. The resulting 57,662 acres of undeveloped beach and wetlands, known as Canaveral National Seashore, offer sanctuary to 1,000 species of plants and 300 species of birds. The seashore is within the **Merritt Island National Wildlife Refuge**, and is only a fraction of the refuge's 140,000 preserved acres. In preserves like this, you can wander freely among rare and not so rare creatures, and remind yourself that Florida is indeed home to a truly incredible amount of natural beauty.

Then there is **Daytona Beach**. While the city's 850km (530 miles) of flat white sands are a remarkable natural phenomenon, these firm, wide beaches have

The Return of the Spoonbill

Should you find yourself roaming about the Merritt Island National Wildlife Refuge and happen to spot a couple of lanky pink birds, you may be tempted to think that you have just come across the colourful flamingoes that populate so much of Florida's advertising. More than likely, however, you will actually be looking at roseate spoonbills, the only spoonbill species found in the western hemisphere, and the fact that you are able to look at them is the result of a long ongoing campaign to bring the creatures back from near-extinction.

The birds were almost extinguished by avid collectors and hunters in the 1800s, all of whom prized their bright plumage. By the middle of the 19th century the birds' feathers were commonly used to decorate fans and popular hats, and soon the breeding population in the Indian River Lagoon was all but wiped out. It was not until the turn of the century that conservationists began to fight for the protection of the endangered bird. Hunters fought back, even going so far as to kill two wardens hired to patrol vital breeding areas.

The market for the feathers eventually subsided and, thanks to the efforts of conservationists, populations of spoonbills have rebounded all over the state, even appearing where they did not exist before. Throughout the 20th century, the population has grown steadily, and by the mid-1970s researchers counted over 1,200 pairs of spoonbills in Florida Bay. In 1975 they discovered eight more pairs in Tampa Bay, where soon afterwards the population reached 300 pairs. However, it wasn't until the mid-1980s that the first breeding spoonbills returned to Merritt Island's Indian River Lagoon, where once again they can be admired for their beauty.

been an attraction for so many years because people can physically and legally drive on them. During high season, the beaches turn into a main street of sorts, with locals and college students parading their vehicles among the bathing suits. As Fort Lauderdale in the south has tried to retire from the fleeting college crowds, Daytona Beach, for better or worse, has embraced them over the years, taking over as Florida's leading spring break destination. The mix of hotels and motels that line the real main street that parallels the beach beckon to the young tourists, boasting of nightly and weekly deals, and there is no mistaking the fact that the town caters to a seasonal crowd.

Beyond Daytona Beach, the urban areas in this region extend from **Titusville**, which is on the coast just across from the Merritt Island National Wildlife Refuge, on down through **Melbourne** and on to **Port St Lucie**, which marks the southern end of the Central East region. Silence comes at a premium, however. To get well away from the thundering roar of race cars and space shuttles will cost you markedly more. Daytona, according to FAR, with a median price of $222,600 for an existing single-family home at the beginning of 2006, turns out to be at the lower end of the market and similar to the the Titusville–

Case Study: Love at First Sight

Peter and Jean Stanhope had never been to Florida until 1985, when they took a four-day side-trip to Walt Disney World® from a business convention. As they landed in Orlando, they were greeted by the sight of green landscapes filled with palm trees and sparkling lakes. Although this welcoming vision stuck with them long after the trip was over, buying a second home anywhere – much less Florida – could not have been further from their minds at the time.

The 'bug' to buy a holiday home somewhere did not hit them until four years later when they were on holiday in France. At the time, they were both in their 50s and their children had grown up and left home. The Stanhopes decided it was a good time to consider a holiday home. They looked around in the south of France but discovered that property was expensive, the cost of living was high and they were not comfortable with the language barrier.

When they returned home to York from their holiday, Peter noticed a small advertisement in the Sunday newspaper for villas in Orlando, not far from Disney World®. In those days, only one builder was marketing in the UK. Peter and Jean sent off for the information and, when it arrived, they were amazed at the good value available in Florida compared with locations in the Med.

'Within seven days we had attended a presentation in Leeds,' says Peter, 'and within another seven days we were in Orlando taking a "Fly 'n' buy" tour.' Over the five-day trip, the Stanhopes made the decision to buy their very own three-bedroom villa with pool, on a golf course, 20 minutes from Walt Disney World®. 'If we could believe just half of the figures on vacation rental income that the management company had projected,' says Peter, 'then we could make it work as a holiday retreat for us – and a source of rental income, too.' The couple also predicted – quite correctly, as it turned out – that although at the time Spain and France were still popular for the British, 'Florida was the future.'

The Stanhopes bought their holiday home in Florida at a less confusing time, when there was little to choose from. They consider themselves lucky to have had the good fortune to buy from a good builder and have had a good experience despite not knowing the market well. However, they strongly caution others to be wary of unscrupulous salesmen who make outrageous promises.

Once the Stanhopes made their purchase, they realized how little they knew about running a home in Florida. In order to educate themselves, they decided to seek out other people who were in the same position, and ended up creating an informal support group where they could share experiences. The support group eventually became the **Florida Brits Group** (**www.floridabritsgroup.com**), which sponsors information and social get-togethers around the UK for people who own holiday homes in Florida.

'Jean and I are now into our golden years of wintering in Florida,' says Peter. The couple still enjoy the three- or four-month-long 'short-sleeve winters' in the Florida sunshine, as well as all the natural attractions the state has to offer. 'And, yes, we do still occasionally go to Disney World®!'

Melbourne area, where the median price was $219,100 for the same period. Prices appear to go up as you move south into the Port St Lucie area, where the median price is $261,500.

The South

Southern Florida is where the 'northerners' come to play, relax and lose their inhibitions, or simply lose themselves. This is the Florida of baseball spring training, of impossibly beautiful people parading in South Beach, of mansions by the sea, and of the southernmost point in the land, Key West. Unexpectedly, it is also the Florida of seemingly endless nature that pushes right up to the edge of the continent. Squeezed in between the two populated regions that make up the area, the Southeast and the Southwest, is Everglades National Park, the largest subtropical wilderness in continental USA.

The south is also where the country takes on its most distinctive Caribbean flavour, which comes from the climate and from the mixture of people from every island nation. The weather turns decidedly tropical below Fort Myers and Fort Pierce. The summer can be oppressive at times but the winter is filled with perfect warm days and cool nights. If tropical days and nights are exactly what you are looking for in the Sunshine State, then you will definitely have some company. Clearly, that is what the majority of people are after, because in this part of the state you will find some of the most expensive housing markets in the entire country. While some experts believe that the prices cannot last and that the bubble will burst, the market shows no sign of slowing down and homes continue to appreciate at record levels.

Southwest

The Southwest is made up of five counties – Charlotte, Collier, Glades, Hendry and Lee – that sit just to the west of the Everglades. This strip of coast is home to thousands of permanent retired residents and 'snowbirds' – retirees who migrate each winter to Florida. Compared with the other southern coast, however, this is a relatively relaxed region, with the combined population of its two most developed counties (where Naples and Fort Myers are located) coming in at around three-quarters of a million people. The larger of the two cities, **Fort Myers**, is well known to some for the fact that it's the Boston Red Sox's spring training ground and is where the Minnesota Twins play exhibition games. To others it is well known for being the former winter home of both Thomas Edison and Henry Ford. In fact, the area has something for everyone.

Adding to the mix of history and sports, the Southwest region is also known for its stunningly beautiful and well-preserved barrier islands, most notably

Sanibel and **Captiva**. The two islands are connected to the mainland by a 5km- (3 mile)-long causeway just southwest of Fort Myers, which is located a few kilometres inland on the shores of the Caloosahatchee River. While Sanibel and Captiva's connection to the mainland is the most likely reason why these two have become the most visited of the barrier islands, other islands reachable only by boat, such as **Gasparilla**, have been seeing wintering northerners since the early 1900s. To some extent development has reached all of the islands, but, whether because of the limited accessibility, the resolve of the locals, or the creation of refuges such as the **J. N. 'Ding' Darling National Wildlife Refuge**, overall the barrier islands offer at least a glimpse of a glorious and distant Florida past. At over 6,300 acres, the Darling refuge covers about a third of Sanibel, and is home to several threatened and endangered species, such as eastern indigo snakes, American alligators, bald eagles, wood storks, peregrine falcons, West Indian manatees and Atlantic loggerhead turtles. If chasing wildlife does not appeal, perhaps collecting shells will. Sanibel is considered to be among the best shelling grounds in the world, where you will find people walking the shell-covered beaches and practising the 'Sanibel stoop' as they search for rare prizes.

Naples does not feel so much like a city as it does a series of residences – large-scale gated developments or mansions on or near the beach. The historic downtown area is a fancy intersection of roads lined with expensive cars, pricey stores and upmarket cafés and restaurants. The downtown area and the scale of some of the houses hidden among the streets lined with palm trees suggest that Naples is not the place for just anyone. However, if you head over to the Naples Pier, an old dock reaching out from the busy beach into the Gulf where ships once docked (the pier has been reconstructed), you will find an friendly mix of people. Retirees, whether temporary or permanent residents, predominate, but people of all ages can be found enjoying the day fishing among the numerous and not so shy pelicans.

The most remarkable fact about Naples is the appreciation in property value it has seen over the last decade. Whether it is the international populations that have settled there, or the perception and promotion of it as a Palm Beach on the Gulf, the Naples area has become the most expensive housing market in Florida. According to FAR, at the beginning of 2006, the median price for an existing single-family home was $511,400. At the same time, the area also registered a 31 percentage drop over the previous year in the number of homes sold, suggesting the market may be slowing down.

Perhaps benefiting from the overflow of people priced out of the nearby Naples market, has seen a far smaller drop in the number of homes sold and a 31 percentage increase in the value of those that did sell. Still, at $287,200, the median price for an existing single-family home in the Fort Myers area remains a bargain compared with those in Naples.

Southeast

Everglades National Park dominates much of the southern tip of Florida, almost as if the tip of the state had been dipped in lush green ink. The 1.5 million acre subtropical wilderness has extensive fresh, river and salt-water areas, plus open Everglades prairies, hardwood tree islands, cypress domes, pinelands and mangrove forests. This wilderness is also the only known meeting place of alligators and crocodiles, which do not co-exist anywhere else in the world.

What is more even remarkable is that just to the east of this vast wilderness is an urban wilderness unlike anywhere in the state. Of the five counties that make up the southeast region – Broward, Martin, Miami-Dade, Monroe and Palm Beach – three are the most populated in all of Florida. Nearly a third of the state's population lives in the southeast.

The 'Gold Coast', as the **Palm Beach** area is known, got its name from the treasures recovered from the many sunken shipwrecks off its coast. But the concentration of wealth and *Fortune 500* companies in the area perpetuates

From Another Time and Place

In addition to its notable Art Deco architecture, Miami is also home to a monastery that was built between 1133 and 1141. Considering that there were not a lot of people living in Florida at that time – much less any monks – this simple statement of fact sounds like a riddle. The solution is really quite simple. The Monastery of St Bernard de Clairvaux was actually built in Sacramenia, in the Province of Segovia, Spain. Cistercian monks occupied the monastery for nearly 700 years until a social revolution in the 1830s resulted in the cloisters being seized, sold and converted into a granary and stable. William Randolph Hearst purchased the cloisters and the monastery's outbuildings in 1925. He had them dismantled stone by stone, bound with protective hay, packed in 11,000 wooden crates, numbered for identification and shipped to the USA.

This part of the story should serve as a timeless piece of advice. Because foot and mouth disease had broken out recently in Segovia, the US Department of Agriculture quarantined the shipment when it arrived. Agents broke open the crates and burned the hay, which was a possible carrier of the disease. Before storing the shipment, workmen packed all the stones back into the crates. Unfortunately, they put them in the wrong crates. And then, because of Hearst's mounting financial problems, the stones remained in a warehouse in Brooklyn, New York, for 26 years.

In 1952, one year after Hearst's death, W. Edgemon and R. Moss purchased the stones and spent 19 months and almost $1.5 million dollars reassembling them. Their plan was to turn the monastery into a tourist attraction. Instead, the building returned to its original use and became the Church of St Bernard de Clairvaux, named in honour of the saint who was a leading influence among the Cistercians 847 years ago.

the appropriateness of the nickname. Palm Beach County stretches along many miles of oceanfront, from **Tequesta** in the north to **Boca Raton** in the south. Many of Florida's wealthier retirees make their home along the Gold Coast.

Miami is also a major contributor, in terms of population and wealth, to the region and marks the beginning and end of Florida for some people. For those who consider South Beach to be where life begins and ends, there is not much else that the state has to offer; for those arriving from points south – sometimes illegally – Miami is literally the beginning of a new life in a new country. Whatever it represents and whether people love it or hate it, Miami has a strong personality that is definitely the sum of its disparate parts. The exciting mix of ethnic communities scattered throughout the city and its suburbs is testimony to its status as an international gateway. By far the most recognizable international community is the Cuban one, which is understandable since Cuba is a mere 145km (90 miles) off the coast of Key West.

Today, Miami's South Beach proudly displays its wealth of restored Art Deco architecture and happily bathes itself in pastel colours. Its reputation as the meeting point of the famous and wealthy from North and South America is well established. However, the Miami area has gone through some interesting ups and downs in its history. The area grew steadily at the beginning of the 20th century thanks to the new railway (railroad) and to the thriving citrus industry, but when the south Florida land rush hit in the 1920s Miami found itself bursting at the seams with people arriving sometimes at the rate of 6,000 a day. The city also soon found itself at the centre of countless shattered dreams as many of the new arrivals discovered they had spent their life savings on a plot of swampland. Many people remained despite this unfortunate discovery. Not until the end of the Second World War did the city go through another remarkable expansion, when its population nearly doubled, after which things quieted down for a bit.

The city gained a certain exotic notoriety in the early 1980s when it became the backdrop for a popular television show called *Miami Vice*. The show highlighted the colourful style of the city and portrayed it as an exciting place – one that would fall entirely into the hands of South American drug lords were it not for the efforts of two stylishly dressed undercover police officers. The questionable fame suggested by the show helped promote the city to those who had not yet discovered it, and the current series of *CSI: Miami* continue reinforcing its popularity and glamour. Young people now flock to Miami in search of excitement and liberation, a far cry from the post-war retirees and vacationers who came in search of peace and warmth. What was once a seasonal destination or in many cases a final destination has become a year-round playground.

The Keys are sometimes categorized as a region in their own right – often by the locals in the self-appointed capital of the island chain, **Key West** – but technically they are part of the Southeast region, which should be very happy to have them. This chain of beautiful islands, in a brilliant Caribbean blue setting,

The Conch Republic

Occasionally, you may hear the Florida Keys referred to as the Conch Republic. The 'legal' boundaries of this republic extend from its capital, Key West, northward to 'Skeeter's Last Chance Saloon' in Florida City. All territories north of Key West are referred to as 'The Northern Territories'. The nation's boundaries were established in 1982. The northernmost boundary point was selected because it was the site of the US border patrol blockade that triggered the 'secession'.

The blockade was set up on Route 1, at Florida City, the gateway to the Keys and the only way on or off the islands by land. The Conch Republic was established by secession from the USA on 23 April 1982 in response to the blockade. Citizens of the Keys claimed that the government act had isolated them and had portrayed them as non-US citizens who had to prove their citizenship in order to drive on to the Florida mainland.

The mayor of Key West at the time, Dennis Wardlow, along with a few others, went to the federal court in Miami to seek an injunction to stop the federal blockade. As he left the courthouse, and having failed in his mission, he announced to the assembled reporters that the Florida Keys would secede from the Union the following day at noon.

At the appointed time, Wardlow read the proclamation of secession and announced that the Conch Republic was an independent nation separate from the USA. The Conch Republic's first and only act of civil rebellion occurred when the mayor – who had now proclaimed himself prime minister – broke a loaf of stale Cuban bread over the head of a man dressed in a US Navy uniform. One minute later, Prime Minister Wardlow surrendered to the Union forces by turning himself over to the admiral in charge of the Navy base in Key West. The prime minister then demanded one billion dollars in foreign aid and war relief to rebuild his nation.

The Conch Republic even has its own 'official' passport. Although some government members, notably the Secretary General of the Conch Republic, claim that they have used it for travel to several European and Caribbean nations, you should not abandon your UK passport just yet!

extends 120km (75 miles) south and west from the Miami area and ends in Key West, which falls almost longitudinally in line with Naples.

This stretch of Route 1 is also known as the Overseas Highway and runs across the islands over an impressive series of bridges that connect 45 of the Keys to the mainland. Mile Marker 0 in Key West is the end of the line for the north–south route and is also a popular photographic spot with tourists. However, it is not where the Keys end; 70 nautical miles west of Key West is **Dry Tortugas National Park**, a group of seven additional islands. Amid the 259 square km (100 square miles) of shoals, water and coral gardens of these distant keys is **Fort Jefferson**, a 19th-century American coastal fort. Fort Jefferson is not only the largest fort of its kind, but its setting in the middle of a beautiful blue emptiness guarantees that it is one of the most extraordinary.

When it comes to real estate, location is important, but so is supply. In the case of the Keys, the combination of a stunning location with limited supply inevitably equals a very expensive housing market. In 2005, the average price of all the homes sold in the Keys was $393,000. At the top end of the scale is Key West where the average price for a single-family home was $481,000. In the Upper Keys, the price was $389,100; in the Middle Keys, $417,600; and in the Lower Keys, $302,200.

As exclusive as the Keys appear to be, Palm Beach county is even more so. The county includes Boca Raton, Delray Beach, Jupiter Island and West Palm Beach and, taken as a whole, its median housing price (this includes new and old homes and condominiums) was $220,000 at the start of 2006 – not the most expensive area in the state but definitely at the top end of the market. This figure is a bit surprising, however, considering that Jupiter Island is among the top 10 richest towns in the USA.

Key Lime Pie: The Official Dessert of Key West

Key lime pie is a delicacy that was born out of necessity. You will find the dessert all over the country today in all kinds of variations and colours (sometimes it is dyed green) but for the original – deep yellow in colour – you must travel to Key West where the recipe originated during leaner times.

Before the arrival of the railroad in 1912, it was hard to get fresh milk in isolated Key West. Canned condensed milk, invented in the mid-19th century, was a common substitute because it could travel and could stay fresh for long periods of time. Combined with the juice of the very sour Key lime, condensed milk made a good custard-like filling for pies without the need for cooking because the sour juice curdled the milk and egg yolks into just the right consistency. It is likely that pie crusts were used originally but eventually the Graham cracker crust became the standard. Today most places bake the pie through fear of salmonella poisoning from the eggs. One interesting variation is dipping the pie in chocolate.

There is some debate over the merits of topping the dessert with meringue or whipped cream, but one of the most important signs of authenticity is that it be made with actual Key limes, which is rare outside Key West. Until the 1926 hurricane wiped out the citrus groves, Key limes were grown commercially throughout southern Florida and the Florida Keys. Persian lime trees, whose fruit is the larger, sturdier lime you see in supermarkets today, replaced the Key lime trees because they are hardier, easier to harvest and the fruits are more durable. You will still find many Key lime trees throughout the Keys but they are mostly in private gardens (backyards). Commercial production is extremely limited, which means of course that the fruit comes at a premium.

It would seem fair to assume that there must be a considerable supply of inexpensive properties in the county to make up for Jupiter Island's $5.6 million median home price. However Jupiter Island's small population of 620 fails to make too much of a financial impression in the county and moreover the area has not yet finished appreciating in value; the West Palm Beach–Boca Raton area is also among the top 20 metropolitan areas with the highest rated appreciation in house prices. Of the 11 Florida entries in the list, the West Palm Beach–Boca Raton area is seventh.

It is also interesting to note that the tenth of the 11 Florida entries in the top 20 highest rates of house price appreciation is **Fort Lauderdale**, which is also in the Southeast region. It would have been hard to believe a few years ago that this small city 45 minutes north of Miami would have become one of the highest priced markets in the state, let alone the country. Real estate values have escalated 125 per cent in Broward county since 2000, and at the beginning of 2006 the median sales price for an existing single-family home in Fort Lauderdale was over $370,500. For the same period, the median price in Miami was $376,300.

Selecting a Property

04

It's time to select a property. If you thought we had left all the questions behind in the last chapters, you're wrong. At this point, you may know why and where you are buying, but there are still plenty of things you need to ask yourself before you are ready to put your money down. What style of house suits you? What can you afford? In this chapter you will discover that selecting a property is about much more than location alone.

Travelling to Florida

The large body of water separating the UK from the USA leaves visitors to the Sunshine State with only two travel options: air and sea. As yet, no ferry service exists between the two countries, which means that going by sea would involve taking a cruise line. If time is short – which it may well be if you are travelling to visit property or else wanting to spend as much of your vacation as possible in your new home – then air travel is really the only option. Fortunately, with 13 international airports and six regional airports, not to mention countless smaller local airports, Florida is extremely accessible by aeroplane. As always, with a bit of planning, air travel can be quite affordable.

Air

Many US airlines have been claiming that they are on the verge of going out of business as a result of falling national tourism. In some cases this has resulted in more competitive fares as the airlines try to lure travellers back, but it has also meant that some carriers have reduced the frequency of their services. Be sure to check the latest rules and regulations on the airline's website regarding what items are permitted in hand luggage – UK–USA flights have the most strngent regulations.

Several airlines offer a non-stop service to Miami, Orlando and Tampa but if you are travelling to smaller cities and towns you will probably have to go through another airport first. Some flights are more direct than others and you might be involved in some stopovers along the way – particularly in New York, Newark, Washington and Atlanta – but others, such as Chicago, will take you halfway across the country and add a bit to your travel time.

In addition to scheduled services, a wide number of charter operators offer cheap flights to Orlando from most of the major UK airports, with a particularly good selection of flights available from London Gatwick, Manchester and Birmingham. Additionally, low-cost carrier Flyglobespan (**t** 08705 561 522; **www.flyglobespan.com**) offesr daily flights to Orlando from Glasgow.

Be sure to check all airports close to your destination. It may make sense to fly into an airport that is a bit further away but which offers non-stop service. For example, not all flights from the UK into St Petersburg are direct, while Tampa, just across the bay, offers non-stop service to London.

The main carriers are:

- **US Airways (t 08456 00 33 00; www.usairways.com)** serves most major Florida cities from London Gatwick with daily flights via Philadelphia, Pittsburgh or Charlotte and direct flights to Orlando and Tampa.

- **Virgin (t 0870 380 2007; www.virgin-atlantic.com)** flies to Orlando from London Gatwick (daily) and from Manchester (six days per week) and daily from London Heathrow to Miami.

- **United Airlines (t 08458 444 777; www.unitedairlines.co.uk)** has daily flights out of London Heathrow to New York and Washington DC, where there are connecting flights to many Florida airports including Jacksonville, Palm Beach International, Fort Lauderdale-Hollywood, Miami, Tampa, Fort Myers and Orlando.

- **Lufthansa (t 08457 737 747; www.lufthansa.co.uk)** offers daily flights from Dublin, Edinburgh, London City, London Heathrow and Manchester to Frankfurt where you can take a connecting flight to Chicago, Washington or Charlotte and then another to Miami or Orlando.

- **British Airways (t 0870 850 9850; www.britishairways.com)** flies direct from London Gatwick to Orlando (daily); Tampa (five per week); and from London Heathrow to Miami (daily).

- **British Midland/BMI (t 0870 607 0555; www.flybmi.com)** offers daily flights to Orlando International from Manchester via Chicago.

- **Air France (t 08701 42 43 43; www.airfrance.com/uk)** flies daily from London Heathrow via Paris to Miami or via Paris and Atlanta to most major Florida airports.

- **American (t 0845 778 9789; www.aa.com)** flies from London Heathrow and Manchester to Miami (both daily).

- **Continental (t 0845 607 6760; www.continental.com/uk)** flies from Birmingham, Bristol, Edinburgh, Glasgow, Manchester, London Gatwick to New York (Newark) for connecting flights to Florida.

- **KLM/Northwest (t 08705 074 074; www.klm.com)** KLM and its partner Northwest service most major cities in Florida via Amsterdam and New York or Atlanta.

- **Delta (t 0800 414 767; www.delta.com)** flies from Edinburgh, London Gatwick and Manchester to Atlanta for connecting flights to most major Florida airports.

Travelling around Florida

Unless you have already picked out exactly where you want to live, selecting a property is going to involve some travel around the state. At about 140,000 square km (54,000 square miles) in size, the state is a little over half the size of the UK. This makes for a relatively manageable piece of land to travel around in.

If you are on a tight schedule and have picked out a few specific spots you wish to visit as quickly as possible, travelling by air may be the most efficient way to go. However, if you have a bit of time, the best way to experience all the glories of the state is from the road. Staying close to the ground is also a good way to get lost, which may additionally lead to discovering areas that you never knew existed.

Air

Most of the major American carriers featured above will take you around the state as well as getting you there in the first place. The websites listed for the American carriers are for the UK market but they are linked to their American counterparts, where you will find information about flights within the USA. Some of the carriers will use partner airlines or subsidiaries for shorter trips, such as those within a state, but you can still book online through the main site.

In addition to the major carriers there are a couple of smaller airlines that service select areas in Florida. The main carrier is **Gulfstream International Airlines** (t 800 525-0280; **www.gulfstreamair.com**), which services Miami, Fort Lauderdale, West Palm Beach, Tampa, Tallahasse, Fort Walton, Pensacola, Gainesville, Orlando, Jacksonville, and Key West.

If you plan to move around by air, then you will have to get to know the location and availability of airports in each area. For a comprehensive list of the commercial airports in Florida and for links to each of their sites, visit **www.airnav.com/airports/us/FL**. Most of the airport sites also list the airlines that fly into it.

Rail

The railways (railroads) played a vital part in the history of the USA; they connected the east and west coasts and opened up entire parts of the country to development, including Florida. Sadly, today rail travel in the USA is almost a last resort for the majority of people. There are stretches of track along the east coast, from Washington to New York, for example, that do see their fair share of passengers, but for most journeys it is cheaper and faster to go by air.

The railroad's lack of popularity – or perhaps its poor management – is most apparent in the ongoing financial struggles of the nation's primary passenger service, Amtrak. Even after sizeable government subsidies, this semi-public

Henry Flagler and the Florida East Coast Railway

In 1912, the first train to travel the full length of Florida East Coast Railway's newly completed overseas connection arrived in Key West. The company's founder, Henry Flagler, was on board, and his triumphant arrival at the end of the line represented the pinnacle of everything he had put into linking the entire east coast of the state. He had built hotels at strategic points along the railway line and had developed Florida's agricultural and tourism industries in order to give his trains a reason to exist.

The amazing thing is that he did all this in his retirement years. Before he had turned his attention to Florida, Flagler had helped found the Standard Oil monopoly, an empire so powerful that it eventually drew the attention and anger of the US government.

Flagler visited Florida for the first time in 1878, and immediately recognized its growth potential, as well as its lack of hotel accommodation. Seven years later he began construction of a grand hotel, the Hotel Ponce de Leon, in St Augustine (today the building is home to Flagler College). Knowing that a solid transportation system was the key to development, he purchased the Jacksonville, St Augustine and Halifax River Railroad, and immediately converted it to a standard gauge track so that it could connect up to other rails. The line served the northeastern region of the state, and was the seed for Flagler's future Florida East Coast Railway Company. Flagler single-handedly brought back to life the largely abandoned city of St Augustine by building schools, churches, hospitals and, most importantly, a modern railroad depot that could accommodate travellers to his resorts.

Flagler bought up more railroads, and by the spring of 1889 his network extended from Jacksonville to Daytona. He also continued to develop hotels

organization that was created in the 1970s to offer national passenger service still struggles to compete with the airlines.

The railroad used to run the full length of Florida, all the way down to Key West. However a particularly severe storm in the 1930s washed away sections of the track along the Keys, toppling railroad cars and claiming many lives. In the end it proved too costly for the financially struggling railroad to restore the service to Key West. The magnificent railroad bridges that connected the string of islands and which remained relatively intact after the storm were soon converted to vehicle (automobile) use. Should you drive down to the southern-most point in the land you might notice the remains of some of those bridges running parallel to the road you are driving along.

Relative to other forms of transportation, rail travel may not be the most popular way to move around but it is still a very pleasant way to travel. You stay close to the ground yet don't have to worry about looking for the correct highway exit. In its attempts to lure back travellers, Amtrak has upgraded its trains and your journey can now be quite comfortable.

that would give tourists a reason to board his trains. When landowners south of Daytona begged him to extend the system 80 miles south, he obtained a charter from the state allowing him to build a railroad along the Indian River all the way to Miami. In 1892, he began laying new tracks, and towns and cities, such as New Smyrna and Titusville, began to blossom along the way. In two years, the system reached what is today West Palm Beach, where he built magnificent hotels, as well as Whitehall, his 55-room, 60,000sq ft winter home. Flagler's conspicuous commitment to the area marked the beginning of its influx of wealthy winter residents.

Despite his original decision not to continue the line any further south, a number of factors convinced him otherwise. He incorporated the Florida East Coast Railway Company in 1895, and a year later its rails reached Biscayne Bay, the east coast's largest harbour. As he had done in other areas to encourage development, he invested heavily in Miami, building streets, dredging a channel, installing water and power systems, and financing its first newspaper. Miami's grateful citizens even offered to rename their town 'Flagler' in his honour when it was incorporated in 1896, but he convinced them to keep the old Indian name.

Now that he had got this far, the restless Flagler decided to go all the way. Key West, a distant city of almost 20,000 people separated from the mainland, was already of strategic importance for Cuban and Latin American trade. Its importance grew significantly when it was announced in 1905 that the Panama Canal would be built. Construction took seven years and used an incredible amount of resources but when it was completed it proved that Flagler had gone as far as he could. Key West was the end of the line for him metaphorically as well. Flagler died one year later.

Amtrak (**www.amtrak.com**) runs the Silver Service/Palmetto from New York to Miami, stopping at many major cities including Washington DC, Charleston, Savannah, Jacksonville, Orlando and Tampa. In addition to Amtrak, there is also Tri-Rail (**www.tri-rail.com**), a commuter train that services the southeast region from Miami International Airport to Fort Lauderdale and on to West Palm Beach and points between.

Road

For sheer efficiency, it is hard to beat travelling around the state by car. Getting around Florida is relatively easy if you have a good map. On the whole most destinations are well signposted, and the roads (highways) are wide and well maintained with plenty of rest stops. Just like train travel, car travel has the advantage of being a good way of familiarizing yourself with potential new neighbourhoods. Driving also gives you more flexibility.

Highways are clearly the most direct route from A to B, but smaller state roads offer hidden pleasures that might make the slower route worthwhile. There are some truly gorgeous drives that will take you along the coast where you can look out of the window and see the brilliant waters of the Gulf of Mexico, or where you can stare out at the green wilderness of the Everglades. Just try and keep your eyes on the road at the same time.

However, be careful not to get caught in peak traffic hours around urban areas. Florida is no exception to the worldwide urban problem of sheer volume of traffic trying to get to work or home. The congestion can be exacerbated by the numerous narrow bridges where traffic tends to bottleneck. Whenever possible, try to avoid travelling into or out of cities 8–10am and 4–7pm.

If you plan to spend a fair amount of time on Florida's highways, you could invest in the state's automated toll-payment system called SunPass (**www.sunpass.com**) which allows you to get through the toll booths quickly. The system has been implemented throughout most of Florida's toll systems and can save you money as well as the hassle of digging for change.

In business or residential areas the speed limit is 30mph. Florida still observes the 55mph limit on most highways but on certain rural, limited-access inter-state roads the speed goes up to 70mph. However, don't assume that if you don't see a lot of other cars on the road and the area seems rural the limit is 70mph. Speed limits are strictly enforced and fines can be quite heavy. In addition, always be sure to wear your seatbelt. It is against the law not to when driving and as a result of a new, highly publicized advertising campaign, law enforcement officers are on the lookout for offenders. (In fact most US cars have a loud, persistent warning system if you have forgotten to fasten your seatbelt.)

Car Hire

The process of hiring a car is universally similar, and very little is different in the USA from in the UK, or anywhere else for that matter. Booking ahead can save you some money and time, although it never seems to guarantee that you are going to get that car you reserved.

If you plan to cover a lot of ground, make sure that the company offers unlimited mileage. Also, read over the hire contract carefully and be wary of additional insurance coverage, which is often unnecessary. Check with your credit card company to see if they offer their own additional insurance coverage.

You do not need an international driving licence to hire a car in the USA and your UK licence (provided it is in date) is sufficient.

At most Florida airports you will find the major companies represented, such as Avis (**www.avis.com**) and Hertz (**www.hertz.com**), as well as smaller ones, such as National (**www.nationalcar.com**) and Alamo (**www.alamo.com**).

If you are unfamiliar with driving an automatic (and most US cars have automatic gear shifts) take a little time to familiarize yourself with the various safety mechanisms before you try and drive away. Some automobiles only allow you to move the gear stick after you have released the foot brake.

Bus and Coach

While cities receive state funding for public transportation, each one runs its own system through its own transportation authority. Each of these systems can look and feel different, with a few creative approaches to moving the masses. Jacksonville, for example, has introduced the Skyway, an automated transit system that runs on an elevated guideway and crosses the St Johns River, while Tampa has revived the electric trolley car system (**www. tecolinestreetcar.org**). Miami, which is home to the largest public transit system in Florida, also runs a good-sized underground train system.

Bus

Because local bus systems are run on a regional basis without state supervision, the quality and range of service can vary widely from area to area. This means that fares will vary, as will the way in which you pay for your ride. It is best to track down each city's transportation authority for detailed schedules, routes and information. The following is a listing of the state's major transit systems.

- BCT – Broward County Transit (**www.broward.org/bct**).
- Collier County Transit (**www.colliergov.net/transadmin/atm/operations/ cat/index.htm**).
- ECAT – Escambia County Transit Authority Bus and Trolleys (**www.goecat.com**).
- HARTline – Hillsborough Area Regional Transit (**www.hartline.org**).
- JTA – Jacksonville Transportation Authority (**www.jtaonthemove.com**).
- LeeTran – Lee County (**www.rideleetran.com**).
- LYNX – Central Florida Regional Transportation Authority (**www.golynx.com**).
- MCAT – Manatee County Area Transit (**www.co.manatee.fl.us**).
- Miami-Dade Transit (**www.co.miami-dade.fl.us/transit**).
- PalmTran – West Palm Beach (**www.palmtran.org**).
- PCPT – Pasco County Public Transportation (**www.pascocountyfl.net/ pubser/comser/PublicTrans/PTMAIN.htm**).
- Pinellas Suncoast Transit Authority (**www.psta.net**).
- RTS – Regional Transit System, Gainesville (**www.go-rts.com**).
- SCAT – Sarasota County Area Transit (**http://scat.scgov.net**).
- SCAT – Space Coast Area Transit (**www.ridescat.com**).

Profiles
of the Regions

The North

1

2

Florida's three northern regions –
Northwest, North Central and Northeast
– share a quiet, rural beauty. Even
though the state capital of Tallahassee
is at the centre of it all, along with the
sprawling city of Jacksonville to the east,
a small-town charm is still predominant
from the 'panhandle' in the Northwest
to the bustling areas of the Northeast.
Crowds have been slow to discover the
region's southern hospitality and
spectacular Gulf Coast beaches, but that
is changing fast.

Northern Florida is a land of surprising
contrasts. Visitors will be just as likely to
encounter canopied country roads
leading to old mansions as they will
boardwalks reaching out to brilliant blue
waters over snow-white beaches. They
will find Spanish military forts that
pre-date the founding of the United
States, as well as racetracks humming
with the latest automotive technology.
The north is also home to a mixture of
architecture, from antebellum mansions
to cosy beach cottages with wrap-
around porches. Except where ancient
oaks rule, palm trees sway above
everything, a constant reminder of
the tropical climate.

1 Old City Hall, Tallahassee
2 Private house, Seaside
3 Beachfront gazebo, Seaside
4 Supreme Court, Tallahassee
5 Corner restaurant, Pensacola
6 Ironwork detail, Pensacola

7 *Beach, Pensacola*
8 *Private house, Pensacola*
9 *Red clay road, near Tallahassee*

The Northeast

The Northeast region is the urban centre of northern Florida. It also boasts the biggest and the oldest: Jacksonville is geographically the largest city in the contiguous United States, and St Augustine is the country's oldest.

1 Castillo de San Marcos National Monument, St Augustine
2 Daytona International Speedway, Daytona Beach

3

4

3 Skyline, Jacksonville
4 Waterfront, Jacksonville
5 Inn, St Augustine
6 Spanish Quarter, St Augustine

1 2

The Centre

Like the north, the centre consists of three distinct regions: Central West, Central and Central East. However, since the Walt Disney company built an enormous amusement park here in the early 1970s, the central region has had most of the attention. What was once predominantly farmland now attracts homebuyers who want to be close to all the fun and excitement – or who want to capitalize on the millions of tourists who visit each year by investing in rental properties. To accommodate all the crowds, Orlando has rapidly grown to become a significant urban hub. Not wanting to be left out of the booming real estate business, the Disney company built itself a cosy picture-perfect hometown called Celebration, not far from the park that started it all.

The beauty of the centre, like many other parts of Florida, is that nature is never too far away even in the more densely populated areas: generous wildlife refuges along the coasts ensure that rare birds and other creatures will always have a home of their own. Not far from one of the state's larger wildlife refuges, visitors will also find another of Florida's well-established icons: the space shuttle, which launches spectacularly from the Kennedy Space Center on the east coast.

1 Office, Orlando
2 Merritt Island National Wildlife Refuge
3 Shopping arcade, Celebration
4 Apartment building, Orlando

5

5 *Merritt Island National Wildlife Refuge*
6 *Private house, Orlando*
7 *Café and shops, Celebration*
8 *Orlando*
9 *Corner café, Celebration*
10 *Skyline, Orlando*

6

7

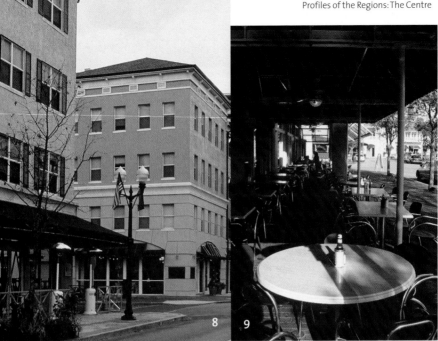

8 9

10

Tampa Bay Area

The Tampa Bay area, which includes St Petersburg across the bay, is what brings Florida's Central West region together. The metropolitan area has steadily been growing more popular – and populated – as homebuyers search for alternatives to the more densely settled east coast. A variety of ethnic neighbourhoods, such as Ybor City in Tampa, make for a surprisingly diverse population throughout the region. Since its early days as a Native American fishing village, Tampa has also witnessed

its fair share of history. Explorer Hernando de Soto came through here looking to claim more land for Spain, and so did Theodore Roosevelt many years later on his way to Cuba to fight those Spaniards who remained. The Caribbean influence can be found in places such as Ybor City, which was named after a Cuban exile who relocated his cigar business here from Key West. Other cigar manufacturers soon followed, moving their factories to the area and creating a vibrant community of Spanish, Italian, German and Cuban workers. Until the rise of Fidel Castro and the embargo on Cuban tobacco, Ybor City was known as the 'Cigar Capital of the World'.

1 Intersection, Ybor City, Tampa
2 Bar, Ybor City
3 Barber shop, Ybor City
4 Store and apartment, Ybor City

5

6

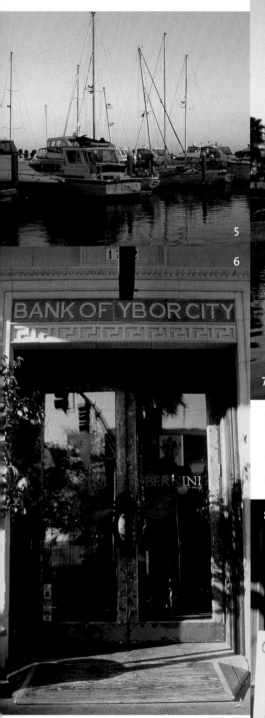

7

5 Harbour, St Petersburg
6 Bank converted to restaurant, Ybor City,
  Tampa
7 Apartments overlooking the harbour,
  St Petersburg
8 Restaurant, Ybor City, Tampa

8

The South

Southern Florida is divided into the Southwest and the Southeast regions, both of which share the natural splendour of the Everglades. Plenty more natural beauty can be found just off the coast of the Southwest region, where some of the state's most stunning and well-known islands, including Sanibel and Captiva, are located. Compared with the well-developed Southeast region, the Southwest seems relatively quiet, but parts of it are home to an equally affluent population.

Naples, Florida, the centre of the state's Southwest region, adopted its name

1 Private home, Naples
2 Pelicans, Naples Pier

3

4

5

after numerous writers who had discovered the area's mild climate in the late 1800s repeatedly described its bay as more beautiful than the one in Naples, Italy. A couple of investors from Kentucky purchased most of the town in 1887 and built an enormous T-shaped pier that could accommodate large ships, and which helped the town develop into a popular winter resort. The pier, which stretches far out over the Gulf of Mexico, has been destroyed and rebuilt several times during the city's history and still exists, but today is a popular attraction in its own right, where people gather to fish and enjoy the sun.

6   7

3 Private home, Naples
4 Beach, Naples
5 Retail strip, Naples
6 Naples Pier, Naples
7 Fishing, Naples

The Keys

The Florida Keys are officially a part of the Southeast but they exist in a world all of their own. Spanish explorers stumbled upon the stunning islands early on in their discovery of the New World, and during the ensuing years artists and writers have been drawn here, perhaps attracted in part by remote Key West's edge-of-the-earth feel. Ernest Hemingway is one of the better-known names associated with Key West, where he wrote *A Farewell to Arms*. His home is a popular tourist destination, and it is said that descendants of the writer's six-toed cat still roam the grounds. Tourism, sponge-harvesting, tobacco-manufacturing and citrus-farming all brought astounding wealth to the area, but the Great Depression and the Second World War brought the good times to an end. The arrival of commercial shrimp-farming and the establishment of a US Naval base brought the area back to life in the second half of the 20th century, and tourism soon picked up again.

1 Guide post, Key West
2 Local decoration outside bar, Key West
3 Inn, Key West
4 Old cigar-roller's house, now a rental property, Key West
5 Private garden, Key West

3

4

5

9

8

6

7

PEPE'S CAFE ELDEST EATING HOU

6 Old timberframe house, Key West
7 Abandoned bridge, The Keys
8 Old restaurant, Key West
9 Private home, Key West
10 Artist's store, Key West
11 Antique shop, Key West
12 Old theatre, Key West

1

2

3

The Southeast

Without question, the Southeast region of Florida is its most densely populated. Palm Beach county, together with the Orlando area, is what keeps Florida in business. Here is where visitors will find the travel-poster version of Florida, which includes more than just the photogenic Keys. Miami, as it has done

for decades, draws the beautiful and famous to its seaside hotels, while cities such as Boca Raton attract well-established older residents. Fort Lauderdale has emerged in the past decade from its origins as a spring break destination for college students, growing into a less expensive alternative to Miami, only a short drive away.

1 Entrance to beach, Fort Lauderdale
2 Delano Hotel, Miami Beach
3 Beachfront hotel and shops, Fort Lauderdale
4 Umbrellas, Miami Beach

5 Umbrella, Miami Beach
6 Lifeguard station, Fort Lauderdale
7 Beachfront restaurant, Fort Lauderdale

- TalTran – Tallahassee (**www.talgov.com/residents/transport.cfm**).
- VOTRAN – Volusia County's Public Transit System (**www.votran.org**).

Coach

There are only a handful of major coach companies in the USA and Greyhound (**www.greyhound.com**) is probably the most extensive. It makes stops throughout the state at or near most major destinations. Sometimes, however, the stop may be nothing more than an unmarked petrol station, so you will have to inform yourself beforehand about the location of stops.

Sea

Fortunately for the preservation of many island refuges, not every stretch of water has been bridged in Florida, and to get to small islands such as Cedar Key and some of the Barrier Islands you have to take a boat. You may be surprised, however, by how many are connected to the mainland by causeways. But, thanks to the energy and passion of some local preservation groups, some of these islands still feel as if they are not quite accessible by all and sundry.

You will soon discover that, like public transport, the boat service between mainland Florida and its many small islands is not state-run. In some of the less popular spots, you may have to charter a boat, while in others a regular service of sorts will already be in place. However, the lack of any kind of state-run services means that it is hard to find information on how to get to your desired island until you actually reach your destination.

One of the more remote islands off the coast of Florida is Fort Jefferson, which is roughly 70 miles west of Key West and is accessible by boat or seaplane. Seaplanes of Key West (**t** 800 950 2359; **www.seaplanesofkeywest.com**), as the name suggests, flies out of Key West and will take you to the island in approximately 35mins each way. The ferry option is provided by Yankee Fleet, which takes about 2hrs 30mins each way (**t** 800 634 0939; **www.yankeefleet.com**).

Climate and Geography

Florida is a narrow, teardrop-shaped peninsula that drips 800km (500 miles) southwards between the Atlantic Ocean and the Gulf of Mexico until it dips into the Caribbean Sea. The state is mostly a flat and rolling landscape with its highest point of 105m (345ft) located in the northwest region.

The state has just over 140,000sq km (54,000sq miles) of land. Add in another 11,650sq km (4,500sq miles) of water and you have nearly 152,000sq km

The First Floridians

As you look at a map of Florida, you might wonder about the origins of place names like Apalachicola or Okeechobee. A lot of names throughout the state are taken from the Seminole language (see p.68). Today the Seminole tribe of Florida has nearly 3,000 members who live on five reservations across the peninsula at Hollywood (formerly Dania), Big Cypress, Brighton, Immokalee and Tampa. However, long before the Europeans arrived in this part of the country, ancestors of the tribe may have numbered in the hundreds of thousands. Their numbers were eventually greatly reduced by disease, which came ashore with the Spaniards in the 16th century.

In the second half of the 18th century, when the first English-speakers arrived, they found hundreds of tribes such as the Euchee, Yamasee, Timugua, Tequesta, Abalachi and Coça living across the head of the Florida peninsula, on the Alachua savannah (today Alachua County). In Maskókî, the core language, *istî siminolî* meant that they were 'free people' because they had never been dominated by either the Spaniards or the English. The new arrivals ignored any separate tribal affiliations and called them all Seminolies, or Seminoles.

Once the USA had been officially established, white settlers began to gradually move southwards. A clash between the white immigrants and the native inhabitants was inevitable. The new US government began taking or buying land from the native tribes in the northeast and the Atlantic seaboard states, and in 1813 some of the Maskókî tribes in Alabama rose up. The conflict came to be known as the Creek War of 1813–14 and resulted in the loss of over two million acres of Indian land. The Maskókî people migrated southwards by the

(59,000sq miles) of wilderness, lakes and beaches to explore. Running along the perimeter of all that land is roughly 1,900km (1,200 miles) of striking and beautifully varied coastline, the majority of which is along the Gulf of Mexico.

Despite its nickname, Florida is actually among the wettest states in the USA. With a fair amount of regional variation, most areas of the state receive at least 1,270mm (50 inches) of rain a year – the panhandle being the wettest and the Keys the driest.

The state is very wet for other reasons as well. It is quite literally soaked through and through. In addition to being surrounded by huge stretches of water, it is dotted with numerous lakes, including Lake Okeechobee, the fourth largest natural lake in the entire USA. Although Okeechobee covers 1,800sq km (700sq miles) across five counties, it is actually very shallow. Adding to the wetness are Florida's 17,000km (10,550 miles) of streams, and 26 billion litres of water pumping through the state's natural underground system of springs.

In terms of climate, the state is classified as a hot-humid region, which sounds worse than it is but which means that for six months of the year temperatures can be above 90°F (32°C) and relative humidity can be 50 per cent or higher. The thousands into Spanish Florida, where they joined the Seminoles in resisting the ongoing settlement.

From 1814 to 1858 the US government and the native Americans fought a series of bloody battles that came to be known as the Seminole Wars, which drove the Indians deeper into the Florida peninsula. Although neither side could claim any real victory in the wars, over 3,000 native Americans had been forcibly removed from Florida to the Western territories of Arkansas and Oklahoma. Perhaps 300 remained, and they took refuge in the inhospitable swamps of the Everglades, where their descendants remained isolated until the late 1800s. With the development boom starting in the 1920s in southern Florida, the Seminoles lost more and more of their hunting lands. They then became agricultural workers in the vegetable fields of south Florida, as well as tourist attractions in their unique and colorful patchwork clothing.

The US Congress passed the Indian Reorganization Act in 1934, which reversed earlier policies and encouraged tribes to form their own governments. Soon after, Congress also set about cutting off aid to tribes across the country. The Florida Seminoles chose to adopt a constitutional form of government that would allow them to operate in the non-native world. On 21 August 1957 a majority of Seminoles voted to establish an administrative entity called the Seminole Tribe of Florida. However, not all of the Seminole people in Florida chose to participate in this new organization. In 1962, after several years of negotiations, a group of Mikisúkî-speakers with camps along the Tamiami Trail created the Miccosukee Tribe of Indians of Florida. Today, there are about 500 members of this tribe.

hot-humid climate is helped along by the plentiful sunshine, the vast stretches of water, and an average rainfall of 1,520mm (60 inches) per year.

Florida is divided into three climatic zones: northern Florida, which because of its latitude tends be somewhat cooler than the rest of the state, with a significant number of days between November and March when temperatures are quite low; central Florida, which perhaps because it is less exposed to cooling breezes tends to have a longer periods of high temperature, high-humidity days; and south Florida, which enjoys comfortable temperatures during much of the year because it is exposed to daytime onshore breezes.

For detailed temperature and rainfall charts, see **References**, p.241.

When to Go

When it comes to house-hunting in the USA, the great thing you will find is that everyone is pretty much open for business all year round. Like the rest of the country, Florida does not shut down for entire months at a time, and if one business does, there is usually someone there to take its place. If you run your

Learn Seminole

The Seminole Indians have two languages still in use today, neither of which is traditionally written. Muscogee (Creek) and Miccosukee are related but not mutually intelligible. Both languages contain sentence structures and sounds that do not exist in English and are difficult to pronounce using the English language. With some words the two languages seem to mirror each other; and sometimes the two lingos are quite different. For example, the English word for bread would be pronounced 'tak-la-eek-i' in the Muscogee dialect and 'pa-les-tee' in Miccosukee. 'Dog' is 'ef-fa' in Creek, 'ee-fe' in Miccosukee. 'Cow' is 'wa-ka' in Creek 'waa-ke' in Miccosukee. Many Seminoles are fluent in both languages; some only speak one or the other.

The names of many Florida cities, counties, places, rivers and lakes are taken from Seminole words, both Creek and Miccosukee.

Apalachicola	place of the ruling people
Chattahoochee	marked stones
Hialeah	prairie
Immokalee	my camp
Miami	that place
Ocala	spring
Palatka	ferry crossing
Yeehaw	wolf
Pahokee	grassy water
Apopka	potato eating place
Okeechobee	big water
Homosassa	pepper place
Thonotosassa	flint place

A Few Seminole Words

ee-cho	deer
ya-laahe	orange
o-pa	owl
hen-le	squirrel
sho-ke	pig
laa-le	fish
yok-che	turtle
chen-te	snake
ke-hay-ke	hawk
nak-ne	man
coo-wah-chobee	big cat

own business this can make for a very competitive environment, as you always have to be on your toes and will find yourself reluctant to take time off. As a consumer, however, you are free to shop around until you find the business or service that suits your needs and schedule. It is important to remember, however, that Florida is a tropical location and therefore the weather should be taken into account when you plan your trip. If you are going to be moving around from house to house, looking for the perfect home in southern Florida, you might not want to go in the middle of summer, even though it would be an informative trip just to see how hot Miami can get in August. For more information about climates, *see* **References**, p.241.

Choosing a Location

Choosing the location of your property is, without a doubt, the most important decision you will make with regard to the purchase. Buying a home is a serious investment and it is important to take your time to really get to know a place and allow a bit more time for the dreamy clouds to lift from your eyes before you hand over your money. This may sound like obvious advice but you should always keep in mind that, if you are only visiting for short periods at a time, and are suddenly enchanted with a particular spot, it is only too easy to be convinced by overly aggressive salespeople that you must act immediately or lose the opportunity of a lifetime.

The Virgin One account, a joint venture between the Royal Bank of Scotland and Virgin, has drawn on the experiences of hundreds of people who have gone through the process of buying a second home and compiled a valuable list of tips for buying abroad:

1. Buy with your head and not your heart – a property with rustic charm and in need of 'some' renovation could become a bottomless money pit.

2. Speak to other British people who have bought in the area – they will know the pitfalls.

3. Work out the overall journey time to your dream home – weekend breaks may not be feasible.

4. Make friends with the locals before you buy and get to know the area – you need to feel welcome and like the surroundings.

5. Make sure your home has access to amenities. It's no good being miles from the nearest shop or beach if you have young children.

6. Include legal fees, travel costs and repairs in your budget. You don't want to be hit with unexpected bills.

7. Find a good, local lawyer to represent you, one who knows the local legal language – foreign conveyancing contracts are just as complicated as ours.

8. Remember your second home will be vacant for long periods. Ask friendly neighbours to keep an eye out and make sure security is adequate – your insurance company will insist on that anyway.

9. Visit your chosen location at different times of the year – a remote hamlet in a shady valley may be idyllic in the summer but cold and blustery in the winter.

In Florida, you are unlikely to end up with a property that is cold and blustery in winter, but you might end up with one that is hit by tropical storms precisely when you wish to be there, or one that is overrun with seasonal traffic rushing to the beach or Disney World®, which makes moving about for the slightest errand a nightmare.

Huge crowds on their way to see Mickey and his friends in central Florida are hard to avoid but you can factor them in to the selection of your location. The Orlando area remains incredibly popular with home-buyers – especially those who are buying to let. It is important to keep in mind that Disney World® traffic will affect your own travel whether you work in the area or are just trying to get around. Make sure that there are plenty of alternatives to the main routes that are close to your potential home and that take you to the places you imagine yourself most likely to be visiting.

Waterfront property comes at a premium in Florida just as anywhere else in the world. If that is what you have your mind set on, then be prepared to pay for it. However, one of the advantages of living on a narrow strip of land is that you are never too far from a coast, so don't rule out places that are a bit inland which may not have an ocean view from your bedroom window but will still give you easy access to the beach. Stepping back from the coast will also give you the chance to get away from the crowds as they descend.

When it comes to amenities, such as shopping, entertainment, and anything else that you might consider a necessary part of your community, you are never too far from anything in Florida. Unless you manage to find yourself a home on some small, sparsely populated island with limited access – which will in any case cost you dearly – most parts of the state are pretty well developed and you will find almost everything you need even in the smaller towns. In fact, if seclusion is what you are after, the tricky part may be getting away from all the development.

Where the Expatriate Communities Are

The British have been moving into Florida for years now and have become a well-integrated part of American life. Some people estimate that there are about 400,000 currently residing in the state and a staggering 1.2 million visiting each year. Not all of the residents are legal, however, which makes it hard to come by official figures. Suffice it to say that you will find well-established British expatriate communities throughout Florida.

The popularity of **Orlando** as a vacation destination has turned it into a popular location to buy property to let out to others. While there are a lot of UK owners in this area, you might not find as strong a resident community as in other parts of the state. **Fort Lauderdale** on the other hand is, and has been for some time, home to one of the biggest resident expatriate communities.

More recently, the **Tampa Bay** area, which covers St Petersburg, Clearwater, Tampa and all the beach areas in between, as well as Sarasota, has seen a surge in popularity with UK investors, and the area has been developing a strong community of its own.

The British community in Florida is also well represented online. There are several sites that are dedicated to bringing together people who have settled in the Sunshine State. One of the most popular is the **British in Florida** site (**www.sunnybrits.com**) which offers all kinds of information and resources as well as an invaluable chat forum for British people already living in Florida providing helpful advice to the newly arrived and to those contemplating relocating. Another site, the **Florida Brits Club** (**www.floridabritsclub.com**) similarly offers support to new residents and includes a property (real estate) division as well.

Florida Homes

For many, Florida architecture means one thing: **Art Deco**. Miami's shameless ability to inject its distinctive architectural style into almost anything ever written about the Sunshine State has overshadowed the state's numerous other architectural contributions, which don't necessarily come in pastel colours.

Miami's promotional savvy should not reflect negatively on it, however, for its fame is well deserved in terms of this particular architectural style. The long line of original Art Deco hotels that run along the shore on Miami Beach are a national treasure and a sight to behold, day or night. During the day, the buildings glow in painted-on pinks, yellows and blues, and at night they are lit up in equally glorious colours. While the oceanfront hotels are for the most part the playground of the rich today just as they were in the first half of the 20th century, you will discover that the Art Deco tradition is spread throughout Miami Beach and Miami proper – and that it is not out of the question to own your own piece of it.

If you can forget about Miami for a minute, you will soon discover what else the state has to offer. Florida's northern region has a lot in common with the southern USA, including its architecture. Here you will find a more subtle and less colourful world. This is the region of the **plantation home**, a style of architecture that, like the grand hotels of Miami Beach, is left over from another era. The grand, columned antebellum homes tucked away among old pine trees are a magnificent example of the southern architecture tradition in Florida.

If you leave behind the Art Deco hotels, plantation homes and other better known architectural gems of Florida, you will find that there is a building tradi-

Addison Mizner and the Spanish Revival

As an architect, Addison Mizner had a few shortcomings: for one thing, he had no formal training, and, for another, he was unable to draw blueprints. Clearly, he made up for what he lacked by knowing the right people and selling them his vision of what original architecture should be. His introduction of the Spanish Revival style is widely credited with launching a 'Florida renaissance' and inspiring architects throughout the rest of the country.

Mizner began his career in San Francisco, where he achieved some recognition, and spent some time in New York, but it was his move to Palm Beach – for health reasons – at the age of 46 that would make his name.

His first commission was a house that would come to be called El Mirasol. When it was finished it had 37 rooms, half a dozen patios, an illuminated pool and a 40-car underground garage. His next project was even more ambitious.

Boca Raton was a tiny, unincorporated town when Mizner arrived. He envisaged a 1,000-room hotel, golf courses, parks and a street wide enough to fit 20 lanes of traffic, and he said as much in his promotional materials. In 1925 he founded the Mizner Development Corporation and bought more than 1,500 acres, including two miles of beach. Famous investors included Irving Berlin, Elizabeth Arden, W. K. Vanderbilt II and T. Coleman du Pont.

Boca Raton eventually became everything that Mizner had said it would, thanks to other developers who took his lead. Unfortunately, Mizner himself was unable to weather a collapse in land values, and within two years of founding his company he was bankrupt. He abandoned architecture for writing. It proved to be a short second career. In 1933, he died aged 61 of a heart attack.

tion that is equally 'southern' but which has more humble origins. This building tradition is known as the **vernacular**. In Florida, these simple buildings are sometimes known as 'folk' or 'cracker' architecture. Their purpose is quite straightforward: to provide basic shelter. Because these buildings were built in areas without any established architectural styles, and were usually built by the occupants themselves with whatever materials were available, the style is distinctly pragmatic. The buildings are by necessity dynamic as well, since they were required to adapt to the ever-changing circumstances of their occupants, such as adding on to accommodate a growing family.

According to *Florida History & the Arts*, a magazine dedicated to the state's heritage, there are several major types of vernacular houses still to be found throughout Florida. Some of them are hidden away in rural areas, while others may be out in the open along highways or even located in urban areas. Unfortunately, because of the humble origins of many of these buildings, it has taken a long time for them to gain the architectural recognition they need in order to be properly preserved and restored. If you are interested in acquiring a little piece of local, down-home architecture, then be prepared to work; you will probably find that many of the homes are in very poor shape and need a lot of attention.

The single- or double-pen home is one of the oldest types of house built by early Florida settlers. The dwelling consisted of a single-room or single-pen house built of logs packed with moist clay and which supported a gable roof. A single fireplace at one end provided fire for warmth and cooking, and one or more porches were built off the side. A **single-pen house** became a **double-pen** by the addition of another room. If the addition was made to the wall opposite the chimney, the house is classified as a double-pen; if it was made against the chimney wall, the house became a 'saddlebag'.

The '**dog-trot**' is a more sophisticated version of the double-pen house, and is often considered the classic example of Florida 'cracker' architecture. The difference between the regular double-pen home and the dog-trot is that the additional room of the dog-trot is separated from the original by an open breezeway, creating two rooms surrounded by an H-shaped arrangement of two porches joined by a walkway.

The **Gulf Coast cottage** is a very popular type of vernacular house in Florida and is sometimes called a **raised Creole cottage**, thanks to its New Orleans origins (although it also bears some similarities to Caribbean architecture). This house was set on piers and divided into four equal-sized rooms flanking a wide central hallway. A steeply pitched gable roof sheltered both the house and its porches.

The '**shotgun**' **house** is an example of urban vernacular and is quite common. The origin of the design has been traced to Africa, from where it made its way to the New World via the Caribbean. The name comes from the linear arrangement of the house's rooms and doors from the front porch to the back door, which would allow a round of shot fired through the front door to exit the back without hitting anything. Each of the rooms opens from one to the next along one side of the building and the house has no hallway. A single home made up of two of these houses connected side by side is sometimes called a **double-barrel**.

Although interest is growing in the beautiful simplicity of the vernacular architecture, pure examples of it are fast disappearing to make way for more modern houses and for the **high-rise apartment buildings** that are now largely the stereotype of Florida architecture. While some may protest at the dominance of the high-rise along Florida's coast, there is a certain democratic quality to these buildings in that they make it possible for many to own a little bit of oceanfront property. The style and quality of the high-rises varies, of course, from Miami's super-cool creations by the 'hottest' architects, to the lingering examples of 1960s architecture that often house some of their original tenants. Some high-rise condominiums offer valuable amenities and, if you are only in your home for short periods of the year, the fact that there is always someone there to keep an eye on things is a definite advantage.

Case Study: Retirement Blues

In the late 1980s, Jean and Ted Kerr found themselves contemplating a major change in the direction of their lives as they entered their 50s. They were hoping that retirement was just seven or eight years away. They feared that the lack of the stimulation provided by a busy working life might lead to a quiet, insular existence and growing old before their time. Thoughts of the long, dark days of an English winter didn't help either. They considered exploring the world through cruises and extended holidays, but, having spent a lot of time travelling in their jobs, they were not enthusiastic about spending their retirement years in airport lounges, aircraft seats and hotel bedrooms. One thing was for sure: they not did want to spend their days looking out of the window at dark, rainy mornings wondering what to do with themselves. They looked at Spain, and even considered France, but some years earlier they had fallen in love with America, and Florida in particular. They had already spent at least one holiday each year in the Sunshine State, and liked the people very much and felt comfortable there. The lifestyle agreed with them.

Jean came across a newspaper article about buying property abroad and soon afterwards the Kerrs attended a seminar organized by an American developer. The couple were impressed by the presentation and found themselves carried away by the image of a beautiful Florida home. The company offered all kinds of incentives – assisted air fares, free accommodation – to persuade people to go out and have a look at their properties. They were even offered a free American fridge/freezer just for attending the seminar if they placed an order for one of the company's homes. The die was cast.

They flew to Orlando and the next morning they were shown a range of model homes and potential building sites. They saw four models and both fell

Property Types

The following is a list of some of the property types you might find on the market today.

• **Town-home development**: The town-home development is an example of the varying success of applying economies of scale to architecture. In general these are groups of homes that are clustered together and built with minimal, if any, variation in the floor plans. In some cases, the homes are connected and in others they will be separated by a small strip of land. What they may lack in individuality, they might make up for in affordability.

• **Condominium**: A condominium is not a housing style so much as it is a real estate arrangement. Since it is usually a part of a larger building, this type of housing tends to be associated with urban areas or central suburbs. Generally, a condominium is a separately owned unit, the boundaries of which are its interior surfaces: walls, floors and ceilings. In addition to receiving title to the in love instantly with the same one. They indicated that their beloved model was a 'possible' choice and were then taken to see a number of vacant plots (lots). Basing their selection on Ted's business background in multiple retailing, they quickly picked out their ideal plot and were immediately told it was a prime site that carried a considerable premium. The news brought them down from their euphoric state. After lunch, they entered into negotiations that ultimately brought the price down to a more sensible level. That evening they suddenly found themselves to be the exhausted prospective owners of a brand-new Florida home.

The next day involved meeting all of the different players involved in putting the meat on the bones of their acquisition. They met the sales person who would deal with the exterior design issues and the interior upgrades, the mortgage broker, the bank manager, the insurance broker, the interior designer, the furnishing-package supplier (they supplied everything from teaspoons to beds), and the management company that would represent them and run the home after it was built. Four months later the Kerrs were the proud owners of a beautiful home.

Looking back, the couple say they could have decided to look at several builders and suppliers in order to widen their options. However, they acknowledge that this would have been a very long, protracted process from England. Going through the whole procedure with several different companies would probably have proved much more expensive without any guarantee that the outcome would have been dramatically different.

Twelve years later their original Florida home is fundamentally still their pride and joy, with a few improvements, of course. But that's part of the fun of owning your own home.

particular unit, the owner also has a proportionate interest in certain of the common areas.

• **Co-operative**: The co-operative shares a lot of physical similarities with the condominium except that it is a different kind of legal relationship. In this case, a corporation or business trust holds title to the larger property and grants occupancy rights to shareholders by means of proprietary leases or similar arrangements. Co-operative arrangements tend to come with more restrictions on what owners can do with their property.

• **Plantation home**: The definition of a plantation home comes, in part, from its land. Today it is unusual to find examples of this distinctly 'southern' property that still include the acreage that would have been needed to plant the cash crops – such as tobacco or cotton – that made it possible to afford such homes. Across northern Florida the grand homes remain, often sitting on a fraction of their original land. What distinguishes a plantation home from a farmhouse is its grand style. These homes were clearly not built for modest farmers who worked their own land, but for wealthier landowners who would oversee others working the land.

• **Cottage**: Because cottages were originally built to be secondary residences, they tend to be quite modest. The floor plans are simple, consisting of perhaps a couple of rooms off one large central area. Originally the dwelling would have been free of excess ornamentation, but as new owners converted them to year-round residences they have taken on additional architectural flourishes.

• **Bungalow**: A bungalow is a one- or one-and-a-half-storey, single-family house with a low-pitched roof and, often, a front porch or a sun room with a bank of windows. At the turn of the 20th century, it was one of the most popular styles of home. For the sake of efficiency, this kind of home was designed to include numerous built-in features, such as bookcases, sideboards and breakfast nooks.

• **Farmhouse**: Working farms still exist in Florida, even though their number and size is greatly reduced. The traditional farmhouse, unlike the plantation home, is generally a simple wood-frame dwelling, sometimes among a cluster of similarly utilitarian buildings.

• **Gated community**: In response to some buyers' demands for greater security, and sometimes exclusivity, developers began creating gated communities. Like other town-home developments, these communities include houses of minimal variation. The difference is that this type of community tends to face inward and is walled off from the rest of the world.

• **Loft**: The loft apartment traditionally is an industrial space converted to residential use and is usually associated with New York City. However, as real estate developers have discovered the popular appeal of these kinds of raw spaces, they have begun to build loft-style apartments from scratch. Over time, the word has come to mean simply a large, airy space with an unfinished look. In truth, the new lofts may look industrial but are often filled with luxury amenities.

• **Manufactured home**: This kind of home is usually associated with trailer park communities of mobile homes with a simple, linear floor plan. The homes in these communities may look as if they could be hitched to a car and towed away, but usually after their initial voyage to the site they tend to stay put. The manufactured home has evolved considerably over time and is now simply defined as a home that is constructed elsewhere and moved to its site. In fact, manufactured homes can be rather elaborate, as new additions are purchased and clicked into place like Lego pieces.

• **Duplex**: When two single-family residences are attached and share a common wall, either a garage wall or a house wall, the building is known as a duplex. Both residences may be located on individually owned lots, but typically both homes will be contained within the same building rather than side-by-side.

• **Ranch home**: Ranch homes represent the 'modern' American home and a break from traditional architecture. The low profile and open floor plan of this style of house developed from the theories of architect Frank Lloyd Wright, who believed that a building should grow out of and blend into its surroundings. In response to the box-like homes that most Americans lived in at the time, Wright created his prairie-style houses, which became the model for the modern ranch home. In keeping with Wright's preference for the suburbs and large lots, ranch homes are not traditionally urban dwellings and usually include at least a small bit of land.

Guide Prices

The following is a list of prices provided by the Florida Association of Realtors (FAR) at the beginning of 2003.

Florida Sales Report – January 2006 (Single-family, Existing Homes)

	Realtor Sales			*Median Sales Price*		
Metropolitan Statistical Area (MSA)	January 2006	January 2005	percent change	January 2006	January 2005	percent change
STATEWIDE	12,815	15,745	−19	$248,600	$205,100	21
Daytona Beach	569	719	−20	$222,600	$172,800	29
Fort Lauderdale	552	864	−36	$370,500	$310,500	19
Fort Myers –Cape Coral	751	829	−9	$287,200	$219,800	31
Fort Pierce –Port St Lucie	343	448	−23	$261,500	$228,800	14
Fort Walton Beach	234	343	−32	$225,500	$226,500	0
Gainesville	182	289	−37	$223,100	$140,400	59
Jacksonville	1,002	1,002	−2	$197,900	$169,200	17
Lakeland–Winter Haven	382	396	−4	$163,300	$111,300	47
Melbourne–Titusville –Palm Bay	296	532	−44	$219,100	$190,600	15
Miami	580	803	−28	$376,300	$298,800	26
Naples	264	384	−31	$511,400	$497,900	3
Ocala	428	284	13	$166,200	$119,600	39
Orlando	2,116	2,257	−6	$254,100	$187,800	35
Panama City	127	147	−14	$223,300	$188,100	19
Pensacola	317	417	−24	$158,100	$139,800	13
Punta Gorda	194	236	−18	$227,400	$196,000	16
Sarasota–Bradenton	511	976	−48	$353,500	$287,100	23
Tallahassee	332	295	13	$175,500	$158,800	11
Tampa–St Petersburg –Clearwater	2,749	2,995	−8	$219,700	$172,800	27
West Palm Beach –Boca Raton	586	957	−39	$393,700	$361,800	9

Mmm... Alligator

The following are a couple of updated old recipes taken from Jonathan Millen's *A Taste of St Augustine: Recipes of the Ancient City*.

Alligator Pilau

After 20 years of protection, the alligator has made a remarkable comeback and alligator meat is available again. Since the body meat is too tough to eat, only the tail meat is used. The best way to prepare alligator tail is to slice the meat across the grain into ¼- to ½-inch strips. While good lightly breaded and fried, try this dish that includes datil pepper, which gives it some heat.

2lb alligator tail, sliced or cubed
¼ cup olive oil
2 large onions, chopped
1 large bell pepper, chopped
4 cloves garlic, minced
4 bay leaves
1 cup diced tomatoes
1 cup long grain rice
2 cups chicken stock
½ fresh datil pepper or 1 tsp pepper sauce
½ tsp salt
¼ tsp black pepper
¼ tsp dried thyme

Note that all these are merely average guide prices. Within each MSA, home prices can vary considerably. For example, in Palm Beach county you might find a home for $100,000, as well as one for $5 million.

These figures can also change quickly, especially if you take into account the fact that Florida has eleven MSAs in the 'top 20' nationwide with the highest rate of house price appreciation, according to the Office of Federal Housing Enterprise Oversight.

Research and Information Sources

Hunting for a home overseas has been made much easier by the arrival of the internet. Of course, all the usual caveats apply to using the Internet, and whenever possible it should not replace seeing something with your own eyes. As a source of general information, however, it is invaluable. An incredibly useful online resource is the site of the **Florida Association of Realtors** (**www.fl.living.net**). The site offers not only property listings, but also a directory of estate agents (realtors) that can be searched by area and by speciality. In addi-

Sauté alligator meat in a small amount of olive oil until tender and set aside. In a Dutch oven, cook onions, bell pepper and garlic in remaining oil until soft. Add tomatoes, bay leaves, datil pepper or sauce and seasonings and simmer over low heat for five minutes. Add chicken stock and well-rinsed rice and simmer for 20 mins. Add the alligator meat, stir well, taste and adjust seasonings. Simmer an additional 5 mins to combine flavours.

Gopher Tortoise Stew

Also known as the 'Hoover chicken', the gopher tortoise was a staple in the diets of Minorcans, Florida natives and Depression-era families. The exact composition of Gopher Tortoise Stew depended on what ingredients were available at the time, but this is a typical recipe. Today, the gopher tortoise is a protected species, but you can substitute alligator or pork.

Cut meat into 2-inch pieces and simmer in salted water until tender. In a large Dutch oven, fry some salt pork until crisp and the fat is rendered. Add meat and brown. Add a generous amount of chopped onion, some chopped bell pepper, minced garlic, diced tomatoes and simmer for 20mins. Then add the water the meat was cooked in, some diced potatoes, a few bay leaves, salt and black pepper to taste, and a fresh datil pepper or a dash of datil pepper sauce. Simmer for 1½ to 2 hours over low heat. If necessary, thicken stew with a little flour dissolved in water, or some mashed hard-boiled egg yolks. For those that could afford the luxury of dry sherry, a dash would be added just before serving.

Serve piping hot with rice and corn pone.

tion, you will find truly useful tips and advice about buying and selling. To find detailed information about specific counties, including prices and climate, go to their 'Cities and Towns' section.

The official site of the **National Association of Realtors (www.realtor.com)** is broader in scope, covering the USA. However, you can search by city and state, or by post (zip) code, and the site provides many other home-buying resources such as links to mortgage lenders, removal companies and real estate news.

Florida Brits Realty (**www.floridabritsrealty.com**), the property sales division of the Florida Brits Group, which was started by a British couple over a decade ago (*see* p.49), offers seasoned advice from people who have actually gone through the very process you are about to embark on.

If you are not interested in old homes, the site of the **National Association of Homebuilders (www.homebuilder.com)** will let you search exclusively for new homes by state and region. Another site dedicated specifically to new homes is **www.newhomenetwork.com**.

One way to avoid dealing with agents is to go to **www.owners.com**, which lists only properties that are For Sale By Owner (FSBO).

Property Exhibitions

If you are looking for information that goes beyond what is available on the Internet, or you want to speak to someone in person but you are not quite ready to make a trip to the USA, then you might go to a property exhibition. Not only will you find information about specific properties, but you will also meet experts in the field. The events also sometimes include home-buying seminars that can be quite helpful.

Several companies organize such events in the UK, which means that you can do some extensive research before you even get on an aeroplane. Have a look at **Homes Overseas (www.homesoverseas.co.uk)**, which promises to bring developers, real estate agents, mortgage lenders and international lawyers together in one place. A similar event is the **International Property Show (www. internationalpropertyshow.com)**.

Estate Agents

Real estate agents (realtors) are a necessary fact of life when you are buying a home. There are no guarantees when dealing with them and it would be unfair to make generalizations about their ethics. If you are lucky you may have a wonderful experience with the first agent you contact. In other cases, the realities of a competitive market may mean that the person you are dealing with will not always have your best interests in mind.

One of the first things to look for when selecting a real estate agent (after you have made sure that they are licensed by the necessary authorities, of course) is their affiliation with a trade group such as the National Association of Realtors or the Florida Association of Realtors. This affiliation is no guarantee but it does offer some measure of assurance that the agent follows certain professional conduct standards. Most regions in Florida have their own trade group. There are too many to list here but if you go to the FAR site (**www.fl.living.net**) under 'Cities and Towns' you will find a list of areas, each of which includes the name of the related association.

Trade groups also offer special credentials and designations that indicate that a member has achieved a higher level of professional skill, much like a postgraduate degree. Initials indicate an agent's level of achievement. For example, the National Association of Realtors (NAR) offers GRI (for Graduate Realtors Institute), CRS (Certified Residential Specialist) and CRB (for Certified Real Estate Brokerage Manager, the brokers' counterpart to the CRS). Less than half of 1 per cent of association member brokers have achieved the CRS level. NAR also sanctions specific international sales expertise.

A little caution and a bit of research will go a long way to help the process go smoothly. The more you know about the intricacies of the home-buying process, the better off you will be. By the time you talk to an agent, you should have a pretty clear idea about the location of your ideal home, as well as the limitations of your financial situation and your legal rights.

If you have a mind for legislative language, you could start by reviewing Florida's Real and Personal Property statute at **www.flsenate.gov/statutes**. Another place to familiarize yourself with the regulatory aspect of Florida real estate is the Real Estate Division of the Department of Business and Professional Regulation (**www.myflorida.com/dbpr/re/index.shtml**).

If you click on the 'real estate' section of the legal reference website Nolo (**www.nolo.com**) you will find, among other valuable tips, detailed information about working with realtors. One important thing always to bear in mind is that real estate agents are not salaried but instead work on commission. This means that they only get paid once your home search is over. It is usually the seller, not the buyer, who pays the real estate agent's commission, with most listing brokers getting sellers to pay 5–7 per cent of the sales price (sometimes lower in the case of an expensive home or a competitive market). The commission is then split, usually 50-50, between the two brokers involved in the transaction – one for the buyer and one for the seller – and the salesperson in each office who handled the transaction also gets a share.

When choosing an agent, make sure you get two or three recommendations from trusted sources, preferably ones that have recently bought a home. Do not work with anyone whose credentials and experience you haven't checked out. Florida will only license agents who meet minimum levels of state-mandated education, training and testing.

Because the seller pays the commission of the real estate salesperson who helps the buyer locate the seller's house, a buyer's agent or broker has a built-in conflict of interest since he won't get paid until you buy a home, unless you have agreed to pay him separately. In addition, the more you pay for a house, the bigger the agent's cut.

There are two ways of avoiding the conflict of interest: you can work with a buyer's agent who represents you exclusively or you can use a discount broker who will charge you a reduced commission as small as one per cent. Some discount companies such as Help-U-Sell (**www.helpusell.com**) offer 'fee for services' rates where you select from a menu of services, such as preparing the written offer, and pay only for those you need.

Once you've narrowed the field down to a few agents, make an appointment to talk to each in person or on the telephone. Nolo, the legal research website, suggests that you discuss the following issues with your prospective agent.

- **The number of homes the agent found for buyers and sold for sellers.** Get the agent to list actual properties, including addresses, and look for homes similar in price to what you can afford. If the homes are in the general neighbourhood or community where you are looking, discuss what you can expect for your money and the pros and cons of the area.

- **Unsold listings**. Let the agent explain why the properties haven't sold, but don't blame him or her for overpriced homes and sellers who refused to reduce the price to a fair market value.

- **Names of past clients**. The list should include both buyers and sellers who can provide references.

- **Financing**. Discuss mortgages, including special and new loan programmes, creative financing, mortgage brokers and lenders and other financial details specific to your needs. Don't forget to talk about insurance and taxes.

- **Management and communication tools**. Ask the agent to explain how he or she gets the real estate transaction done, both online and off. Find out how often the agent would report to you on sales activity or buying leads. Once a week is a minimum in a stable market but a hot market might require daily check-ins. Get the agent to share logs, checklists, worksheets and other tools or documents he or she uses to keep track of the details for the entire home-buying process.

- **Representation**. Discuss the intricacies of dual agency. Will the agent be representing sellers with homes you may want to buy? If he or she is representing you exclusively, ask if a contract with fees is required. Also ask about fees in lieu of commissions and the duration of any contracts.

Viewing Trips

The length of your visit will dictate the amount of time you will have for shopping for a home in Florida. You may be in the fortunate position of having unlimited time, but more than likely you will not wish to spend your entire vacation running from house to house.

If you set aside a specific period for your viewing, you should take care to be as efficient and thorough as you can during that time. Come prepared: bring a notepad and a camera (a digital or Polaroid camera will give you immediate results if you are pressed for time) and be sure to map out the area so that you don't get lost searching for a particular house.

Take plenty of notes and jot down anything and everything that is good and bad about each property, carefully identifying each house so that you will be able to sort it all out when you are done for the day. Based on the information you've collected, you can create a pros and cons list and begin eliminating those properties that don't match your criteria. You might also find yourself identifying desirable amenities that you hadn't thought of. Make a note of them. With all your information in front of you, you can begin the process of elimination and, most importantly, choosing the right home for you.

What Questions to Ask

The questions never seem to end, but once you have bought your house you will be glad you asked yourself so many questions before rather than wondering after: 'Why didn't I see this coming?' So, here are a few more.

• **What is your budget, and can your finances support it?** Generally, people spend 1.5–2.5 times their annual income on a second home.

• **Do you need to secure a loan?** You may want to investigate whether you qualify for a loan in the USA, since rates can be quite competitive, or you may want to take out equity on your home in the UK. Be sure to find out first whether your bank will mortgage your home for property abroad. For more information see **Making the Purchase**, pp.92–100.

• **Do you plan to remodel or renovate?** Factor the cost of any alterations into your budget.

• **Should you spend money on a home inspection?** Absolutely. The first thing you should do is make an appointment with a surveyor to check all the important areas of the house, including plumbing, roofs and floors.

• **If you are buying a condominium, what are the building's financial reserves?** Should any major repairs have to be done to public areas, if the building does not have enough money to cover the work the financial responsibility will fall on condominium owners.

• **Are there outstanding mortgages, loans or taxes on the property?** Previous debts can unexpectedly fall into your hands if you're not careful.

• **What is the water situation?** Check to make sure there is adequate water supplied to the property, especially if it is in a remote area. You could end up having to drill a new well.

• **Is the property protected by any historic preservation laws?** Alterations to a listed (protected) property can be costly – if they are allowed at all.

• **Have you checked the zoning?** Converting a property to a different use, whether residential or commercial, requires it to be zoned appropriately.

• **Have you accounted for closing costs?** Completion (closing) costs in the USA tend to be higher than in the UK. Be sure to budget for them.

• **Are you dealing with a licensed estate agent?** Check credentials.

Temporary Accommodation

There are plenty of affordable options for a short stay in Florida. After all, it is a state that thrives on tourism. Motels and small hotels are everywhere and their rates, especially if you get away from the main roads, can be quite reasonable. In fact, even close to many attractions you can find some reasonable prices as long as you don't expect too much. However, if you are staying for a few weeks, you might want to look into an extended-stay facility. Several hotel chains have set up locations specifically designed for guests who are staying for longer than just a few nights. Sometimes they will offer spacious suites that include a small kitchen. A good place to start is the Extended Stay Network (**www.extended-staynetwork.com**), which lists hotels and offers special discounts.

Renting Before Buying

One more option as far as temporary accommodation goes is a short-term rental. Renting is not only more cost-effective than staying in a hotel, it is also a good way to get to know an area before you buy and to get to know the world of Florida real estate, since you will probably have to use an agent.

The National Association of Realtors (**www.realtor.com**) includes on its website a section on renting, as does the Florida Association of Realtors (**www.fl.living.net**). There is no shortage of online sites that offer rental information but be very wary. If you search for 'Florida rentals', you will literally get hundreds of thousands of sites and there is no way of distinguishing a good from a not-so-good one. Ideally, especially if you are not that familiar with Florida, you should try to find someone who can recommend a reputable rental office or at least can advise you on locations. If you don't have anyone who can guide you, there are always online message boards where you can post your questions. The British in Florida site (**www.sunnybrits.com**) hosts a popular board populated with friendly and informed people.

Most importantl, you should be well aware of your rights as a tenant under Florida law. Even if you are staying for only a month, get to know the law before you sign any contract. Once you sign that contract, you are bound by it. Ask all your questions before putting your name to anything. Just as you are responsible for paying rent on time, the landlord is also responsible for certain things that may or may not be spelt out in the contract. Know what these responsibilities are, because it is within your rights to withhold payment if they are not fulfilled. The Division of Consumer Services has summarized the state's landlord/tenant laws on its website (**www.800helpfla.com/landlord_text.html**).

It is highly likely that the landlord will require you to pay a security deposit – sometimes the equivalent of one month's rent – as well as one month's rent in advance before letting you move in. There is no predetermined amount to these deposits, so they will vary depending on who you are dealing with. Try to avoid putting any money down unless you are absolutely sure that you want to rent somewhere, because you may not be entitled to a refund if you change your mind. If a deposit is non-refundable, however, it should be stated clearly in the rental agreement.

The security deposit is meant to cover any damages on the part of a tenant, so be sure to inspect the property with the landlord and take plenty of notes about damaged items or areas. To avoid disputes later, give a copy of your notes to the landlord and keep one for yourself.

At the end of the lease, the landlord has 15 days to return your security deposit (plus interest, if applicable) unless he or she intends to make a claim on it. If the landlord intends to keep all or some of the deposit, he or she has 30 days from the end of the lease to justify the action in writing by certified mail to your last-known address. Otherwise, the landlord forfeits his or her right to any claim on the deposit.

Buying to Let

Buying property for income-generation is fast becoming a popular option with foreigners. As a foreigner yourself in Florida, you will know what will meet other foreigners' needs. You can advertise your property from home, send out brochures, set up your own website and pass news of your rental property on to friends and work colleagues to secure short-term tenants. With around 1.48 million British visitors to Florida every year, you should never be short of tenants. When the property is not occupied, you can use it yourself. It's a business that anyone can run and which virtually runs itself.

There are however a few basic guidelines for letting your property (for more information, see **Letting Your Property**, pp.191–206). To begin with, the shorter the stay, the more you must charge per night to cover cleaning and laundry expenses. You will need to find a cleaning agency who can take care of getting the property ready for the next set of tenants. Find out how much they will charge and then factor those expenses in to determine a fair rent (also based on location, time of year and the size of your property).

You should also calculate for how long you need to let your property in order to earn back your initial capital investment. Add the cost of the property plus renovation expenses to find out when you are going to be in profit. Many people who have taken out a mortgage to buy a second home let out their property as a way of paying the mortgage.

Building from Scratch or Renovation

As mentioned several times, when looking at a property that you hope to reno-vate, check the building's historic status. If the home is in clear need of restoration but has some kind of historic designation, any repairs you embark on could be bound by costly legal requirements. However, if a do-it-yourself project is what you want to get your hands on, then there are plenty of properties in Florida that will keep you busy for years. Fortunately for you, the USA is the land of giant do-it-yourself stores like Home Depot where you can find everything you need to build yourself a house from scratch. Unfortunately, these mega-stores have driven a lot of small stores out of business and so, inversely, you will have a hard time finding a local corner hardware store to buy a box of nails.

Case Study: Securing Your Own Construction Loan? Don't!

There are countless horror stories circulating in the American real estate industry. You may even encounter the same tale told by different people in different states. Some sound suspiciously like urban legends and others have just enough detail to be good advice whether they are true or not. In fact, you could think of them as cautionary fables.

One common story involves a man named 'Joe' who wanted to build a house. He contacted an apparently well-regarded builder and to save money Joe arranged to secure his own construction loan. The builder agreed to draw on the construction loan as the house was being completed. For a while, everything went fine. Then Joe started noticing that the builder was never on the site and that the subcontractors would only come in sporadically. Following a series of repeated delays, Joe was served notice that the builder had filed for bankruptcy. Bank records showed that the builder had drawn the construction loan down more than the stage of construction would warrant. The house was valued at $400,000.

It turned out that the builder was a very good friend of the appraiser responsible for inspecting the construction and reporting back to the bank, which meant that the appraiser was in charge of the amount of money the builder could withdraw. Instead of inspecting the job himself, the appraiser took his friend's word on what percentage of the house was finished. In the end, the builder took 35 per cent more than he had completed. On a $400,000 house with a $300,000 construction loan, the builder had completed only 25 per cent of the job but had received 60 per cent of the money. Joe would need $200,000 out of his own pocket to finish construction. However, even if he did come up with the money, the house is stuck in months of litigation because the builder is in bankruptcy proceedings.

The bottom line? Never get your own construction loan. Let the builder do it. If the builder is not strong enough to obtain the loan, don't use that builder. If you insist on getting your own construction loan, then you should request that the appraiser notify you when he's going out to the site to verify the degree of completion. Ask him lots of questions and make sure the percentage of draw equals the average rate of construction. No matter what, you should always check out the builder very carefully. Get references from people who used him two years ago, one year ago, and currently.

If you don't plan to do it all yourself, you will need to find someone who can do it for you. An all-purpose handyman may be good for small jobs, but if you are going to be doing major renovations you are going to need to call in the experts. Picking a name out of a telephone directory is a gamble, of course. If that is your only option, then you should allow enough time to shop around for estimates, get references and, most importantly, follow up on those references. If an estimate is too low, then there is probably a good reason. Beware of hidden costs and, if you are paying by the hour, make sure that you keep track of how each hour is being spent.

If possible try to find other homeowners in the area who can offer a referral. Again, it might be a good idea to go to the online message boards for help with this. Other British people who have gone through similar experiences can offer the most valuable perspective. Another option is to try an online directory such as Service Magic (**www.servicemagic.com**), which claims to screen all of the contractors it lists on its site and which matches them to your needs. In addition to connecting you with thousands of local service providers – identified by zip code and searchable by speciality – the site also includes helpful articles and tips on renovating and remodelling.

If you prefer to start from scratch rather than spending your precious days trying to fix the mistakes of others, then you are looking at quite a different story. No doubt there is something very appealing about having some control over every detail of a house built from nothing, not least of which is the fact that you can customize it to your preferences and include amenities that you might not find in older properties. In addition, new homes tend to be more energy-efficient, which may save you some money down the road. Of course, you will soon discover that there are a few problems inherent in building a home in another country. For a start, it is not so easy to supervise construction when you live thousands of miles away.

There are a couple of websites that offer a lot of good tips and advice about building a home. One belongs to the Association of Homebuilders (**www.home builder.com**) and the other is an affiliated site (**www.homeplans.com**). The first one includes a searchable database of builders who are connected to the association, as well as detailed articles about what to look for in a builder and what to expect once the project gets going. The second site includes similarly informative articles, but also offers customizable home plans and blueprints that you can purchase and use as the basis for your new home.

If you are looking at buying into a development that is already in the process of being built, you should keep in mind that it is the developer you are buying and not the house. Find out everything you can about the quality and reputation of the builder by talking to owners who live in the same development or in another development by the same builder. You might want to consider bringing in an experienced contractor or home inspector to examine the quality of construction in a completed home. If you do buy into the development, try to get your contractor or inspector to make periodic visits to the construction site of your home to examine various areas as they are completed. You should also enquire about complaints filed against the developer with the state or local licensing or consumer protection agency that oversees contractors, as well as the local Better Business Bureau.

Beware of optional add-ons. You may be lured into looking at a home in a development because of its relatively low price, but as the salesperson starts to add on costly amenities you might see the price rising by anywhere between 5 and 20 per cent. Be sure to take care of essentials first, such as a fenced yard and additional electrical outlets. You can also negotiate and ask the developer to throw in something for every couple of things you buy.

To avoid getting stuck with a house that falls apart soon after you move in, be sure to buy from a reputable developer who includes a new house warranty from an independent insurance company. The warranty should cover workmanship and materials for one year; plumbing, electrical, heating and air-conditioning systems for two years and major structural defects for 10 years. You should get everything in writing, especially when dealing with sales representatives who promise you what will be done and when.

Making the Purchase

John Howell and Marcell Felipe

05

Buying a property in Florida is as safe as buying a property in England, but caution is always the order of the day. A book such as this – which must explain the potential pitfalls if it is to serve any useful purpose – can make it seem a frightening or dangerous experience. But if you go about the purchase in the right way, it is not dangerous and should not be frightening. The same or similar dangers arise when buying a house in England. If you are in any doubt, look briefly at a textbook on English conveyancing and all the dreadful things that have happened to people in England. You don't worry about those dangers because you are familiar with them and, more importantly, because you are shielded against contact with most of them by your solicitor. The same should be true when buying in Florida. Read this book to understand the background and why some of the problems exist, ask your lawyer to advise you about any issues that worry you, and then leave him or her to avoid the landmines!

Law

This book is intended primarily for people from England and Wales. For this reason I have drawn comparisons with English law. Scottish law is somewhat different. Where the points apply also to Scottish law, I have tried, depending on the context, to refer to either UK or British law. The law is, except where otherwise stated, intended to be up to date as at 1 January 2006.

Disclaimer

Although we have done our best to cover most topics of interest to the buyer of a property in Florida, a guide of this kind cannot take into account every individual's personal circumstances, and the size of the book means that the advice cannot be comprehensive. The book is intended as a starting point that will enable people who are thinking of buying property to understand some of the issues involved and to ask the necessary questions of their professional advisers. **IT IS NO SUBSTITUTE FOR PROFESSIONAL ADVICE.** Neither the authors nor the publishers can accept any liability whatsoever for any action taken or not taken as a result of this book.

Finding a Property in Florida

At the moment we are in a property 'boom'. It is, in most popular areas, a seller's market. Property – and, in particular, attractive, well-located and well-priced property – sells very quickly, although many good purchases are area-specific. A few years ago it was fairly simple to go to Florida, look around, see a few properties and then come back to England to ponder which to buy.

Today someone doing this could well find that the house they wanted to make an offer on had sold to someone else in the few days since they saw it.

As a result, people who are serious about buying property in Florida should do some research and make some preliminary preparations *before* they go on a visit to look at property. When they visit, they should do so with the intention that, if they see something that they really like, they will make a 'contingent offer' and commit themselves to the purchase while they are still on the spot. A contingent offer is one which allows the purchaser to withdraw from the offer if all the conditions of the contigencies are not met.

What Preparation Should You Make?

Understand the System

The system of buying and selling property in Florida is, not surprisingly, different from the system of buying property in England or Scotland. On balance, it is neither better nor worse, just different. It has some superficial similarities, which can lull you into a false sense of familiarity and over-confidence. *The most important thing to remember is that buying a home in Florida is just as safe as buying a home in Cardiff – providing that you take the right professional advice and precautions when doing so.* If you do not take such advice, there are many expensive traps for the unwary.

It is essential to surround yourself with the following qualified and referred local professionals: a lawyer, an accountant, a banker, a mortgage broker and a real estate agent.

See a Lawyer

It will save you a lot of time and trouble if you see your lawyer *before* you find a property. There are a number of preliminary issues that can best be discussed in the relative calm before you find the house of your dreams rather than once you are under pressure to sign some document to commit yourself in the purchase. These issues will include:

- **Who should own the property, bearing in mind the Florida and British tax consequences of ownership; i.e. in whose name the title will be held.**
- **Whether to consider mortgage finance, and if so what amount.**
- **What to do about buying the dollars needed to pay for the property, i.e. currency conversion, wire transfers.**
- **How to structure your purchase to minimize present and future taxes and costs.**
- **If you are going to be living in Florida, sorting out the tax, pension and investment issues that will need to be dealt with *before your move* if you are to get the best out of both systems.**

Only UK lawyers who specialize in dealing with US and specifically Florida laws, or US lawyers who understand UK laws, will be able to help you fully. Your usual English solicitor will know little or nothing of the issues of US law and an American lawyer is likely to know little or nothing about the British tax system or the issues of English or Scottish law that will affect the way the transaction should be arranged. A local lawyer may also be able to recommend realtors (estate agents), architects, surveyors, banks, mortgage lenders and other contacts in the area where you are looking.

A physical meeting is still the best way to start an important relationship. It has a number of advantages. It allows you to show and be shown documents and to wander off more easily into related topics. Most importantly, it is usually easier to make certain that you have each understood the other in a face-to-face meeting. But, these days, 'seeing' your lawyer does not need to involve an actual meeting. If it is more convenient to you, it could be done by telephone conference call, by videoconference or over the Internet.

Decide on Ownership

Who should be the owner of your new home? This is the most important decision you will have to make when buying a property. Because of the combination of the US and British tax systems, getting the ownership wrong can be a very expensive mistake indeed. It can lead to unnecessary tax during your lifetime and on your death. Even on a modest property this can amount to tens of thousands of pounds. This subject is dealt with more fully later, see pp.100–103.

Get an Offer of Mortgage/Finance

These days, with very low interest rates, more and more people borrow at least part of the money needed to buy their home in Florida. Even if they don't need to do so, for many it makes good business or investment sense.

If you want to borrow money to finance your purchase, it is better to get clearance or a preliminary approval *before* you start looking at property. Your lawyer should be able to get a preliminary mortgage offer within about 2–4 weeks.

Raising Finance to Buy a Property

In these days of low interest rates, many more people are taking out a mortgage in order to buy property abroad.

If the property is viewed simply as an investment, a mortgage allows you to increase your benefit from the capital growth of the property by 'leveraging' the investment. If you buy a house for £200,000 and it increases in value by £50,000 that is a 25 per cent return on your investment. If you had only put in £50,000 of your own money and borrowed the other £150,000, then the increase in value represents a return of 100 per cent on your investment. If the rate of increase in the value of the property is more than the mortgage rate, you have won. In recent years property values in the most popular areas have risen in value by much more than the mortgage rate. The key questions are whether that will continue and, if so, for how long.

If you decide to take out a mortgage, you can, in most cases, either mortgage (or extend the mortgage on) your existing UK property or take out a mortgage on your new US property. There are advantages and disadvantages both ways. Perhaps most useful are mortgage brokers who can discuss the possibilities in both the UK and the USA.

Many people buying property in the USA will look closely at fixed-rate mortgages so they know their commitment over, for example, the next five, 10 or 15 years. Again there are advantages and disadvantages.

Mortgaging Your UK Property

At the moment there is fierce competition to lend money and there are some excellent deals to be had, whether you choose to borrow at a variable rate, at a fixed rate or with one of the hybrid schemes now on offer. Read the Sunday papers such as the *Sunday Times* or the specialist mortgage press to see what is on offer, or consult a mortgage broker.

It is outside the scope of this book to go into detail about the procedures for obtaining a UK mortgage.

Advantages
• **The loan will probably be very cheap to set up.**

You will probably already have a mortgage. If you stay with the same lender there will be no legal fees or land registry fees for the additional loan. There may not even be an arrangement fee. If you go to a new lender, many special deals may mean that the lender will pay all fees involved.

• **The loan repayments will be in sterling.**

If the funds to repay the mortgage are coming from your sterling earnings, then the amount you have to pay will not be affected by fluctuations in exchange rates between the sterling and the dollar. At the time of writing (summer 2003) most experts are predicting that the pound may fall somewhat in value against the dollar (a correction from the recent decline of the dollar).

If sterling falls in value, then your debt as a percentage of the value of the property decreases. Your property will be worth more in sterling terms but your mortgage will remain the same.

• **You will be familiar with dealing with British mortgages.**

• **You can easily take out an endowment mortgage, a pension mortgage or an interest-only mortgage.**

Although in the USA it is possible to find interest-only mortgages and some programmes which resemble the pension mortgage, these are not common, though if you hunt hard you will be able to find what you want, as the USA does provide a litany of mortgage structures to fit virtually every situation.

• **You will probably need no extra life insurance cover.**

This can add considerably to the cost of the mortgage, especially if you are getting older.

Disadvantages

• **You will have a mortgage on your UK property without gaining any specific benefit over a mortgage on your second home. That is, you will pay UK interest rates which, at the time of writing are pretty much comparable to US rates.**

Crude rates (which, in any case, may not be comparable as they are calculated differently in the two countries) do not tell the whole story. What is the total monthly cost of each mortgage, including life insurance and all extras? What is the total amount required to repay the loan, including all fees and charges?

• **If sterling increases in value against the dollar, a mortgage in dollars would become cheaper to pay off.**

For example, your loan of $60,000 (worth about £31,800 at $1 = £0.53p) would only cost about £24,000 to pay off if the pound rose 20 per cent to about £0.40.

• **If you are going to let the property, it will be difficult or impossible to get US tax relief on the mortgage interest unless properly structured as an expense from the beginning.**

• **Many people do not like the idea of mortgaging their main UK home – a debt they may only just have cleared after 25 years of paying off an earlier mortgage!**

• **Some academics argue that, in economic terms, debts incurred to buy assets should be secured against the asset bought and that assets in one country should be funded by borrowings in that country.**

All in all, we believe that a UK mortgage is generally the better option for people who need or wish to borrow relatively small sums and who will be repaying it straight out of UK income.

US Mortgages

A US mortgage is one taken out over your US property. This will either be from a US bank or from a British bank that is registered and does business in the USA. You cannot take a mortgage on your new US property from your local branch of a UK building society or high street bank.

The basic concept of a mortgage to buy property is the same in the USA as it is in England, Wales or Scotland. It is a loan secured against the land or buildings. Just as in the UK, if you don't keep up the payments the bank will repossess your property after due notices.

Main Differences Between an English and a US Mortgage

• US mortgages are almost always created on a repayment basis. That is to say, the loan and the interest on it are both gradually repaid by equal instalments over the period of the mortgage. Endowment, pension and interest-only mortgages do exist, but they are not common.

• There are some US loan programmes that impose penalties for early payment of the loan.

• Most US mortgages are usually granted for 15 or 30 years, not 25 as in England. In fact the period can be anything from five to 30 years.

• The maximum loan is generally 95 per cent of the value of the property, but for foreign nationals, with no US credit history, 75 per cent or less is more common. As a planning guide, we suggest that you think of borrowing no more than 70 per cent of the price you are paying.

• Fixed-rate loans – with the rate fixed for the whole duration of the loan – are more common than in England. They are very competitively priced.

• The way of calculating the amount the bank will lend you is different from in the UK. As you would expect, there are detailed differences from bank to bank but most banks do not lend you more than an amount the monthly payments on which amount to 30–40 per cent of your net disposable income. *See* below.

How Much Can I Borrow?

Different banks have slightly different rules and different ways of interpreting the rules. Generally they will lend you an amount that will give rise to monthly payments of up to about 30–40 per cent of your net available monthly income.

The starting point is your net monthly salary after deduction of tax and National Insurance but before deduction of voluntary payments such as those to savings schemes. If there are two applicants, the two salaries are taken into account. If you have investment income or a pension, this will be taken into account. If you are buying a property with a track record of letting income, this may be taken into account. If you are buying an investment property, then the rental income can usually be taken into account.

If your circumstances are at all unusual, seek advice, as approaching a different bank may produce a different result.

e.g.		
Mr Smith – net salary per month	£3,000	
Mrs Smith – net salary per month	£2,000	
Investment income per month	£1,000	
Total income taken into account	£6,000 per month	

The maximum loan repayments permitted will be 30 per cent of this sum, less your existing fixed commitments.

i.e. Maximum permitted loan repayment £6,000 x 30% = £1,800 per month

Regular monthly commitments would include mortgage payments on your main and other properties, any rent paid, HP commitments and maintenance (family financial provision) payments. Repayments on credit cards do not count. If there are two applicants, both of their commitments are taken into account.

e.g.   Mr and Mrs Smith – mortgage on main home   £750
        Mr and Mrs Smith – mortgage on UK country cottage   £400
        Mrs Smith – HP on car   £200
        Total pre-existing outgoings   £1,350 per month

i.e. Maximum loan repayment permitted = £1,800 – £1,350 = £450 per month. (This would, at today's rates, equate to a mortgage of about £60,000 over 15 years.)

If you are buying a property for investment (rental) the bank may treat this as commercial lending and apply different criteria. Generally, in commercial lending, the income history of the property is the dominant factor. In most cases the rental income history must exceed the mortgage obligation by a certain ratio. For example, some banks will require that your mortgage obligations be less than 80 per cent of the property's net rental income (after all expenses have been calculated).

Applications for a US Mortgage

Once again, the information needed will vary from bank to bank. It will also depend on whether you are employed or self-employed.

Applications can receive preliminary approval (subject to survey of the property, confirmation of good title and confirmation of the information supplied by you) within a few days.

The Mortgage Offer

Allow four weeks from the date of your application to receiving a written mortgage offer, as getting the information to them sometimes takes a while. It may take longer.

Once you receive the offer you will generally have 30 days from receipt of the offer in which to accept it, after which time it will lapse. Have the mortgage explained to you in detail by your lawyer.

Payments for New Property

In the USA, when buying a new property, one normally makes payments gradually, as the development progresses, and takes title at the end. This can pose problems for banks, as you do not own anything you can mortgage until you make the final payment and take title. In most cases the mortgage will therefore only be granted to cover the final payment. As this is often 80 per cent (in the case of pre-construction contracts for new developments) this is seldom a problem.

In some cases (i.e. custom-made or semi-custom homes), if the earlier payments are more substantial than that, the banks will offer a credit facility to make the earlier payments. Once the property has been delivered to you (and thus the full loan has been taken) the normal monthly payments will begin.

Property Needing Restoration

Not all banks will finance such property. Many of those that do will consider the loan as a construction loan.

The Cost of Taking Out a Mortgage

This will normally involve charges amounting to about 1–2 per cent of the sum borrowed. These charges are in addition to the normal expenses incurred when buying a property, which normally amount to about 3–5 per cent of the price of the property.

Hidden Costs

You will probably be required to take out mortgage insurance, although this may be waived if your down-payment is significant (i.e. 20 per cent or more). You will be required to have title insurance, but you would probably have done this anyway. You will also be required to insure the property and produce proof of insurance – but you would probably also have done this anyway.

You will also be required to have an appraisal of the property conducted by an approved, licensed appraiser.

Early Redemption Penalties

The offer may be subject to early payment penalties. Read every paragraph of the offer carefully. Try to get an advance copy to read and review before signing.

The Exchange-rate Risk

If the funds to repay the mortgage are coming from your sterling earnings then the amount you have to pay will be affected by fluctuations in exchange rates between the pound and the dollar. Do not underestimate these variations. In recent times, the US dollar has been as high as $1.5 = £1 and as low as $1.7 = £1. This means that sometimes the amount of sterling you would have had to send to the USA to pay the mortgage would have been almost double the amount at other times. This is less of a worry if you have income in dollars, for example from letting the property.

Saving Money on your Dollar Repayments

Your mortgage will usually be paid directly from your US bank account. Unless you have sufficient rental or other dollar income going into that account, you will need to send money from the UK in order to meet the payments.

Every time you send a payment to the USA you will face two costs. The first is the price of the dollar. This, of course, depends on the exchange rate used to convert your sterling. The second cost is the charges that will be made by your UK and US banks to transfer the funds – which can be substantial.

There are steps that you can take to control both of these charges. As far as the exchange rate is concerned, you should be receiving the so-called 'commercial rate', not the tourist rate published in the papers. The good news is that it is a much better rate. The bad news is that rates vary from second to second and so it is difficult to get alternative quotes. By the time you telephone the second company, the first's rate has changed! In any case, you will probably want to set up a standing order for payment and not shop around every month.

There are various organizations that can convert your sterling into dollars. Your bank is unlikely to give you the best exchange rate. Specialist currency dealers will normally better the bank's rate, perhaps significantly. If you decide to go through a currency dealer you must deal with one that is reputable. They will be handling your money and, if they go bust with it in their possession, you could lose it. Ask your lawyer for a recommendation.

Another possibility for saving money arises if you 'forward-buy' the dollars that you are going to need for the year. It is possible to agree with a currency dealer that you will buy all your dollars for the next 12 months at a price that is, essentially, today's price. You normally pay 10 per cent down and the balance on delivery. If the dollar rises in value you will gain, perhaps substantially. If the dollar falls in value – well, life is hard!

The main attraction of forward-buying is not so much the possibility for gaining on the exchange rate – though at the moment this seems likely – but the certainty that the deal gives you. Only enter into these agreements with a reputable and, if possible, bonded broker.

Bearing in mind the cost of conversion and transmission of currency, it is better to make fewer rather than more payments. You will have to work out whether, taking into account loss of interest on the funds transferred but bank charges saved, you are best sending money monthly, quarterly or six-monthly.

Tax Implications

There are also certain US tax advantages that may be obtained by having a US mortgage. The extent and applicability of such advantages will vary from person to person.

See **Financial Implications**, 'Taxation', pp.124–41, but you should also consult your lawyer and a qualified certified public accountant (CPA).

Mortgaging your US Property: Summary

The following are some issues to discuss and confirm with your consultants.

Advantages

• **You will pay US interest rates which, at the time of writing (2006) are pretty muchcomparable with UK rates, without having to mortgage your UK property.**

US interest rates have been rising in the USA over recent quarters, but are expected to stop or slow again due to the cooling of the real estate market. Make sure you compare the overall cost of the two mortgages. Crude rates (which, in any case, may not be comparable as they are calculated differently in the two countries) do not tell the whole story. What is the total monthly cost of each mortgage, including life insurance and all extras? What is the total amount required to repay the loan, including all fees and charges?

• **If you are going to let the property you will usually be able to get US tax relief on the mortgage interest.**

See 'Tax on Rental Income', pp.132–3.

• **The loan repayments will usually be in dollars.**

If the funds to repay the mortgage are coming from rental income paid to you in dollars, this will give you something to spend them on!

• **Many people do not like the idea of mortgaging their main UK home – a debt they may only just have cleared after 25 years of paying a mortgage.**

• **Some academics argue that, in economic terms, debts incurred to buy assets should be secured against the asset bought and that assets in one country should be funded by borrowings in that country.**

Disadvantages

• **There may be higher set-up fees, as compared with your UK mortgage.**

• **Interest-only mortgages are difficult to find.**

• **The loan repayments will usually be in dollars.**

If the funds to repay the mortgage are coming from your sterling earnings then the amount you have to pay will be affected by fluctuations in exchange rates between the pound and the dollar. At the time of writing (summer 2003) most experts are predicting that the pound may fall marginally in value against the dollar. If the pound were to fall in value, then your debt as a percentage of the value of the property would increase in sterling terms. Your property would be worth more in sterling terms but your mortgage would also have increased in value.

• **You will be unfamiliar with dealing with US mortgages. Seek advice from at least three qualified sources.**

Generally speaking, US dollar mortgages will suit people letting their property on a regular basis.

Foreign Currency Mortgages

It is possible to mortgage your home in the USA by borrowing not in dollars but in pounds – or euros or Swiss francs or Japanese yen.

Who Should Own the Property?

There are many ways of structuring the purchase of a home in the USA. Each has significant advantages and disadvantages. The choice of the right structure will save you possibly many thousands of pounds of tax and expenses during your lifetime and on your death. Because some states will force you to give part of your estate to your surviving spouse, titling concerns are particularly important for people in second marriages.

The Options

Sole Ownership

In some cases it could be sensible to put the property in the name of one person only. If your husband runs a high-risk business, or if he is 90 and you are 22, i.e. there is a wide divergence of age between you, this could make sense. It is seldom a good idea from the point of view of tax or inheritance planning.

Joint Ownership

If two people are buying together they will normally buy in both their names. There are three forms of co-ownership: joint tenancy, tenancy in common and tenancy by the entirety.

A **tenancy by the entirety** is presumed to exist in any conveyance to a husband and wife. In this type of ownership, each spouse has a right to the undivided whole estate and a right of survivorship. It can be terminated by divorce or mutual accord. On dissolution of marriage, each owner in a tenancy by the entirety will own the property as a tenancy in common. It cannot be terminated by involuntary partition (i.e. your spouse's creditor cannot take it from you).

In a **tenancy in common**, each owner has a distinct, proportionate, undivided interest in the property. There is no right of survivorship. On your death your half will be disposed of in accordance with your will and or the laws on intestacy (inheritance rules). A person who owns property in this way, even if they own by virtue of inheritance, can, in many states, insist on the sale of the property. So if your stepchildren inherit from your husband they could insist on the sale of your home.

In a **joint tenancy**, the rights are very similar to those found in a tenancy by the entirety, except that the two co-owners need not be husband and wife, and a creditor of one of the parties can attach that party's interest in the property, and in many states force a sale of the same.

In all cases, it is important to note that in some states, including Florida, your *main home* cannot be taken by any creditors – save the Internal Revenue Service (IRS), your spouse or your mortgage company in the event of a default.

It is very important to seek clear advice from your lawyer about the form of ownership that will suit you best with regard to the consequences in the USA and in the UK.

Adding Your Children to the Title

If you give your children the money to buy part of the property and so put them on the title from the outset, you may save them quite a lot of inheritance tax. On your death you will only own (say) one-fifth of the property rather than one-half. Only that part will be taxable. It may be such a small value as to result in a tax-free inheritance. This only works sensibly if your children are over 18. Of course, there are drawbacks; for example, if they fall out with you they can insist on the sale of the property and on receiving their share.

Putting the Property in the Name of Your Children Only

If you put the property only in the name of your children (possibly reserving for yourself a life interest – *see* below) then the property is theirs. On your death there will be little or no inheritance tax and there will be no need to incur the legal expenses involved in dealing with an inheritance. This sounds attractive. Remember, however, that you have lost control. It is no longer your property. If your children divorce, their husband/wife will be able to claim a share. If they die before you without children of their own, you will end up inheriting the property back from them and having to pay inheritance tax for the privilege of doing so. A life interest is the right to use the property for a lifetime. So, on your death, your rights would be extinguished *but* your second wife or partner, who still has a life interest, would still be able to use the property. Only on their death would the property pass in full to the people to whom you gave it years earlier. This device will not only protect your right to use the property but also save large amounts of UK inheritance tax, particularly if you are young, the property is valuable and you live for many years. As always there are also drawbacks, not least being the fact that after the gift you no longer own the property. If you wish to sell you need the agreement of the 'owners', who will be entitled to their share of the proceeds of sale and who would have to agree to buy you a new house.

If you wish to do this, you must structure the gift carefully. Otherwise it could be taxable in the USA *either at once, or when you die.*

Limited Company

For some people, owning a property through a limited company can be a very attractive option. You own the shares in a company, not a house in the USA. There are various types of company.

US Corporations (Corp or Inc.) and Limited Liability Companies (LLC)

Corporation

Ownership through a company will mean that the income from letting the property is taxed in the usual way for companies – basically, you pay tax only on the profit made, rather than at the flat rate applicable in the case of an individual owner who is not tax-resident in the USA. This can reduce your tax bill. It also allows your property-based liabilities to be limited to your investment in the company (your property). As such, should you be sued by someone who was injured or killed in your property as a result of some alleged negligent act, they could not enforce a judgment against any of your other assets.

Limited Liability Company

Ownership through a limited liability company will provide the same limitations on liability as the traditional corporation, but from a tax point of view it is transparent. That is, the LLC will file an information-only report with the Internal Revenue Service, indicating what its income and expenses were for the year and what it finally ended up with as profits or losses. The IRS then looks to its owners to include their proportionate share of the company's profits or losses in their individual tax returns.

Conclusion

Ownership in the form of a corporation or an LLC gives rise to expenses such as accountancy and filing tax returns. Buying through a US company gives rise to a host of potential problems as well as benefits. In some cases, it is the best strategy, while in others it may constitute an unnecessary expense. The plan needs to be studied closely by your professional advisers so that you can decide whether it makes sense in the short, medium and long term.

UK Company

It is rare for a purchase through a UK company to make sense for a holiday home or single investment property. This is despite the fact that the ability to pay for the property with the company's money without drawing it out of the company and paying UK tax on the dividend is attractive. Once again you need expert advice from someone familiar with the laws of both countries.

Offshore (Tax Haven) Company

This can work in select cases. From the US perspective, a US property which is owned by a US company, which is in turn owned by an offshore company, has a number of income and inheritance tax advantages. However, these advantages may be entirely eliminated by other laws in the UK. The expenses of setting up these structures will also make them impractical in the majority of vacation property purchases. They could, however, make sense in cases where the property values and/or rental income is high. You must consult a competent attorney, with knowledge in both US and UK tax law, to give you proper advice. Your best source for such counsel is the bar association in the country where the property is located and three referrals.

The Use of Trusts

A trust can be a good vehicle for avoiding costly and timely probate process in the USA. In many ways, it can serve as a partial replacement to a will. As in England, trusts are widely used in the USA and recognized by law. Particularly common are 'revocable trusts' by which the owner keeps the right to terminate the trust at any time. Although these trusts do not have any tax benefits (its assets are treated as your own for tax purposes), they will allow you to avoid burdensome and costly probate proceedings.

Again, careful specialist advice is essential.

Which is Right for You?

The choice is of fundamental importance. If you get it wrong you will pay far more tax than you need to, during your lifetime and on your death. The tax consequences arise not only in the USA but also in your own country. For each buyer of a home in the USA one of the options set out above will suit perfectly. Another might just about make sense. The rest would be an expensive waste of money. The trouble is, it is not obvious which is the right choice. You need *in every case* to seek professional advice. If your case is simple, the advice will be too. If it is complex, the time and money spent will be repaid many times over.

The Process of Buying a Property

The Law

As you would expect, this is complicated. A basic textbook on US property law might extend to 500 pages. There are certain basic principles which it is helpful to understand.

• **The main legal concepts relating to property law are similar to those in the UK, as the two legal systems are based on common law principles. As in the English concept of real and personal property, real property includes land and buildings, but not the shares in a company that owns land and buildings.**

• The sale of real property located in the USA must always be governed by the law of the state where the property is located. Fortunately, these laws tend to be quite similar. The form of ownership of land is generally in 'fee simple'. This is similar to what we would call 'freehold ownership'.

• It is possible to own the buildings – or even parts of a building – on a piece of land separately from the land itself. This is of particular relevance in the case of long-term land leases, but it is generally a rare situation in the USA.

• Where a building or piece of real property is physically divided among a number of people, a condominium is created. The real property is divided into privately owned parts – like an individual flat – and communally owned areas. The management of the communally held areas is up to the owners of the privately held area, but can be delegated to someone else. Most states have legislation providing for the rights and duties of condominium associations and their members (the property owners).

• Transfer of ownership of property (real estate) is done by deed, but the process usually begins with a simple written agreement. The agreement needs to be in writing to be enforceable. The agreement will usually be subject to a number of contingencies such as a satisfactory home inspection, the buyer qualifying for a mortgage, and proper title examination. It will generally also include the real estate agent's commission (in Florida, 6 per cent is typical), and a stipulated completion (closing) date.

• Ownership can also be acquired by possession, usually for 30 years. Other rights – short of ownership – can exist over land. These include rights of way, tenancies, life interests, mortgages and option contracts. Most require some sort of formality in order to be valid against third parties but are always binding as between the people who made the agreements.

General Procedure

The general procedure when buying a property in the USA seems, at first glance, similar to the purchase of a property in England: sign a contract; do some checks; sign a deed of title. This is deceptive. The procedure is very different and even the use of the familiar English vocabulary to describe the different steps in the USA can produce an undesirable sense of familiarity with the procedure. This can lead to assumptions that things will be the same as they would in England. This is a dangerous assumption. Work on the basis that the system is totally different.

Choosing a Lawyer

Your real estate lawyer is the only person who represents your interests and your interests only in the home-buying process. All other parties concerned have a vested interest in having the transaction consummated, regardless of whether it is in your best interests or not.

Primarily, your attorney's job is to help you:

- **Fully understand exactly what you're committing yourself to when you look at homes for sale in Florida.**
- **Make sure that, when the transaction is over, you get what you think you are agreeing to.**
- **Ensure that you are buying a house from the right person – one who does not have 'baggage' that could harm you down the road.**

For the English buyer, there is no substitute for using the services of a specialist UK lawyer familiar with US law and international property transactions. This is the clear advice of every guidebook, of the US and British governments and of the Federation of Overseas Property Developers, Agents and Consultants (FOPDAC). It is therefore baffling why so many people buying a property in the USA do not take this necessary step.

US Lawyers

Most Americans buying a home in the USA will use the services of a lawyer, although they won't always know it. This is because, when buying with borrowed funds, if a buyer does not indicate that he desires an independent attorney, the bank will appoint one. Of course, the bank's attorney will look to make sure there is clean title to the property, but he or she will not advise you on other issues which may be germane to your acquisition. For example, he or she will not advise you on the contract, nor will he or she advise you on the propriety of the bank's charges, or on the implications of buying in your name versus a corporate name, or on whether you are entitled to receive your deposit back if something goes wrong.

For these reasons, it is common for Americans to appoint their own attorney when buying a home in the USA, in addition to the bank's attorney who is compulsory.

English Lawyers (Solicitors)

For English people the services of a US lawyer alone are unlikely to give them all the information or help they need to buy a home in the USA. They will often require advice about UK tax implications of their purchase, mortgages, currency exchange, etc. They should retain the services of a specialist UK lawyer familiar with dealing with these issues.

The buyer's usual solicitor is unlikely to be able to help, as there are only a handful of English law firms with the expertise.

The Price

This can be freely agreed upon between the parties. Depending on the economic climate, there may be ample or very little room for negotiating a reduction in the asking price. At the moment the scope is limited for reasonably priced properties in the main cities and tourist areas, which are in short supply. Note however, that real estate cycles do change and that normally the summer period is the best time to negotiate price and terms on a contract.

Where Must the Money be Paid?

The price, together with the taxes and fees payable, is usually paid by the buyer to the closing agent (usually an attorney). The closing agent then disburses all the funds directly to the different parties involved. For example, the closing agent will generally pay the realtor's commission directly, and then deduct these sums from the sums paid to seller. The closing agent will generally also arrange for payment of escrow charges (*see* p.110). This is the best and safest way to deal with this. You can, in fact, agree to pay in whatever way and wherever you please. So, for example, in the case of a British seller and a British buyer the payment could be made in sterling by bank transfer.

In the case of a seller who is not tax-resident in the USA, the buyer is generally obliged to retain and adjust 30 per cent of the price and pay it to the taxman on account of the seller's potential tax liabilities. *See* below for more details.

General Enquiries and Special Enquiries

Certain enquiries are made routinely in the course of the purchase of a property. These include, in appropriate cases, a check on the planning situation of the property. This zoning classification will reveal the position of the property itself but it will not, at least directly, tell you about its neighbours and it will not reveal general plans for the area. If you want to know whether the authorities are going to put a prison in the village or run a new bus route through your back garden (both, presumably, bad things) or build a motorway access point or railway station two miles away (both, presumably, good things), you will need to ask. There are various organizations you can approach but, just as in England, there is no single point of contact for such enquiries. If you are concerned about what might happen in the area then you will need to discuss the position with your lawyers at an early stage. There may be a considerable amount of work (and therefore cost) involved in making full enquiries, the results of which can never be guaranteed.

Normal general enquiries also include a check that the seller is the registered owner of the property and that it is sold (if this has been agreed) free of mortgages or other charges. Additionally, ordinary enquiries will include a full home inspection to determine if there is any major damage to the property. A site survey is usually performed as well.

In order to advise you what special enquiries might be appropriate, your lawyer will need to be told your proposals for the property. Do you intend to let it out? If so, will you do this commercially? Do you intend to use it for business purposes? Do you want to extend or modify the exterior of the property? Do you intend to make interior structural alterations?

Agree in advance the additional enquiries you would like to make and get an estimate of the cost of those enquiries.

Your Civil Status and Other Personal Details

This is something you will have given no thought to. For most of the time it is not a matter of importance in the UK. It is something the Americans get very worked up about.

When preparing documents in the USA you will be asked to specify your civil status. This comprises a full set of information about you. They will not only ask for your full name and address but also, potentially, for your nationality, passport number, and maiden name. If appropriate, you will also declare your marital status at this point.

Tax Identification Number

To own a property in the USA you generally need to obtain a tax identification number (TIN or ITIN). This is obtained from the IRS office and you will need to fill in a simple form. Alternatively, your lawyer can obtain this for you.

The Homeowners' Association

When a number of people own land or buildings in such a way that they have exclusive use of part of the property but shared use of the rest, then a home-owners' association (HOA) is created to carry out the maintenance of the common areas and to enforce any agreed-upon rules for the community such as architectural design restrictions. Houses on their own plots with no shared facilities will not have a HOA.

In a HOA the buyer of a house or an apartment owns his own house or apart-ment outright – as the English would say, 'freehold' – and shares the use of the remaining areas as part of a community of owners. It is not only the shared pool that is jointly owned but (in an apartment) the lift shafts, corridors, roof, foun-dations, entrance areas, parking zones, etc.

The members of the HOA are each responsible for their own home. They collectively agree the works needed on the common areas and a budget for those works. They then become responsible for paying their share of those common expenses, as stipulated in their title.

The community is managed by an elected committee and appoints a president and secretary – both of whom are residents in the community. Day-to-day management is usually delegated to an administrator, who need not be a resident in the community.

The charges of the HOA are divided in the proportions stipulated in the deed creating the HOA. You will pay the same HOA fees whether you use the place all year round or only for two weeks' holiday. You do not have the option of non-participation in the HOA.

The HOA should provide not only for routine work but, through its fees, set aside money for periodic major repairs. If it does not – or if the amount set aside is inadequate – the general meeting can authorize a supplemental levy to raise the sums needed.

The rules set by the HOA are intended to improve the quality of life of residents. They could for example deal with concerns about noise (no radios by the pool), prohibit the use of the pool after 10pm, ban the hanging of washing on balconies, etc. More importantly they could ban pets or any commercial activity in the building. These rules and by-laws form an important document. Every buyer of a property in a community with a HOA should insist on a copy of the rules prior to signing any written agreement. In many states, a buyer will have three days from receipt of the HOA rules and by-laws to cancel a real estate purchase agreement.

Initial Contracts

In the USA, most sales start with a preliminary contract. The type of contract will depend on whether you are buying a finished or an unfinished property. Signing any of these documents has far-reaching legal consequences, which are sometimes different from the consequences of signing a similar document in England. Whichever type of contract you are asked to sign, always seek legal advice before signing.

Who Prepares Them?

Generally the preliminary contract is prepared by the estate agent's regulatory board (they are professionally qualified in the USA) or, in the case of new or unfinished property, by the developer. Estate agent's contracts are often based on a pre-printed document in a standard format. Many realtors' contracts have so many options to 'check' that it would be unwise to dive into a contract without proper advice from your lawyer. In the case of new or unfinished property (also called pre-construction property) the contracts are extremely one-sided, giving the developer – the seller – all the rights and taking away all the rights of the buyer. It is important that these contracts are not just accepted as final. In every case they will need to be modified, in some cases extensively.

If You Are Buying a Finished Property

You will be invited to make an offer by signing a contract, which, if accepted by the seller, will bind you to its terms. In most parts of the USA it is the most common type of document. It is an agreement that commits both parties. The seller must sell a stated property at a stated price to a stated person on the terms set out in the contract. The buyer must buy.

This is a far-reaching document and so it is particularly important that you are satisfied that it contains all the terms necessary to protect your position. Take legal advice. Remember that, under US law, by signing and completing this contract you become, in some senses, the owner of the property, although you will need to sign a deed of sale and register your ownership to be safe as far as third parties are concerned.

The contract will contain a variety of 'routine' clauses:

- **The names of seller and buyer should both be stated fully.**
- **The property should be described fully, both in an everyday sense and by reference to its land registry details.**
- **A date for the signing of the deed of sale will be fixed or the contract will permit either party to require the signing of the deed at any point by giving notice to the other.**
- **A statement will be made as to when possession will take place – normally, on the date of signing the title.**
- **The price is fixed.**
- **A receipt for any deposit is given.**
- **The property should be sold with vacant possession.**
- **The property should be sold free of any charges, debts or burdens and all bills should be paid up to date before signing the deed.**
- **It will provide for who is to pay the costs of the purchase.**
- **It may confirm the details of any agent involved and who is to pay his or her commission.**
- **It will set out what is to happen if one or both of the parties break the contract.**
- **It will establish the law to cover the contract and the address of the parties for legal purposes.**

If the buyer or seller drops out of the contract or otherwise breaks it, various arrangements may be made.

A special deposit (**escrow**) might be payable by the buyer. If the buyer fails to complete, he or she will lose the deposit. If the seller fails to complete, the buyer will have a 'cause of action for specific performance', i.e. the transfer of the deed. This is one of the reasons why it is important for buyers to have their own independent attorney who will serve as escrow agent and who is unlikely to agree readily with a seller's claim that the buyer has defaulted. For example, most developer contracts, if unchanged, will name the developer's attorney or some other affiliated company as the escrow agent for the deposit. If closing is delayed for any reason, these escrow agents are more likely to interpret such delay as a default on your part.

Alternatively, the contract may provide for a deposit to be paid as a simple part of the price of the property. The contract can provide for all or part of this deposit – and any other sums paid up to the relevant moment – to be lost if the buyer does not proceed.

If the parties fail to comply with their obligations there is the ultimate remedy of seeking a court order. As in any country, this is very much a last resort, as it is costly, time-consuming and (also as in any country) there is no guarantee of the outcome of a court case. If a court order is made in your favour, this order can be registered at the land registry.

If You Are Buying an Unfinished Property (Pre-construction)

There are three stages of the purchase.

Reservation contract: In these cases there is usually a preliminary contract. This is the reservation contract. This allows you to reserve a plot or unit when you see it and allows you time to sign one of the other types of contract when you have made the necessary enquiries. In some cases, it will be non-binding; in others you can lose your deposit if you do not comply with its terms. It is important to get your lawyer to give it a careful read.

Contract 'on plan': You agree to buy a property once it has been built and agree to make payments in stages as the construction progresses. Sometimes the payments are dependent upon the progress of the building works. On other occasions they are due on set dates. The latter are now the more common, though less attractive to the buyer.

Deed of sale: Once the property has been built you will sign the **deed of sale** and pay the balance of the price. It is only then that you become the owner of the property and register your title. Until then, if the builder goes bust you are simply one of many creditors.

There are, however, things you can do to protect yourself. For instance, you can insist on having the contract modified so that all your deposits and payments are made not to the builder himself, but to the escrow agent (usually your attorney or realtor), *see* above. If this happens, the builder only gets the money if and when the property is completed. If the builder goes bankrupt, your deposit is not subject to the claims of his creditors.

In most cases in the USA, builders agree to have the funds placed in escrow, although they will insist on having them held by their lawyer, not yours. In some cases, however, particularly in 'hot' developments, builders simply refuse to give such a guarantee and will use your deposits to build the property. 'I am your guarantee. I am a man of honour. I have been building for over 30 years!' Remember that big companies and honourable men go bust: Rolls-Royce, Barings Bank, Enron.

A common practice in some areas is to have the first 10 per cent deposit held in escrow, and the second 10 per cent to be available to the builder for the construction of the project. In general, pre-construction deposits range from 10–30 per cent of the total price.

At the end of the construction, you pay the balance. Depending on the contract it may be subject to obtaining a mortgage. However, be careful, as more developers are making their contracts 'cash deals', meaning that if you are not able to obtain a mortgage you must either come up with the whole sum or lose your deposit.

Again, having an attorney look over this type of agreement is very important, as he or she may identify potential abuses by the builder – remember, unlike the standard re-sale contract, the builder's contract has been drafted specifically for him by his attorney. It is not intended to be fair and balanced, but rather is intended to protect the builder from all possible angles. It is up to you and your attorney to say what specific terms are unacceptable to you. Those who do not raise issues end up with a one-sided contract. Those who raise the issues will generally find that, with the exception of particularly 'hot' developments, builders are generally willing to modify their standard contract to make you feel comfortable about the purchase.

Other Documentation

You should be given a full specification for the property, a copy of the community rules and constitution if the property shares common facilities, and a copy of any agreements you have entered into regarding management or letting of the property. All are important documents. Pay particular attention to the specifications. One thing to watch out for are the models and the 'available' options, and another are the 'standard' options. For instance, all marketing material and models may have marble floors, but these may be available only at an extra charge, and your basic model may come only with carpet.

Checklist – Signing a Contract

Property in the Course of Construction   **Existing Property**

Are you clear about what you are buying?

Have you taken legal advice about who should be the owner of the property?

Have you taken legal advice about inheritance issues?

Are you clear about boundaries?

Checklist – Signing a Contract (*cont'd*)

Property in the Course of Construction	Existing Property

Are you clear about access?

Have you seen the seller's title?

Have you seen an up-to-date land registry extract?

Are you sure you can change the property as you want?

Are you sure you can use the property for what you want?

Is the property connected to water, electricity, gas, etc.?

Is the property in a hurricane zone?

Is insurance available?

Have you had a survey done?

Have you made all necessary checks or arranged for them to be made?

Have you included 'get-out clauses' for all important checks not yet made?

Is your mortgage finance arranged?

Is the seller clearly described?

If the seller is not signing in person, have you seen a power of attorney/mandate to authorize the sale?

Are you fully described?

Is the property fully described? Identification? Land registry details?

Is the price correct?

Are there any possible circumstances in which it can be increased?

Are extras described fully?

Property in the Course of Construction	Existing Property
Are the stage payments fully described?	Does the contract say when possession will be given?
Are the arrangements for stage payments? satisfactory?	Is there a receipt for the deposit paid?
Is the date for completion of the work agreed?	In what capacity is the deposit paid?
Is your deposit paid to an escrow account, or will it be used by the builder for construction, i.e. is it at risk?	Does the property have a habitation licence?

Is the date for signing the deed agreed?

Does the contract provide for the sale to be free of charges and debts?

Does the contract provide for vacant possession?

Who is to act as closing agent?

Is the estate agent's commission dealt with?

What happens if there is a breach of contract?

Are all the necessary special get-out clauses included?

Does the contract allow for assignment or sale prior to taking title?

Steps between Signing the Contact and Signing the Deed

Power of Attorney

Very often it will not be convenient for you to go to the USA to sign the deed in person. Sometimes there may be other things that, in the normal course of events, would require your personal intervention but where it would be inconvenient for you to have to deal with them yourself.

Just as often you will not know whether you will be available to sign in person. Completion dates on US property are notoriously fluid and so you could plan to be there but suffer a last-minute delay to the signing that makes it impossible.

The solution to this problem is the power of attorney. This document authorizes the person appointed to have power of attorney to do whatever the document authorizes on behalf of the person granting the power. The most sensible type of power to use will be the US-style of power of attorney that is appropriate to the situation. The power will be signed in front of a notary either in the UK or in the USA. If it is signed in front of a UK notary it has to be ratified by, of all people, the Foreign and Commonwealth Office for use overseas. This sounds very grand but is actually quick and simple.

The type of US power of attorney that you will need depends on what you want to use it for. Your specialist English lawyer can discuss your requirements with you and prepare the necessary document. Alternatively you can deal directly with the US lawyer who will ultimately need the power. In theory an English-style power should be sufficient, but in practice the cost and delay associated with getting it recognized are likely to be unacceptable.

Even if you intend to go to the USA to sign, it is sensible to think about granting a power of attorney just in case. It is not something that can be done at the last moment. From decision to getting the document to the USA will take at least seven and more likely 10 business days. If you are able to go, the power will not be used.

Even if you have granted a power of attorney, if you get the opportunity to go to the USA at the time of the signing it is worth doing so. It is quite interesting but, more importantly, you will be able to check the house to make sure that everything is in order before the deed is signed.

If you do not wish to grant a power of attorney, and cannot go to the USA, you may have the closing documents delivered to you in England for you to sign, notarize and return to the USA. This, however, will generally delay the closing by at least one week, and hence it must be planned carefully in advance, as any slight mix-up or mistake in the documentation will require that the whole process be repeated.

Getting the Money to the USA

There are a number of ways of getting the money to the USA.

Electronic Transfer

The most practical is to have it sent electronically by SWIFT transfer from a UK bank directly to the recipient's bank in the USA. This costs about £20–35 depending on your bank. It is safer to allow two or three days for the money to arrive in the bank, despite everyone's protestations that it will be there the same day.

Europe has now introduced unique account numbers for all bank accounts. These incorporate a code for the identity of the bank and branch involved as well as the account number of the individual customer. These are known as IBAN numbers. They should be quoted, if possible, on all international currency transfers; US banks have ABA numbers. You should get specific wiring instructions from the person to whom you are sending the funds. You can send the money from your own bank, via your lawyers or via a specialist currency dealer.

For the sums you are likely to be sending you should receive an exchange rate much better than the 'tourist rate' you see in the press. There is no such thing as a fixed exchange rate in these transactions. The bank's official inter-bank rate changes by the second and the job of the bank's currency dealers is to make a profit by selling to you at the lowest rate they can get away with. Thus if you do a lot of business with a bank and they know you are on the ball you are likely to be offered a better rate than a one-off customer. For this reason it is often better to send it via your specialist UK lawyers who will be dealing with large numbers of such transactions. This also has the advantage that their bank, which deals with international payments all the time, is less likely to make a mistake causing delay to the payment than your own bank, for which such a payment might be a rarity.

You or your lawyers might use a specialist currency dealer such as Moneycorp to make the transfer of funds instead of a main UK bank. Such dealers often give a better exchange rate than an ordinary bank. Sometimes the difference can be significant, especially compared to your local branch of a high street bank. Although these dealers use major banks to transfer the funds, you need to make sure that the dealer you are dealing with is reputable. Your money is paid to them, not to the major bank, and so could be at risk if the dealer is not bonded or otherwise protected.

However you make the payment, be sure you understand whether you or the recipient is going to pick up the receiving bank's charges. If you need a clear amount in the USA you will have to make allowances for these, either by sending a bit extra or by asking your UK bank to pay all the charges. As mentioned above, make sure you have the details of the recipient bank, its ABA number, its customer's name, the account codes and the recipient's reference precisely right. Any error and the payment is likely to come back to you as undeliverable – and may involve you in bearing the cost of it being converted back into sterling. You should consider receiving also a verbal confirmation of receipt from the bank branch manager.

The bank in the USA will make a charge – which may be substantial – for receiving your money into your account.

Banker's Drafts

You can arrange for your UK bank to issue you with a banker's draft (bank certified cheque) which you can take to the USA and pay into your bank account. Make sure that the bank knows that the draft is to be used overseas and issues you with an international draft. There are long holds on such instruments once deposited in the USA.

Generally this is not a good way to transfer the money. It can take a considerable time – sometimes weeks – for the funds deposited to be made available for your use. The recipient bank's charges can be surprisingly high. The exchange rate offered against a sterling draft may be uncompetitive, as you are a captive customer.

Cash

This is not recommended. You will need to declare the money on departure from the UK and on arrival in the USA. You must by law do this if the sum involved is US$10,000 or more. You are well advised to do so for smaller amounts. Even then, if you declare £200,000 or so they might think you are a terrorist or drug dealer. That suspicion can have far-reaching consequences in terms of listings in police files on 'dodgy people' and even surveillance. To add insult to injury the exchange rate you will be offered for cash (whether you take sterling and convert there or buy the US dollars here) is usually very uncompetitive and the notary may well refuse to accept the money in his account. Don't do it.

Exchange Control and Other Restrictions on Moving Money

Other than the requirement to declare the transport of any sums exceeding $10,000, the USA has no exchange control when taking money to or from the USA. There are some statistical records kept showing the flow of funds and the purpose of the transfers.

When you sell your property in the USA you will be able to bring the money back to the UK if you wish to do so (after you've paid your taxes on any gain resulting from the sale).

Final Checks about the Property

All the points outstanding must be resolved to your satisfaction, as must any other points of importance to you.

Fixing the Completion Date

The date stated in the contract for signing the deed could most charitably be described as flexible or aspirational. Often it will move, if only by a day or so. For this reason it is not sensible to book your travel to the USA until you are almost sure that matters will proceed on a certain day.

Checklist – Steps Before Completion

Property in the Course of Construction	Existing Property
Prepare power of attorney	
Check what documents must be produced on signing the deed	
Confirm all outstanding issues have been complied with	
Confirm all other important enquiries are clear	
Confirm arrangements (date, time, place) for completion with your lender if you have a mortgage	
Confirm arrangements (date, time, place) for completion with the closing agent	
Send necessary funds to the USA	
Receive rules of community	
Insurance cover arranged? (If you do not, the bank will arrange it or require it)	
Sign off work or list defects	Proof of payment of community fees
	Proof of payment of other bills

The Deed of Sale

This must generally be signed in front of a US notary public either by the parties in person or someone holding power of attorney for them. Although it is technically possible to sign it in front of a UK notary and have the deed 'legalized', this will generally delay the process.

Formalities

Certain procedures are followed at the signing of the deed.

The parties are identified by their passports, driver's licence, social security cards or tax identification numbers. This will normally be done, initially, by the closing agent and/or his assistant, usually a notary public.

The closing agent may also go through the content of the deed with the parties. This tends to be very superficial. More importantly, the closing agent will review the 'closing statement' in detail with both parties. This important document summarizes all of the charges and prorations associated with the transaction. It will include an itemization of bank charges, attorneys' fees, estate agent's fees, taxes, stamps, utilities, etc.

After the Deed Has Been Signed

The deed and any mortgage must be registered with the land registry and the taxes and stamps must be paid. The closing agent will arrange for this. This should be done as quickly as possible. Whoever registers first gets priority in most cases. These rules will actually vary from state to state, but in general this is not something to be delayed.

After several months the land registry will issue a certificate to the effect that the title has been registered.

The Cost of Buying a Property

There are fees and taxes payable by a buyer when acquiring a property in the USA. They are sometimes known as completion expenses or completion costs, but more commonly they are known as closing costs. They are impossible to predict with total accuracy at the outset of a transaction. This is because there are a number of variable factors that will not become clear until later. However, you will generally be looking at a minimum of 3–5 per cent of the purchase price. *These costs are calculated on the basis of the price paid for the property.*

As a general guide:

• **Loan fees**: This includes loan origination fees or 'points', and charges for the appraisal, checking your credit and processing your loan application. Generally, these total about 1–2 per cent of the total price, but can add up to 3 per cent of the amount you borrow.

• **Private mortgage insurance**: Determined based on the type and amount of loan taken out.

• **Title insurance**: Can range from a few hundred to over a thousand dollars, depending on the sale price of your home. Generally, however, it is less than 1 per cent of the value of your home. Virtually all property in the USA has title insurance. It is required if a mortgage is involved.

• **Homeowner's insurance**: This varies depending on the area. For example, if your home is in a flood zone or high-risk area (such as a hurricane area) it will be higher. For an idea of prices in your area, contact the State's Department of Insurance and ask for information on insurance rates.

• **Property taxes**: Usually 1.5–2 per cent of the appraised value of your home as determined by the county property appraiser. These are annual fees; they are not transactional. However, upon purchasing your home, your lender will require you to deposit a portion of this payment in escrow with them so as to make sure that you will not default. As such, you won't generally need the full amount available for closing.

- **Inspections**: Based on purchase price and square footage, the range is $250–450 for home inspections and $60–125 for termite inspections.

- **Recording**: There is a fee for recording the **deed** and **mortgage** for local public records. Typically you will be charged on a per-page basis. Although the fees vary from place to place, in Florida you will generally pay $10 for the first page plus $8.50 per each additional page.

- **Document stamps on the deed**: Some states charge a tax when property is transferred from one party to another. In Florida, the tax is $7 for every $1,000 of the purchase price, i.e. $700 for a $100,000 home.

- **Tax on mortgage**: Again, although this varies, if you were buying in Florida you would pay $5.50 for every $1,000 of purchase price, i.e. $550 for a $100,000 home.

- **Home warranty insurance**: Covers repairs for individual parts of the home for a certain length of time and costs vary depending on the condition of the home, its proximity to the ocean or water and if it is in a flood zone. Due to the recent spate of hurricanes in 2004 and 2005, numerous Floridan insurance companies have opted not to renew home policies; some have left the state entirely, preferring not to be subject to such risk. Therefore it is critical that a firm insurance commitment in writing be obtained before title is conveyed.

- **Initiation fees**: Condominiums and homeowners' associations often charge these fees. Costs vary depending on the property or neighbourhood.

- **Legal fees**: Range from $500–600 for a $100,000 home to $750–950 for a $200,000 home. The fees are lower if your attorney issues the title insurance policy, as the title insurance company will generally pay the attorney for his opinion.

Key Points

Property Under Construction

When buying a new property, these are the key points to look out for:

- **Make sure you understand exactly what you are buying. How big is the property? What will it look like? How will it be finished? What appliances are included? What facilities will it enjoy?**

- **Think about who should own the property so as to minimize tax and inheritance problems.**

- **Make sure the contract has all the necessary clauses required to protect your position.**

- **Make sure you are paying your deposits to an escrow account if you are buying 'pre-construction'.**

- **Be clear about the timetable for making payments.**

- **Think about whether you should buy currency in advance.**

Case Study Round-up

You should never take pleasure in the misfortunes of other, but you can learn from them. The following tips are based on lessons learned the hard way.

• **Conduct the final inspection as close as possible to the closing (completion)**: Check all appliances thoroughly, run the furnace and air-conditioner, run the hot water, flush the toilets, try the lights, check the basement for standing water, test each electrical outlet for power by plugging a hairdryer into it, inspect the carpet in areas formerly covered by furniture, and locate any necessary electronic gadgets such as garage door openers. **Here's why**...a couple who wanted to show off their new house soon after the closing discovered that the sellers had stripped it of absolutely everything: light bulbs, electrical fixtures (including plastic switch-plate covers), curtain rails, cabinet knobs and all the drawers in the garage work bench. They had even siphoned all the oil out of the fuel tank after the gauge had been read for the closing adjustment, and had replaced the new appliances with older models that didn't work. Unfortunately, the sellers had moved out of state, leaving the new owners with $8,000 worth of damages and very little legal recourse.

• **If you plan to buy in a regulated subdivision, read any and all restrictions very carefully before you close**: Whether you like it or not, some development subdivisions have restrictions that are meant to protect the value of the property in your neighbourhood. Make your contract subject to your review and approval of the restrictions. **Here's why**...a family purchased a home on a heavily wooded lot in an upscale subdivision. They liked the house more than they liked the trees, and six weeks after closing they called in a tree company and within a few hours 43 trees had been cut and removed from the yard. Later in the day

• When you take possession of the property, consider carefully whether it is worth incurring the expense of an independent survey to confirm that all is in order with the construction and to help draft any 'snagging list'.

Resale Properties

When buying a resale property, these are the key points to look out for:

• Make sure you understand exactly what you are buying. Are the boundaries clear? What furniture or fittings are included?

• Think about whether to have the property surveyed, especially if it is nearly 10 years old and its warranty will soon be expiring.

• Think about who should own the property so as to minimize tax and inheritance problems.

• Make sure the contract has all the necessary clauses required to protect your position.

the developer drove by on his way to another project. When he saw what they had done he was furious, and informed the family that the subdivision restrictions prohibited the cutting of any trees unless they were diseased or dead or were a threat to a house. Should a homeowner cut down any trees unnecessarily, then they would have to replace them with trees of similar size. Mature trees are expensive, to say the least, and the family ended up spending over $45,000 to replace trees they hated in the first place.

• **If you are purchasing a house that has a septic system, before you close, be sure to obtain a copy of the original septic permit to investigate whether the system was installed properly and is large enough for the size of the house**: If something doesn't look right, call the Department of Environmental Control and a reputable septic company immediately to determine whether or not the system is sufficient. You should get the seller to sign a disclosure statement that reveals the existence of any problem and lists the measures the seller took to correct it. **Here's why**...a young couple bought a house that was for sale by the owner, and which was on a septic system. They took the seller's word that there had never been any problems with the system. Six months after closing, the drain field started to puddle and overflow into the yard. The new owners called a septic company to drain and pump the entire system. Six months later, the system overflowed again, this time into the neighbour's yard. Faced with a smelly, overflowing septic problem and angry neighbours, they took the advice of a friend and requested a copy of the original septic permit from the county to be sure that the seller had installed the proper system. They discovered that the seller did have a septic permit, but it was for a three-bedroom home. They had purchased a five-bedroom house with three bathrooms. The existing septic system could never have supported a house that size. A septic company came

• Think about whether you should buy currency in advance.

• When you take possession of the property, make sure that everything agreed is present.

Special Points – Older Properties

When buying an older property – by which is meant a property built more than 50 years ago, for example – there are additional special points to look out for:

• Are you having a survey? Not to do so can be an expensive mistake.

• Are you clear about any restoration costs to be incurred? Do you have estimates for those charges?

• Are there any planning problems associated with any alterations or improvements you want to make to the property? Will the local authorities allow you to re-build it, and if so at what standards?

out to the house and informed them there simply wasn't enough room to install an adequate system. If notified, the county could have forced the family to move out of the house. Eventually they discovered that the septic system had never performed properly, and the seller had intentionally hidden this from them – a major violation of disclosure law. The new owners have a strong case, but only if they can still locate the seller.

• **Refuse to buy a house without a termite letter, a heat and air letter, a survey and a professional home inspection:** Many mortgage companies do not require termite letters, but every buyer should. Be sure to choose the termite company yourself. In addition, a professional home inspector will find crucial problems such as leaking seals and water damage. You should never use a blank contract supplied by the seller without having a real estate attorney or a good realtor read it and make changes that protect you. **Here's why**...after months spent looking for a house with a series of uncommitted agents, one couple decided to go it alone and soon walked into their dream home. The price was $10,000 less than they had planned to spend. They made an offer immediately and, since the sellers had a blank contract on hand, the couple signed on the spot. A few weeks later they had moved in. While cleaning, the wife soon discovered hundreds of 'ants with wings'. They called an exterminator who explained to them that these were, in fact, termites. Further inspection revealed that the insects were everywhere and had been in the house for quite some time. The original estimate to repair the damage was $5,000. Once the repairs had begun, workmen discovered that all three bathrooms had severe water damage from leaking seals on the lavatories and the entire floor under the bathrooms had rotted away and the floor joists were starting to rot. The total repairs ended up costing $12,400.

• When you take delivery of the property, make sure that everything agreed is present.

• Is the property designated as a historic site?

Special Points – Rural Properties

Such properties have often acquired a number of rights and obligations over the years. Are you clear about any obligations you might be taking on?

• You are probably buying for peace and quiet. Are you sure that nothing is happening in the vicinity of your property that will be detrimental to that?

• If you have any plans to change the property or to use it for any other purposes, will this be permitted?

• If you intend to build on the site, be very clear about minimum permitted plot sizes – which can vary – and other planning limitations.

Special Points – City Properties

City properties will usually be apartments; *see* further overleaf.

- If you intend to use a car, where will you park?

- Unless you are used to living in a city, do not underestimate the noise that will be generated nearby. If you are in a busy area (and you are likely to be), this will go on until late at night. How good is the sound insulation?

- Are your neighbouring properties occupied by full-time residents, are they used as weekday-only '*pied-à-terre*'s or are they holiday homes? Think about security issues.

Special Points – Apartments and Houses Sharing Facilities

Have you thought about having a survey of the property? Will it include the common parts? This can be expensive.

- Make sure you understand the rules of the community.

- Make sure you understand all the charges that will be raised by the community.

- Make contact with its administrator. Ask about any issues affecting the community. Are there any major works approved but not yet carried out? Make sure the contract is clear about who is responsible for these.

- Make contact with owners. Are they happy with the community and the way it is run? (Remember that no one is ever completely happy.)

- Understand how the community is run. Once you are an owner, try to attend the general meetings of the community.

Other Things to Do When You Buy a Property

- Insure the property and its contents (but *see* p.118).

- Make a full photographic record of the property. This is useful in the event of an insurance claim and for your scrapbook.

- Make arrangements for your bank to pay automatically your local property tax, water and electricity bills, etc. You can also do it yourself online (even from your UK home).

- Make a will in the US form covering your assets in the USA. This will usually mean making small changes in your existing UK will as well.

- Appoint an attorney and an accountant. Your lawyer should provide you with US legal advice, including tax law advice. Your accountant will put it to work. He will be your point of contact with the IRS. He will also usually complete and file your annual tax return. Your lawyer should be able to suggest a suitable person.

- Develop a working relationship with your banker and estate agent.

Financial Implications

John Howell and Marcell Felipe

06

Taxation

All tax systems are complicated. The US system is no exception. The Americans would say it is even more complex, and certainly more aggressive, than the UK system! Fortunately, most people will have only limited contact with the more intricate parts of the system. For many owners of holiday homes in the USA, their contact with the system will be minimal.

It is helpful to have some sort of understanding about the way in which the system works and the taxes you might face. Be warned: getting even a basic understanding will make your head hurt. You also need to be particularly careful about words and concepts that seem familiar to you but which may have a fundamentally different meaning in the USA. Of course, just to confuse you further, the rules change every year.

There are several points where it is emphasized that the contents are only a general introduction to the subject. There is nowhere where this is more true than in this section. Books (and long ones at that) have been written about US taxation. This general introduction does little more than scratch the surface of an immensely complex subject. It is intended to allow you to have a sensible discussion with your professional advisers and, perhaps, to help you work out in advance the questions you need to be asking them. It is not intended as a substitute for proper, comprehensive professional advice.

Your situation when you have a foot in two countries – and, in particular, when you are moving permanently from one country to another – involves the consideration of the tax systems in both countries with a view to minimizing your tax obligations in both. It is not just a question of paying the lowest amount of tax in, say, the USA. The best choice in the USA could be very damaging to your position in the UK. Similarly, the most tax-efficient way of dealing with your affairs in the UK could be problematic in the USA. The task of the international adviser and his client is to find a path which allows you to enjoy the major advantages available in both countries without incurring any of the worst drawbacks. In other words, there is an issue of compromise. There is no perfect solution to most tax questions. That is not to say that there are not a great many bad solutions into which you can all too easily stumble.

What should guide you when making a decision as to which course to pursue? Each individual will have a different set of priorities. Some are keen to screw the last ha'penny of advantage out of their situation. Others recognize that they will have to pay some tax but simply wish to moderate their tax bill. For many, the main concern is a simple structure, which they understand and can continue to manage without further assistance in the years ahead. Just as different clients have different requirements, so different advisers have differing views as to the function of the adviser when dealing with a client's tax affairs. One of your first tasks when speaking to your financial adviser should be to discuss your basic philosophy concerning the payment of tax and management of your affairs, to make sure that you are both operating with the same objective in mind and that you are comfortable with his or her approach to solving your problem.

Are You Resident or Non-resident for Tax Purposes?

The biggest single factor in determining how you will be treated by the tax authorities in any country is whether you are 'resident' in that country for tax purposes. This concept of 'tax residence' causes a great deal of confusion.

Tax residence can have different meanings in different countries. In the USA, 'residence' for tax purposes is not necessarily the same as residency for immigration purposes. If you are a resident for immigration purposes, you will be a resident for tax purposes, but you may also qualify as a resident for tax purposes even though you are not a resident for immigration purposes. That means you can be classified as tax resident, even when you don't have a tourist visa.

Let us first look at what 'tax residence' does not mean. It has nothing to do with whether you have registered as resident in a country or whether you have obtained a residence permit or residence card (although a person who has a card will usually be tax resident). Nor does it have anything to do with whether you have a home (residence) in that country – although a person who is tax resident will normally have a home there. Nor has it much to do with your intentions.

Tax residence is a *question of fact*. The law lays down certain tests that will be used to decide whether or not you are tax resident. If you fall into the categories stipulated in the tests, then you will be considered a tax resident whether or not you want to be and whether or not it was your intention to be tax resident. It is your responsibility to make your tax declarations each year. The decision whether you fall into the category of resident is, in the first instance, made by the tax office. If you disagree with the decision, you can appeal through the courts.

Because people normally change their tax residence when they move from one country to another, the basis on which decisions are made tends to be regulated by international law and to be pretty, but not totally, consistent from country to country.

You will have to consider two different questions concerning tax residence. The first is whether you will be treated as tax resident in the UK and the second is whether you will be treated as tax resident in the USA.

UK Tax Residency Rules

It is outside the scope of this book to go into any details about UK taxation, but some basic points will have to be dealt with for the explanation of US taxation to make any sense. In the UK there are two tests that help determine where you pay tax. These assess your domicile and your residence.

Domicile

Your domicile is the place that is your real home. It is the place where you have your roots. For most people it is the place where they were born. You can change your domicile but it is often not easy to do so. Changes in domicile can have far-reaching tax consequences and can be a useful tax reduction tool.

Residence

Residence falls into two categories. Under English law, there is a test of simple residence – actually living here other than on a purely temporary basis – and of ordinary residence.

A person will generally be treated as **resident** in the UK if he or she spends 183 or more days per year in the UK. A visitor will also be treated as resident if he or she comes to the UK regularly and spends significant time here. If he or she spends, on average over a period of four or more years, more than three months here per year he will be treated as tax resident.

A person can continue to be **ordinarily resident** in the UK even after he or she has stopped actually being resident here. A person is ordinarily resident in England if his or her presence is a little more settled. The residence is an important part of his or her life. It will normally have gone on for some time.

The most important thing to understand is that, once you have been ordinarily resident in this country, the simple fact of going overseas will not automatically bring that residence to an end. If you leave this country in order to take up permanent residence elsewhere, then, by concession, the Inland Revenue will treat you as ceasing to be resident on the day following your departure. However, it will not treat you as ceasing to be ordinarily resident if, after leaving, you spend an average of 91 or more days per year in this country over any four-year period.

In other words, it doesn't want you to escape too easily!

Note: Until 1993, you were also classified as ordinarily resident in the UK if you had accommodation available for your use in the UK even though you may have spent 364 days of the year living abroad. This very unfair rule was cancelled but many people still worry about it. It is not necessary to do so provided you limit your visits to the UK to less than the 91 days referred to above.

US Tax Residency Rules

If you qualify as a resident 'alien' (this affectionate term generally means anyone who is not a US citizen), you must report all interest, dividends, wages, or other compensation for services, income from rental property or royalties, and other types of income on your US tax return. You must report these amounts whether from sources within or outside the USA, i.e. worldwide. On the other hand, a non-resident 'alien' is usually subject to US income tax only on US source income.

Non-resident 'Aliens'

If you are an alien (not a US citizen), you are considered a non-resident 'alien' unless you meet one of the two tests described below.

Resident 'Aliens'

You are a resident alien of the USA for tax purposes if you meet either the **green card test** or the **substantial presence test** for the calendar year (1 January to 31 December). Even if you do not meet *either* of these tests, you may be able to choose to be treated as a US resident for part of the year if this results in more favourable treatment for you.

The Green Card Test

You are a resident for tax purposes if, pursuant to the immigration laws, you are a lawful permanent resident of the USA at any time during the calendar year. This is known as the green card test.

You are a lawful permanent resident of the USA if at any time you have been given the privilege, according to the immigration laws, of residing permanently in the USA as an immigrant. You generally have this status if the US Bureau of Citizenship and Immigration Services (USCIS, formerly the INS) has issued you an alien registration card, also known as a '**green card**' (after its former colour). You continue to have resident status under this test unless the status is taken away from you or is administratively or judicially determined to have been abandoned.

The Substantial Presence Test

You will also be considered a US resident for tax purposes if you meet the substantial presence test for the calendar year. To meet this test, you must be physically present in the USA on at least:

- **31 days during the current year,** *and*
- **183 days during the three-year period that includes the current year and the two years immediately before that, counting:**
  - **all the days you were present in the current year,** *and*
  - **one-third of the days you were present in the first year before the current year,** *and*
  - **one-sixth of the days you were present in the second year before the current year.**

Example. You were physically present in the USA on 120 days in each of the years 2004, 2005 and 2006. To determine whether you meet the substantial presence test for 2006, count the full 120 days of presence in 2006, 40 days in 2005 (one-third of 120) and 20 days in 2004 (one-sixth of 120). Since the total for the three-year period is 180 days, you are not considered a resident under the substantial presence test for 2006.

Do not count days for which you are an 'exempt individual'. The term 'exempt individual' does not refer to someone exempt from US tax, but to anyone in the following categories:

• **An individual temporarily present in the USA as a foreign government-related individual (i.e. diplomats, usually on an 'A' visa or 'NATO' visa).**

• **A teacher or trainee temporarily present in the USA under a J or Q visa, who substantially complies with the requirements of the visa.**

• **A student temporarily present in the USA under an F, J, M or Q visa, who substantially complies with the requirements of the visa.**

• **A professional athlete temporarily visiting the USA to compete in a charitable sports event.**

Closer Connection to a Foreign Country

Even if you meet the substantial presence test, you can be treated as a non-resident alien if you:

• **are present in the USA for fewer than 183 days during the year,** *and.*

• **maintain a tax home in a foreign country during the year,** *and*

• **have a closer connection during the year to one foreign country in which you have a tax home than to the USA.**

Your tax home is the general area of your main place of business, employment or post of duty, regardless of where you maintain your family home. Your tax home is the place where you permanently or indefinitely work as an employee or a self-employed individual. If you do not have a regular or main place of business because of the nature of your work, then your tax home is the place where you regularly live. If you do not fit either of these categories, you are considered an itinerant and your tax home is wherever you work.

For determining whether you have a closer connection to a foreign country, your tax home must also be in existence for the entire current year, and must be located in the same foreign country to which you are claiming to have a closer connection.

Tax Residence in More than One Country

Remember that you can be tax resident in more than one country under the respective rules of those countries. For example, you might spend 230 days in the year in the USA and 135 days in the UK. In this case you could end up, under the rules of each country, being responsible for paying the same tax in two or more countries. This would be unfair, so many countries have signed reciprocal 'Double Taxation Treaties'. The UK and the USA have such a treaty. It contains 'tie breakers' and other provisions to decide, where there is the possibility of being required to pay tax twice, in which country any particular category of tax should be paid. The US tax residency rules do not override tax treaty definitions of residency. If you are treated as a resident of a foreign country under a tax treaty, you are treated as a non-resident alien in assessing your US income tax. *See* 'Double Taxation Treaty', pp.140–41.

Decisions You Must Make

The most basic decisions you will have to make when planning your tax affairs are whether to cease to be resident in this country, whether to cease to be ordinarily resident in this country and whether to change your domicile to another country. Each of these has many consequences, many of which are not obvious. A second consideration is when in the tax year to make these changes. Once again, that decision has many consequences.

For many ordinary people, getting these decisions wrong can cost them tens of thousands of pounds in totally unnecessary taxation and a great deal of irritation and inconvenience. It is vital that you seek proper professional advice before making these decisions. You will need advice from specialist lawyers, accountants or financial advisers, all of whom should be able to help you.

Taxes Payable in the UK

The significance of these residence rules is that you will continue to be liable for some British taxes for as long as you are either ordinarily resident or domiciled in the UK. Put far too simply, once you have left the UK to live in the USA:

- **You will continue to have to pay tax in the UK on any capital gains you make anywhere in the world for as long as you are ordinarily resident and domiciled in the UK.**

- **You will continue to be liable to pay British inheritance tax on all of your assets located anywhere in the world for as long as you remain domiciled here. This will be subject to double taxation relief (*see* 'Double Taxation Treaty', p.140). Other, more complex rules apply in certain circumstances.**

- **You will always pay UK income tax (Schedule A) on income arising from land and buildings in the UK – wherever your domicile, residence or ordinary residence.**

- **You will pay UK income tax (Schedule D) on the following basis:**

  - **income from 'self-employed' trade or profession carried out in the UK (cases I and II) – normally taxed in the UK if the income arises in the UK.**

  - **income from interest, annuities or other annual payments from the UK (case III) – normally taxed in the UK if income arises in the UK and you are ordinarily resident in the UK.**

- income from investments and businesses outside the UK (cases IV and V) – normally only taxed in the UK if you are UK domiciled and resident or ordinarily resident in the UK.

- income from government pensions (fire, police, army, civil servant, etc.) – taxed in the UK in all cases.

- sundry profits not otherwise taxable (case VI) arising out of land or building in the UK – always taxed in the UK.

- You will pay UK income tax on any income earned from salaried employment in the UK (Schedule E) only in respect of any earnings from duties performed in the UK unless you are resident and ordinarily resident in the UK – in which case you will usually pay tax in the UK on your worldwide earnings.

If you are just buying a holiday home and will remain primarily resident in the UK, your tax position in the UK will not change very much. You will have to declare any income you make from your US property as part of your UK tax declaration. The calculation of tax due on that income will be made in accordance with UK rules, which may result in a different taxable sum than is used by the US authorities. See 'Tax on Rental Income', pp.132–3. The UK taxman will give you full credit for the taxes already paid in the USA.

On the disposal of the property, you should disclose the profit made to the UK taxman. You will get full credit for US tax paid.

Similarly, on your death, the assets in the USA must be disclosed on the UK probate tax declaration but, once again, you will be given full credit for sums paid in the USA.

Should You Pay Tax in the USA?

Under US law it is your responsibility to fill in a tax return in each year that you have any taxable income.

The tax office is generally known as the Internal Revenue Service (IRS). It is a federal agency with its headquarters in Washington, DC, but with far-reaching tentacles that expand not only over the whole USA, but also overseas.

There are four key points to remember:

- Lots of Americans don't pay all the taxes they owe! They tend to forget about cash payments received, and they tend to be creative in classifying some personal activities as a deductible business expenses (i.e. you might find some very wealthy businessman who runs an extremely unprofitable horse-breeding business on his country estate).

- The IRS is perhaps the fiercest revenue collector in the world, with sophisticated investigators and regulations aimed at preventing people from taking deductions for personal activity expenses (i.e. if you do run a horse-

breeding business unprofitably for more than three years, you are examined in detail).

- **The rules are applied more strictly every year.**

- **If you are caught not paying the taxes you owe, the penalties are substantial, and you can be charged with a criminal offence.**

The IRS provides a lot of help and advice on the Internet – including tax forms and guidance notes.

Local US Taxes

Both residents and non-residents pay these taxes. The taxes payable fall into various categories.

Local Real Estate Taxes

These taxes are paid if you own a residential property. They are paid by the person who owns the property on the tax due date, often towards the end of the calendar year. If the property changes hands in one particular year, the tax liability is pro-rated by the closing agent.

The tax is raised and spent by the town hall of the area where you live.

It is calculated on the basis of the assessed value of your property. You can appeal against the valuation decision, but the sums involved are usually lower than the actual value. The amount you will be charged will generally range from 1 to 2 per cent of the value.

Other Local Taxes

Town halls can also raise taxes for other projects and to cover shortfalls.

Payment of Local Property Taxes

A demand for payment is sent each year. The sum claimed must be paid by the specified date (which varies from place to place). Failure to do so incurs a penalty. It is probably simplest to arrange for payment from your bank by direct debit. If your property is subject to a mortgage, your mortgage payment will include a partial pre-payment for this tax. In such cases, your mortgage lender will pay the taxes directly.

Other Taxes Payable in the USA – Non-residents

In general, a person who is non-resident for tax purposes has few contacts with the US tax system and they are fairly painless.

Taxes on Income

The US tax system, like any other tax system, is very complex. What follows, therefore, can only be a very brief summary of the position.

A non-resident alien usually is subject to **US income tax** only on US source income. Under limited circumstances, certain foreign source income is subject to US tax.

The general rules for determining US source income that apply to most non-resident aliens are shown in the table below.

Summary of Source Rules for Income of Non-resident Aliens (non-US Citizens)

Item of Income	Factor Determining Source
Salaries, wages, other compensation	Where services performed
Business income	Where services performed
Personal services	Where services performed
Sale of inventory – purchased	Where sold
Sale of inventory – produced	Allocation
Interest	Residence of payer
Dividends	Whether a US or foreign corporation
Rents	Location of property
Royalties	Location of property
Natural resources	Location of property
Patents, copyrights, etc.	Where property is used
Sale of real property	Location of property
Sale of personal property	Seller's tax home
Pensions	Where services were performed that earned the pension
Sale of natural resources	Allocation based on fair market value of product at export terminal

In practice, these rules translate into taxation on the following types of income:

- **Income generated from land and buildings located in the USA. If you own a building in the USA and let it out, the US government collects the first wedge of tax from you.**
- **Income from US securities and capital invested in the USA.**
- **Income from business activities in the USA.**
- **Earned income if you are employed or self-employed in the USA.**

Provisions Relating to Real Estate

Tax on Rental Income

You will generally be required to pay tax on rents received.

You will be allowed to deduct any expenses associated with the rental of the property. These expenses not only include the obvious management fees, but will include local property taxes, interest payments made on your mortgage, and the 'scheduled building depreciation'. This last item is basically a calculation of how much your building structure has depreciated each year. It is based on a depreciation schedule published by the government. You do not take a depreciation deduction for the land element, as land, according to the IRS, does not depreciate. These items will need to be dealt with by your lawyer and your accountant.

Taxes on Capital Gains

You will pay tax on the capital gain you make on the sale of real estate in the USA or on any other capital gain made from property or a business in the USA.

For non-residents, this is taxed at 30 per cent of the gain, after various allowances, and is also dependent on the time during which the property was held, i.e. the rate may be reduced to 15 per cent if it was held for longer than a year. You may elect, of course, to be treated as a US tax resident and/or to treat your income as 'effectively connected with a US trade or business'. This will generally place you in the same category as US citizens with respect to that income. The price of the purchase – in effect, the price declared in the title – is adjusted by adding the costs and taxes of acquisition, except interest charges. If it is an investment property, the cost is further adjusted to take account of any depreciation deductions you have made in the past. Note: in the USA you can make a deduction for the 'depreciation' of the building component of the property. This depreciation is generally made according to a government schedule.

If the seller is not tax-resident in the USA, the payment of the tax on the gain is partly collected by a withholding deposit of 10 per cent, taken at the time of the sale. The buyer (or actually the closing agent on behalf of the buyer) must pay 10 per cent of the price to the IRS instead of to the seller. The other 90 per cent is paid as usual to the seller. The closing agent provides the seller with the documentation to show that the payment was made to the taxman. To recover any balance due to the seller, he or she will need to submit a tax return. This will usually require a little tax advice.

If the buyer does not pay this 10 per cent retention to the IRS, he or she will be liable for any tax owed by the seller.

Exclusion of Gain From the Sale of Your Main Home

If you sell your main home, residents may be able to exclude up to $250,000 of the gain on the sale of your home. If they are married and file a joint return, they may be able to exclude up to $500,000. Non-residents (foreign nationals), however, do not benefit from such exclusions, though deductions for improvement can be made from the final gain analysis.

Tax Deferral on Gain from Sale of Investment Property

If you owned a property primarily as an investment, you can exclude the gain on the sale of the property if you exchange it for one of equal or higher value.

Whenever you finally 'cash out' of the real estate business, you pay tax on the total appreciation, which takes into account your initial investment in the first property purchased.

These transactions are called '1031 exchanges' (after the Section of the Tax Code that authorizes it). Unless you are actually exchanging the property with another owner, you will require the use of a professional intermediary agent, generally called a '1031 company' or a '1031 agent', as this benefit theoretically only extends to exchanges, not outright sales. The agent's role is to purchase the property you want, exchange it for yours (giving you the tax deferral benefit) and then re-sell yours to your purchaser.

Corporation Tax

A foreign (non-US) company will pay tax on the profits it makes from activities in the USA but not its activities elsewhere. A US company has to pay tax on its worldwide income (subject to a number of credits for foreign taxes paid).

The tests of company residence and these taxes are not dealt with in this book.

Other Taxes on Real Estate Owned by 'Foreign' Companies in the USA

Branch Profits Tax

The Branch Profits Tax will apply to any income received by a foreign company from the activities of its branches in the USA. This tax is in addition to the regular tax on rents. In general, it attempts to place foreign companies in the same category as US companies by forcing them into a double tax regime. It taxes the income at the corporate level and at the shareholder level. There are other exemptions of limited application. If your property is owned in a way that attracts this tax, it is worth seeking advice on how to restructure the ownership to avoid the tax.

Taxes on Wealth

There are no wealth taxes in the USA, but there are gift taxes and estate (inheritance) taxes. See 'Taxes on Death and on Lifetime Gifts' below.

Taxes on Death (Estate Tax) and on Lifetime Gifts

Non-residents pay estate tax in the USA on the value of any assets in the USA as at the date of their death. That means the tax is calculated on the basis of the estate as a whole. Payment is made from the estate, not from individual heirs.

All of the assets will have to be declared for the purposes of UK taxation. Double taxation relief will apply, so you will not pay the same tax twice. UK inheritance tax is outside the scope of this book.

Any debts (including mortgage or overdraft) are deducted from the asset value, as are medical bills and funeral costs.

Some gifts on inheritance are partly tax exempt, such as gifts to spouses and gifts to charitable entities. In addition, each non-resident has an exemption amount for which no estate tax is due. As of 2005, the estate tax exemption amount for non-residents is $60,000. This means that if you own a $200,000 property, and it has a $130,000 mortgage, your US estate will be approximately $70,000. If your funeral and other expenses are $10,000, then your total taxable estate will be $65,000. Because your exemption is $60,000 you would not owe any US estate tax.

It is important to note that even if you had to pay US estate tax, the UK would grant you a credit for such payment. This credit would be used to offset your UK estate tax credit. Some people, however, may have no UK estate tax to offset. In such cases, it may be desirable to plan your US holdings so as to minimize their 'net' value, and hence minimize your US estate tax liability. Your international lawyer and your tax advisers should be able to assist you on this matter. Remember, this will require the co-operation of advisers both in the UK and in the USA.

The top rate on estates of people dying, and gifts made, in the years indicated, will decline as follows: in 2006, 46%; in 2007–2009, 45%.

Unified Gift and Estate Tax Rates

The tax rates on the taxable amount of any gift or inheritance are (subject to the exemption amounts) as follows:

If the amount ($) is: over	but not over	tax ($) is:	+ this %	of the excess over
0	10,000	0	18	0
10,000	20,000	1,800	20	10,000
20,000	40,000	3,800	22	20,000
40,000	60,000	8,200	24	40,000
60,000	80,000	13,000	26	60,000
80,000	100,000	18,200	28	80,000
100,000	150,000	23,800	30	100,000
150,000	250,000	38,800	32	150,000
250,000	500,000	70,800	34	250,000
500,000	750,000	155,800	37	500,000
750,000	1,000,000	248,300	39	750,000
1,000,000	1,250,000	345,800	41	1,000,000
1,250,000	1,500,000	448,300	43	1,250,000
1,500,000	2,000,000	555,800	45	1,500,000
2,000,000	–	780,800	46	2,000,000

Taxes Payable in the USA – Residents

Tax on Income

As has already been stressed, the US tax system is very complex. What follows therefore can only be a very brief summary of the position. The detail is immensely complicated and is made even more so because it is so different from the position in the UK. The following section is written with reference to the person retiring to the USA. Issues arising out of employment or self-employment are not considered and, in any case, they would probably double the length of the book. You are advised to consult your own accountant or tax adviser on these aspects.

Tax Threshold – Gross Income

If your income is less than $7,550 you do not have to file a tax return unless you are running a business or are self-employed. If you are married, the level rises to $15,100. If your income is above these limits you should consider consulting a tax adviser, at least for the first couple of years.

Types of Income Tax

As in the UK, income is divided into various categories. Each category of income is subject to different rules and allowances.

For a married couple, income tax is generally assessed by reference to the income of the household, rather than on sole income. Unmarried couples are assessed as two households. When assessing the income of the household, the income of any dependent children is also included.

As a tax resident, you will generally pay tax in the USA on worldwide income.

Remember that the USA is (taken overall, not just in relation to income tax) a high tax society. Whether for this reason or out of an independence of spirit, many people suffer from selective amnesia as far as the taxman is concerned and significantly under-declare their income. As mentioned above, this is dangerous and carries severe penalties. There are, however, quite legitimate tax-saving devices that you can use to reduce your liabilities. These issues are best addressed *before* you move to the USA as there are then many more options available to you.

Tax Credits and Deductions from Taxable Income

From your gross income you can deduct a number of items, including:

- **Your (or your family members') personal allowances.**
- **Local taxes paid.**
- **Foreign taxes paid.**
- **Contributions to a retirement plan (with certain limitations).**
- **Mortgage interest paid on your principal residence.**

Income Tax Rates

If taxable income ($) is: over	but not over	tax ($) is	+ this %	of the excess over
Single People				
0	7,550	0.00	10	0.00
7,550	30,650	755.00	15	7,550
30,650	74,200	4,220.00	25	30,650
74,200	154,800	15,107.50	28	74,200
154,800	336,550	37,675.50	33	154,800
336,550	–	97,653.00	35	336,550
Married Couples Filing Jointly				
0	15,100	0.00	10	0.00
15,100	61,300	1,510.00	15	15,100
61,300	123,700	8,440.00	25	61,300
123,700	188,450	24,040.00	28	123,700
188,450	336,550	42,170.00	33	188,450
336,550	–	91,043.00	35	336,550
Married Couples Filing Separately				
0	7,550	0.00	10	0.00
7,550	30,650	755.00	15	7,550
30,650	61,850	4,220.00	25	30,650
61,850	94,225	12,020.50	28	61,850
94,225	168,275	21,085.00	33	94,225
168,275	–	45,521.50	35	168,275
Head of Household				
0	10,750	0.00	10	0.00
10,750	41,050	1,075.00	15	10,750
41,050	106,000	5,620.00	25	41,050
106,000	171,650	21,857.50	28	106,000
171,650	336,550	40,239.50	33	171,650
336,550	–	94,656.50	35	336,550

- Investment interest (with limitations).
- Moving expenses.
- Charitable contributions to recognized tax exempt entities.
- Portions of your health insurance premiums (if self-employed).
- Some portions of student loans.
- Childcare expenses.

There are other deductions too. Talk to your tax adviser.

Tax Rates

The tax payable is calculated using the table above. The tax is calculated in tranches. That means you calculate the tax payable on each complete slice and then the tax at the highest applicable rate on any excess.

Most taxes are paid to the federal government. However, most states have their own income tax, although these are generally at lower rates. Some states, such as Florida, have no state-specific income or estate tax, making them very attractive for the wealthy and the retired.

Payment of Tax Due

You must complete your tax form and submit it each year between 1 January and 15 April. Sending it in late incurs a penalty.

Corporation Tax

These taxes are outside the scope of this book.

Taxes on Wealth

There is no wealth tax. There is, however, an estate (inheritance) and lifetime gift tax. *See* 'Taxes on Death and on Lifetime Gifts', pp.134–5.

Taxes on Capital Gains

You will pay tax on your worldwide gains. Gains are generally only taxed when the gain is crystallized, for example on the sale of the asset.

Gains are taxed as part of your income and are generally subject to a maximum rate of 15 per cent (for sales occurring after May 2003), unless the asset is held for less than 12 months, in which case it is treated as regular income and subject to regular (and higher) income tax rates.

Exclusion of Gain From the Sale of Your Main Home

If you sold your main home, you may be able to exclude up to $250,000 of the gain on the sale of your home. If you are married and file a joint return, you may be able to exclude up to $500,000. You must have owned and lived in the home for a minimum of two years.

Tax-Deferral on Gain from Sale of Investment Property

If you owned a property primarily as an investment, you can exclude the gain on the sale of this property, if you exchange it for one of equal or higher value. Whenever you finally 'cash out' of the real estate business, you pay tax on the total appreciation, which takes into account your initial investment in the first property purchased.

These transactions are called '1031 exchanges' (after the Section of the Tax Code that authorizes it). Unless you are actually exchanging the property with

Capital Gains Tax Rates

Capital Gains Category	Rate
Gains on collectibles and small business stock (Section 1202 Stock)	28%
Gain on real property attributable to straight-line depreciation	25%
Gains from property sold before 6 May 2003, not subject to 25% rate or 28% rate from capital assets held over one year	20%
Gains from capital assets held over five years and acquired after 2000 (or property held over five years and for which the taxpayer made the Section 311 election on 2001 Schedule D); does not apply until the 2008 tax year	18%
Gain from property sold on or after 6 May 2003, to the extent taxable income, is taxed at a rate over 15%	15%
Effective rate on gain from small business stock eligible for the 50% exclusion	14%
Gain from property sold before 6 May 2003, and held five years or less, to the extent taxable income, is taxed at 10% or 15%	10%
Gain from property sold before 6 May 2003, if held over five years, to the extent taxable income, is taxed at 10% or 15%. (See the Qualified Five-year Gain Worksheet in the Schedule D instructions)	8%
Gain from property sold on or after 6 May 2003, to the extent taxable income, is taxed at 10% or 15%	5%

another owner, you will require the use of a professional intermediary agent, generally called a '1031 company' or a '1031 agent', as this benefit theoretically only extends to exchanges, not outright sales. The agent's role is to purchase the property you want, exchange it for yours (giving you the tax deferral benefit) and then re-sell yours to your purchaser.

Taxes on Death (Estate Tax) and on Lifetime Gifts

With some exceptions, this tax is similar to the estate tax paid by non-residents (see 'Taxes on Death and on Lifetime Gifts', pp.134–5). The most notable exceptions are: the exemption amount is higher for residents; and residents are subject to such tax on their worldwide holdings.

In the case of non-residents the applicable exclusion amount is $60,000. In the case of residents, the applicable exclusion amount is currently $2,000,000, and it is set to increase progressively to $3,500,000 by 2009.

In the case of residents subject to the provisions of double taxation treaties, tax is paid on your worldwide assets as of the date of your death. In the case of non-residents you are only responsible for the property that is located in the USA.

Residents in the USA who leave their real estate to their husband or wife, or to a charity (including a Family Private Foundation), will not pay any estate tax.

Lifetime gifts are generally subject to the same rules and tax rates as testamentary gifts. There are, however, some differences. You can make a gift of up to $12,000 a year, per recipient, without incurring any gift tax liability. Thus a married couple with four children can give up to $96,000 a year to their children (each parent can give $12,000 to each of the children).

If you are not careful, a transfer of title in property from you to your children can trigger a gift tax liability. You should, therefore, decide at the outset who will own the property before you go ahead and buy. For example, if prior to taking up residence in the USA you give your house purchase money to your children, there will be no US gift tax issues as the gift is between non-residents and consists of non-US property. By contrast, if you buy the property in the USA, and then give it to your children, you have made a transfer of US property, and that will be subject to US gift tax rules, unless it is exempted under some other provision of law.

Other Taxes

There is a miscellany of other taxes and levies on various aspects of life in the USA. Some are national and others local. Individually they are usually not a great burden. These taxes are outside the scope of this book.

New Residents

New residents will be liable to tax on their worldwide income and gains from the date they arrive in the USA. Until that day they will only have to pay US tax on their income if it is derived from assets in the USA.

The most important thing to understand about taking up residence in the USA (and abandoning UK tax residence) is that it gives you superb opportunities for tax planning and, in particular, for restructuring your affairs to minimize what can otherwise be penal rates of taxation in the USA. To do this you need good professional advice at an early stage – preferably several months (or even years if you have a sizeable estate) before you intend to move.

Double Taxation Treaty

The detailed effect of double taxation treaties depends on the two countries involved. While treaties may be similar in concept, they can differ in detail. Only the effect of the US–UK treaty is considered here. The main points of relevance to residents are:

• **Any income from letting property in the UK will normally be outside the scope of US taxation and, instead, will be taxed in the UK.**

• Pensions received from the UK – except for government pensions – will be taxed in the USA but not in the UK.

• Government pensions will continue to be taxed in the UK but are neither taxed in the USA nor do they count when assessing the level of your income for calculating the rate of tax payable on your income.

• You will normally not be required to pay UK capital gains tax on gains made after you settle in the USA except in relation to real estate located in the UK.

• If you are taxed on a gift made outside the USA, then the tax paid will usually be offset against the gift tax due in the USA.

• If you pay tax on an inheritance outside the USA, the same will apply.

Double tax treaties are detailed and need to be read in the light of your personal circumstances.

Tax Planning Generally

Do it and do it as soon as possible. Every day you delay will make it more difficult to get the results you are looking for. There are many possibilities for tax planning for someone moving to the USA. Some points worth considering are:

• Time your departure from the UK to get the best out of the UK tax system.

• Think, in particular, about when to make any capital gain if you are selling your business or other assets in the UK.

• Arrange your affairs so that there is a gap between leaving the UK (for tax purposes) and becoming resident in the USA. That gap can be used to make all sorts of beneficial changes to the structure of your finances.

• Think about trusts. These are very useful in the USA.

• Think about giving away some of your assets. You will have to pay neither gift nor inheritance tax on the gift if structured properly.

Inheritance

The US Inheritance Rules

In many states, Americans cannot do just as they please with their property when they die. Inheritance rules often apply to protect the surviving spouse. These rules generally set out a minimum portion of the estate which must go to the spouse.

Making a Will

It is always best to make a will for your US assets. If you do not, your UK will should be treated as valid in the USA and will be used to distribute your estate. This is a false economy, as the cost of implementing the UK will is much higher than the cost of implementing a US will and the disposal of your estate as set out in your UK will could be a tax disaster in the USA.

If you are not resident in the USA, your US will should state that it applies only to immovable property in the USA. The rest of your property – including movable property in the USA – will be disposed of in accordance with English law and the provisions of your UK will. If you are domiciled in the USA (as to the meaning of which *see* pp.125–9) you should make a USA will disposing of all of your assets wherever they are located. If you make a US will covering only immovable property in the USA, you should modify your UK will so as to exclude any immovable property located in the USA.

Always use a lawyer to advise you on the contents of your will and to draft it. Lawyers love people who make home-made wills. They make a fortune from dealing with their estates because the wills are often inadequately drafted and subsequently give rise to lots of expensive problems.

Making a Revocable Testamentary Trust

A popular US enhancement to the will is the Revocable Testamentary Trust. By titling your US assets under a Revocable Testamentary Trust you avoid the expenses and hassles of probate. Other than that, it is the same as a will.

What if I Don't Make a Will of Any Kind?

A person who dies without a will dies intestate.

This gets complicated. Will the UK rules as to what happens in this event apply (because you are British) or will it be the US rules? This gives rise to many happy hours of argument by lawyers and tax officials – all at your (or your heirs') expense. It really is much cheaper to make a will.

Investments

The Need to Do Something

Most of us don't like making investment decisions. They make our heads hurt. They make us face up to unpleasant things – like death and taxes. We don't really understand what we are doing, what the options are or what is best – particularly when the markets are volatile. We don't know whom we should trust to give us advice. We know we ought to do something, but it will wait until next week – or maybe the week after. Until then our present arrangements will have to do. But if you are moving to live overseas you *must* review your investments. Your current arrangements are likely to be financially disastrous – and may even be illegal.

What Are You Worth?

Most of us are, in financial terms, worth more than we think. When we come to move abroad and have to think about these things, it can come as a shock.

Take a piece of paper and list your actual and potential assets. A suggested checklist can be found in **Appendix 2** at the end of this book.

This will give you an idea as to the amount you are worth now and, just as importantly, what you are likely to be worth in the future. Your investment plans should take into account both figures.

Who Should Look After Your Investments?

You may already have an investment adviser. You may be very happy with their advice and the service you have received. But they are unlikely to be able to help you once you have gone to live in the USA and they will almost certainly not have the knowledge to do so. They will not know either about the US investments that might be of interest to you or, probably, of the many 'offshore' products that might be of interest to someone no longer resident in the UK. Even if they have some knowledge of these things, they are likely to be thousands of miles from where you will be living. Nor is it simply a question of selecting a new local (US) adviser once you have moved. They will usually know little about the UK aspects of your case or about the UK tax and inheritance rules that could still have some importance for you.

Choosing an investment adviser competent to deal with you once you are in the USA is not easy. By all means seek guidance from your existing adviser. Ask for guidance from others who have already made the move. Do some research. Meet the potential candidates. Are you comfortable with them? Do they share your approach to life? Do they have the necessary experience? Is their performance record good? How are they regulated? What security/bonding/guarantees can they offer you? How will they be paid for their work: fees or commission? If the answer is commission, what will that formula mean they are making from you in 'real money' rather than percentages? Above all, be careful.

Where Should You Invest?

For British people, the big issue is whether they should keep their sterling investments. Most British people will have investments that are largely

sterling-based. Even if they are, for example, in a Far Eastern fund they will probably be denominated in sterling and will pay out dividends and so on in sterling.
You will be spending dollars.

As the value of the dollar fluctuates against the pound, the value of your
investments will go up and down. That, of itself, is not too important because
the value won't crystallize unless you sell. What does matter is that the revenue
you generate from those investments (rent, interest, dividends, etc.) will fluctuate in value.

Take, for example, an investment that generated you £10,000 per annum. Rock
steady. Then think of that income in spending power. Let's use US dollars as an
example. In recent times, the US dollar has varied in value from £1 = $1.5 to £1 =
$1.7. Sometimes, therefore, your income in US dollars would have been $15,000
per year and at others it would have been $17,000 per year. This is a big differ-
ence in your standard of living based solely on exchange rate variations.

This is unacceptable, particularly as you will inevitably have to live with this
problem so far as your pension is concerned. In general terms, investments
paying out in dollars are preferable if you live in the USA.

Trusts

Trusts are an important weapon in the hands of the person going to live in the
USA. Trusts offer the potential benefits of:

- **Allowing you to put part of your assets in the hands of trustees so that
they no longer belong to you for inheritance tax and/or probate purposes.**

- **Allowing you to receive only the income you need (rather than all the
income generated by those assets), so keeping the extra income out of sight
for income tax purposes.**

- **Allowing a very flexible vehicle for investment purposes.**

So how do these little wonders work?

Well in advance of moving to the USA, you reorganize your affairs by giving a
large part of your assets to 'trustees'. These are normally professional trust
companies located in a low tax regime. The choice of a reliable trustee is critical.

Those trustees hold the asset not for their own benefit but 'in trust' for whatever purposes you established when you made the gift. It could, for example, be
to benefit a local hospital or school or it could be to benefit you and your family.
If the trust is set up properly in the light of the requirements of US law, then
those assets will no longer be treated as yours for tax purposes.

On your death the assets are not yours to leave to your children (or whoever),
and so do not (subject to local anti-avoidance legislation) carry inheritance tax.

Similarly, the income from those assets is not your income. If some of it is
given to you it may be taxed as your income, but the income that is not given to
you will not be taxed in the USA and, because the trust will be located in a

nil/low tax regime, it will not be taxed elsewhere either. The detail of the arrangements is vitally important. Trusts must be set up precisely to comply with US tax law. If you do not do this, they will not work as intended.

Trustees can manage your investments in (virtually) whatever way you stipulate when you set up the trust. You can give the trustees full discretion to do as they please or you can specify precisely how your money is to be used. There are particular types of trusts and special types of investments that trusts can make that can be especially beneficial in the USA.

Trusts can be beneficial even to US residents of modest means – say £350,000. It is certainly worth investing a little money to see if they can be of use to you, as the tax savings can run to many thousands of pounds. If you are thinking of trusts as an investment vehicle and tax planning measure, you must take advice early – months (even years if you have a sizeable estate) before you are thinking of moving to the USA.

Keeping Track of Your Investments

Whatever you decide to do about investments – put them in a trust, appoint investment managers to manage them in your own name or manage them yourself – you should always keep an up-to-date list of your assets and investments and *tell your family where to find it*. Make a file. By all means have a computer file but print off a good old-fashioned paper copy. Keep it in an obvious place known to your family. Keep it with your will and the deeds to your house. Keep it with either the originals of bank account books, share certificates, and so on, or a note of where they are to be found.

As a lawyer it is very frustrating – and expensive for the client – when, after the parents' death, the children come in with a suitcase full of correspondence and old cheque books. It all has to be gone through and all those old banks contacted lest there should be £1,000,000 lurking in a forgotten account. There never is, and it wastes a lot of time and money.

Settling In

07

Now that you own a Florida home, you need to go and spend some time there. In general, life can be quite simple if you prepare yourself for what's to come. Life in the Sunshine State won't always be sunny, but with a little advance warning you can weather almost anything. Part of the process, of course, is getting yourself and all your belongings over there. This is the one area where you will definitely want to ask yourself and others plenty of questions before you do anything.

Making the Move

There are a few things to keep in mind as you prepare to make your move to Florida and making a list always helps. The following are some items to get you started.

• Are all your necessary visas and stay permits in order (*see* 'Visas and Permits', pp.15–25)?

• Is your passport valid for your entire stay in the USA? Be sure to keep copies of your passport at home and with you, as you will need it when you are filling in official documentation or trying to replace your passport should you lose it. It is also useful as a means of ID as you move around.

• If you are bringing a pet into the USA, it should be accompanied by an Official Certificate of Veterinary Inspection from your local vet. The certificate should state that your pet is free of any signs of infectious or communicable diseases, did not originate in an area under quarantine for rabies, and is not known to have a history of exposure to a rabies-infected animal. The UK is considered a rabies-free environment by the US authorities so your pet will not need to be quarantined, nor will you be required to provide proof of vaccination. *See* pp.185–6 for more details.

• If you are bringing a computer with you that does not have a built-in voltage converter, you will need to acquire a step-down transformer. The voltage in the USA is 120v. You will also want to sign up for a local Internet provider (ISP) once you arrive (*see* 'The Internet', pp.163–4), as it won't be economical to keep your UK provider.

• You may want to look into how easy it is to access your bank from abroad and what fees you will incur for doing so. You may not be able to write cheques on your UK account once you are in the USA but you should be able to use cards connected with it (cheque card, ATM/debit card). It may be easier simply to open an account in the USA. If you bring large sums with you, remember that there is no limit to the amount of currency you can bring with you into the USA, nor do you have to pay duty on currency, but you must declare amounts larger than $10,000.

• If you are moving to Florida permanently, notify your credit card companies and any mailing lists of your change of address.

• Contact the UK post office so that they can forward your mail to your new address.

• Make sure you acquire all necessary British tax forms before they are due.

• Terminate or suspend your utility contracts in the UK.

• Bring British postage stamps with you in case you need to send stamped, self-addressed envelopes back to the UK.

• Check what kind of coverage your health insurance company offers you while you are overseas. Before you leave, arrange a last round of dental and medical appointments.

• Prescription medication can be quite expensive in the USA. Be sure to bring with you ample supplies of your own. However, if your medication contains narcotics or habit-forming drugs, you should bring your prescription or a letter from your doctor with you. You might also want to arrange with your UK doctor for repeat prescriptions and for someone to collect them and send them on to you while you are away. A doctor's letter should accompany anything sent by post and 'Doctor's Letter Attached' should be written on the outside of the parcel.

• Stock up on any of your favourite beauty or other products that may not be available in the USA.

• You will need voltage converters and plug adapters for your electrical appliances. You should also bring a surge protector with multiple outlets so that you can run several of your UK appliances off the same converter. Be aware that the cycles are different in the USA as well (for more details, *see* 'Electricity', pp.156–7). Do not bring your UK television set ,as it won't work in the USA.

Removal Companies

When it comes to moving your belongings to the USA, you obviously do not have the option of driving it all there. This means that you will either have to hire a removal company or carry what you can with you on the plane. Excess baggage rates can vary, so you will have to check with your airline how much it will cost to bring extra luggage. Because of stricter safety regulations on flights into the USA, most airlines no longer allow you to send unaccompanied baggage. Check with your carrier to see if that is an option.

As a visitor or non-resident you are exempt from the duty and internal revenue tax that is imposed on some articles as long as they are for your own personal use, which means you don't intend to sell anything you bring with you.

Moving Tales

A series of articles published by the Milwaukee *Journal Sentinel* in 2002 brought to light a frightening number of horror stories concerning American removal companies. Inadequate federal oversight is one reason why some of these scams are going unpunished. Someone in Washington must have been listening, however, because a couple of months later one of the companies mentioned was fined $98,000 by the US government.

The lead story described how one couple's move ended up costing $8,000 more than the removal company had originally estimated, on top of which their belongings arrived a month late. That wasn't the end of the story. When the movers opened the doors of the truck, the couple discovered that every single item they owned had been damaged.

The couple's story ended up making national news and shedding light on a scam that typically involves someone hiring a removal company through the Internet because of the price is attractive. When the truck arrives and the customer's possessions are loaded, the estimate is increased two, three or four times over the original bid. The movers then inform the customer that, unless the new bill is paid, his belongings will be sold at auction.

The growing number of complaints from consumers about removal companies has prompted a lot of talk about introducing federal legislation in order to regulate an industry that was actually deregulated in 1995. So far, nothing has happened.

Florida, in the meantime, has taken a stand. In 2002, Governor Jeb Bush signed a law that imposes restrictions on removal companies and how they operate. Unfortunately, it applies only to removals within the state of Florida and does not affect interstate laws. Perhaps it's not that surprising that the state has taken the lead: many of the questionable companies mentioned were based in south Florida. All the attention, coupled with the new laws, is forcing some companies to relocate to other states.

For example, you do not have to pay duty on your personal effects – clothes, jewellery, toiletries, hunting and fishing equipment, cameras, portable radios – that accompany you into and out of the USA.

More importantly, you may also import furniture, china, linen, libraries, artwork and similar household furnishings free of duty. The exemption applies as long as the items were in your previous home for at least one year, and, again, as long as you don't plan to sell any of them on your arrival. Your household items don't have to accompany you to the USA to be duty-free; you may have them shipped to your US address later. Depending on the size of the shipment, you can either send it airfreight or seafreight. You should get comparative quotes from several companies. For a small shipment, it may not be much more expensive to send it airfreight and it will almost certainly be faster.

The shipment will have to be cleared through customs at its first port of arrival, unless you have made arrangements with a foreign freight forwarder to have your effects sent 'custody in-bond' (where a third party initially clears customs for you) from the port of arrival to a more convenient port of entry for clearance. Ask your removal company if they offer this service.

There are several documents involved in clearing your belongings through customs, including form 3299, 'Declaration for Free Entry of Unaccompanied Articles'. Your removal company should provide you with all the necessary forms beforehand. You will probably need to sign a power of attorney form giving the company or its agent the ability to clear your belongings on your behalf. The 'Frequently Asked Questions' section of the US customs website (**www.customs.ustreas.gov**) may answer some of your questions. One removal company, Excess International Movers (**www.internationalmovers.co.uk**) has a lot of useful customs regulation information on its site.

See 'Removal Companies', pp.237–8, for a list of firms. There are also a couple of websites that include updated lists of removal companies, such as **www. britsintheus.com** and **www.uk-yankee.com/shipping.html**.

Removal Company Helpful Hints

The Milwaukee *Journal Sentinel* (*see* box, left) listed the following tips for dealing with removal companies.

- **Check out the company's insurance status and safety history through www.safersys.org, operated by the US Department of Transportation. You will need the company's DOT number or motor carrier number.**

- **Get your own insurance and do not trust the mover's coverage.**

- **While you should be very cautious in your use of the Internet when hiring removal companies, it is nevertheless invaluable for research. The Better Business Bureau (www.bbb.org) is a good place to start. Other sites include www.consumeraffairs.com and www.ripoffreport.com.**

- **Use a local removal company. Ties to a community can mean a company has an interest in maintaining a good reputation. At the very least, use one that is based in your state or the state you are moving to.**

- **Get binding estimates in writing. Even a non-binding estimate should be written out. Save every scrap of paper associated with the move.**

- **Know your rights under federal law. A removal company is not allowed to charge for more than the binding estimate unless it is asked to provide services not included in it. Even with a written non-binding estimate, the mover cannot require a customer to pay more than 10 per cent above the original estimate at delivery, excluding extras not in the original estimate. If there is a dispute, the mover is required to unload the furniture and give the customer 30 days after delivery to pay any charges that remain.**

Shopping

The USA prides itself on offering both abundance and convenience. Few activities demonstrate this more clearly than shopping. The end result of the American desire to bring these two concepts together in one place is grocery stores the size of aeroplane hangars and retail malls the size of small towns. You can easily spend hours wandering the towering aisles of these commercial monsters but, in theory at least, you should be able to find anything and everything you could ever need. In recent years, there has been a growing appreciation of the advantages of smaller, 'gourmet' grocers and so 'international' markets have sprung up, as well as more specialized shops such as stand-alone bakeries.

Grocers and Other Food Shops

Most of your grocery shopping will be in the large chains such as Publix. These stores are no different from UK supermarkets, and they have meat, cheese and bread departments as well as rows of aisles stacked high with every conceivable product. Another kind of grocery store chain that has been steadily expanding is Whole Foods Market (**www.wholefoods.com/stores/list_FL.html**). This chain has six locations in Florida and the layout of its stores is ostensibly no different from other chain supermarkets, but its focus is on organic foods.

The so-called 'international' markets can sometimes be found in pricey new developments and stock quality imported products, but usually at a premium. In the ethnic neighbourhoods of big cities, such as Miami and Tampa, you will also find small grocers with a startling array of imported products catering for the local clientele that come at an affordable price.

Outdoor Food Markets

Direct selling of farm products through farmers' markets continues to be an important sales outlet for agricultural producers nationwide. Farmers' markets have continued to rise in popularity, mostly because of the growing consumer interest in obtaining fresh products directly from the farm. The number of farmers' markets in the USA has grown dramatically, more than doubling between 1994 to 2004. According to the 2004 *National Farmers' Market Directory*, there are over 3,700 farmers' markets operating in the USA. This growth clearly indicates that farmers' markets are meeting the needs of a growing number of farmers with small- to medium-sized operations. The Agricultural Marketing Service of the United States Department of Agriculture (USDA) has now become involved in this and their website contains a useful directory of markets at **www.ams.usda.gov/farmersmarkets**.

In response to demand, many US cities have launched outdoor farmers' markets to promote local farm produce. Florida is no different. In fact, because of the state's considerable agricultural past, there has been a strong drive to revive the fortunes of local farmers and bring back a 'simpler' – or nostalgic – time. The Bureau of State Farmers' Market helps promote over 70 public markets throughout the state (**www.florida-agriculture.com**). They have proved popular with increasingly health-conscious consumers, who now have an opportunity to find out exactly where their produce is resourced from.

Other Markets

Everyone loves a bargain and all over the world you will find that flea markets attract the most dedicated bargain-hunters. Florida is no exception. In fact, the large number of tourists that roam the state's dusty back roads – as well as its well-kept highways – make it the ideal climate for the flea market to flourish. As you drive around the state, especially on smaller, rural roads, you will come across all sorts of hand-made signs directing you towards some market or other. Some are well organized, taking place every weekend at set times and places; others just seem to pop up like wildflowers. Miami Beach has its own flea market every weekend that transforms a large section of fashionable Lincoln Road into an outdoor bazaar.

Of course, it wouldn't be America if there wasn't an organization dedicated to the equal representation of the humble flea market. The National Flea Market Association (**www.fleamarkets.org**) helps to promote its members and to foster some semblance of a code of professional conduct. It also offers a state-by-state listing of markets as well as contact information for local associations.

Discount Clubs

If you think ordinary supermarkets are big, wait until you step into a warehouse club such as Costco. Originally wholesale stores for small businesses, these enormous retail establishments began allowing individual consumers (as opposed to just trade) to become members, so they had access to buying wholesale products at discounted prices. The popularity of these stores has led them to expand their range to include everything from cars to appliances.

DIY Shops

As in the UK, the DIY store is also an important part of the American lifestyle. No weekend is complete without a homeowner's trip to Home Depot or Lowe's to pick up timber for their deck project or to bring home a new kitchen sink. The huge size of these stores, like the warehouse clubs and some grocery stores, means that you can find yourself wandering around for ages trying to find a member of staff. For a listing of online DIY resources, visit **www.refdesk.com/doitself.html**.

Clothing

You cannot argue with the fact that, where the latest fashions are concerned, Miami is the place to shop in Florida. Other cities have their fashionable retail strips but nowhere else does the need to see and be seen feel more like a lifestyle choice. Even clothing store chains like Gap, which in other locations can appear quite mundane, have more of an edge here. You will certainly find plenty of shopping in cities like Naples and West Palm Beach but they tend to cater for a wealthier and slightly older crowd than Miami.

Professional Sports

In addition to the state's well-regarded college sports teams (you will find graduates all over the country still following any game they can), Florida has several professional sports franchises in each of the national leagues:

Arena Football League (AFL)
Orlando Predators
Tampa Bay Storm

Major League Baseball (MLB)
Florida Marlins
Tampa Bay Devil Rays

Major League Soccer (USL)
Miami FC
Ajax Orlando Prospects
Bradenton Academics
Central Florida Kraze
Cocoa Expos
Palm Beach Pumas

National Basketball Association (NBA)
Miami Heat
Orlando Magic

National Football League (NFL)
Jacksonville Jaguars
Miami Dolphins
Tampa Bay Buccaneers

National Hockey League (NHL)
Florida Panthers
Tampa Bay Lightning

Retail malls may not be quite as fashionable as the streets of Miami but you will appreciate the convenience of finding everything you need in one place. The fashion-conscious who are also budget-conscious will find that factory outlet stores may satisfy both demands. Most major retailers have an outlet store where they sell their discounted products that are slightly defective or, perhaps, have been discontinued. You can also find bargains at places such as Designer Shoe Warehouse, which sells brand-name shoes.

When shopping, remember that the customer is always right and most stores have a pretty liberal returns policy, so if you are not happy with something you can almost always bring it back. However, this does not usually apply to factory outlet stores, where the customer may still be right, but all sales are final.

Home Utilities and Services

Utilities are regulated in Florida only in the sense that the state oversees them to ensure fair competition. The mission of the state's Public Service Commission (**www.psc.state.fl.us**) is actually to support the policy of deregulation, the theory being that this should lead to competitive prices for consumers. You can also file complaints about specific utility companies with the commission, which oversees hundreds of electric, gas, telecommunications, and water and waste water firms. Many companies are simply resellers of services and you will not be dealing with them directly.

Depending on the size of your market, establishing services in your particular area may involve dealing with more than one company. When choosing a telephone company you will have a choice of not only local service, but also long-distance services, and they don't have to be provided by the same firm.

Payment

Utility bills are similar across the board. You will receive a statement that should include a detailed list of usage and rates. The total due will be clearly displayed along with a due date. The form will include a tear-away section that acts as your remittance slip. Almost every company includes an addressed (but not usually postage-paid) envelope with which to send your payment. It is very rare these days to pay your bills in person at the utility company. Doing so is still an option in some cases, but most companies discourage this since they prefer to reduce costs by not maintaining the extra personnel. Fortunately, there are several other convenient ways to pay for your utilities.

- **Pay by cheque**: Paying bills is a very good reason to open a local bank account. The procedure is no different from that in the UK: use the addressed envelope to send your cheque (or money order), and write your utility account number on the cheque in case it gets lost or separated from the remittance slip when it reaches the company.

• **Pay through your bank**: Before you set up a local bank account, find out if they offer online banking. This service allows you to set up a list of companies that you can pay online, saving not only time but also postage stamps. If a particular bill is always for the same amount, you can also set up an automatic payment online.

• **Pay through automatic withdrawal**: Some companies offer their own automatic billing, which can be set up through your account (called direct debit in the UK). This is different from the online option as it is arranged directly with the utility company. Once you have established it, the company withdraws the money without you being involved. However, you should still receive statements indicating the amount that has been withdrawn.

Keep **customer service numbers** for each utility handy, as this is the number you will need in case of any disputes. Hopefully, in the case of a dispute you will be able to solve the matter by phone. Otherwise, you will have to visit the utility company's main office. Keep all records of usage, as well as any documents relating to your travels, so that you can clearly dispute any high bills for periods when you are out of the country.

With the exception of mobile phones, all utilities can be terminated by calling at least two weeks in advance of when you'd like service to end. Simply let the utility know when you'd like service to stop and a final bill is issued. If you'd like your final bill to be sent to a different address, you should inform the utility company at this time. Enquire about when and how your deposit is refunded.

Electricity

There are five main power-generating companies in Florida – Florida Power and Light Company, Florida Power Corporation, Tampa Electric Company, Jacksonville Electric Authority and Gulf Power Company – which use combinations of coal, petroleum, gas, nuclear and hydroelectric power to produce electricity. However, you will not receive bills from these companies, but from smaller regional companies that buy the electricity from these generators and resell it to the consumer.

In new and relatively new houses, power overload should not be an issue. Ideally, power will be distributed to outlets with some thought as to what will be plugged into them. Window air-conditioning units, for example, will often have their very own outlet so as not to overload the system every time the machine kicks in.

The same goes for kitchen appliances. Older homes use a replaceable, screw-in type of fuse while newer ones will have circuit breakers that need to be reset in the case of overload. The existence of the older kind of fuse box is a good indication that the house's electrical system may not have been upgraded in quite a long time and it may be time to do so.

The voltage in American homes is 120v, compared with 240v in the UK. When dealing with appliances that you may bring out with you, however, there are a few other differences to bear in mind, such as the number of watts the product draws (different for each product) and the frequency (60Hz in the USA and 50Hz in the UK). Of course, the plug on the power cord is also different from the bulky one we know back home.

Clearly, you will be buying any major appliances locally, so the power differences will only concern you for smaller electronic gadgets, which may require a transformer if they don't have a built-in converter. Make sure that the transformer also provides enough wattage for the particular electronic product. The transformer will not convert frequency, but the only products for which this is a problem are those with synchronous motors, such as power drills or hairdryers. Motors that run on direct current, such as portable cassette players and computer disk drives, are not affected. A good source of information on conversion issues is the FAQ page of an American company that specializes in voltage converters (**www.voltageconverters.com/faq.htm**).

Gas

The USA produces the majority of the natural gas that it consumes, which makes for a relatively affordable natural resource. What little the country does import comes from Canada. Florida's use of natural gas has been growing as companies find new uses for this abundant and cost-effective source of energy.

Not only is gas being used in all kinds of high-tech domestic heating systems, it is also used in water heaters, fireplaces, cooking and air-conditioning. Granted, you may not have much use for a fireplace in Florida, but, when it comes to air-conditioning, natural gas can give you considerable cost savings over the long term. Of course, if you are living in a multi-unit building with central heating and air-conditioning you may not have much say over energy sources. If you own a house, though, it may be worthwhile investigating what kinds of natural gas options are available from the local provider.

A few rural homes may not be connected directly to gas pipes and may instead have refillable storage tanks, but the majority of residents are close enough to the lines to establish service.

Water

Florida may be surrounded by water but that doesn't mean it always has enough. Despite heavy annual rainfalls and a considerable number of underground springs, the state has the occasional drought in some regions, especially in the south.

In thinking about your home, some of the issues to be aware of when it comes to water are the size of your boiler, the existence or need for a well, and the existence or need for a septic tank. Water boilers are usually tucked away in the basement and handle all the hot water needs for the whole house. You should make sure that yours is big enough for the number of people living in your house. The need for a well or a septic tank – which treats sewage before releasing it into the environment – depends on how rural an area you are living in. Most homes now have access to plentiful water supplies but these could be matters to consider if your dream home happens to be in the middle of nowhere.

Swimming pools are a major water-related consideration. A lot of newer homes in Florida already have one, and, if you are building your home, choosing a pool may be no more of a decision than choosing a refrigerator. However, if you plan to add a pool to your home, while you may not have trouble locating a reasonably priced builder, you should keep in mind the long-term costs of keeping it filled and maintained.

Like other utilities, water is **metered** individually, so you will be responsible only for your own usage. However, you should be aware of the **Water Management District Tax**. Florida has five water management districts, which were created to preserve and conserve the state's waters. The districts also monitor water pollution, regulate the drawing of water from underground sources and buy environmentally sensitive land to be put in the public domain. District operating funds come from a tax on property owners and 'documentary stamp taxes' (levied on certain documents including property transfers).

Water management districts and the counties they oversee are:

- **Northwest Florida (Havana)** (**www.nwfwmd.state.fl.us**): All or parts of Bay, Calhoun, Escambia, Franklin, Gadsden, Gulf, Holmes, Jackson, Jefferson, Leon, Liberty, Okaloosa, Santa Rosa, Wakulla, Washington.

- **St Johns (Palatka)** (**sjr.state.fl.us**): All or parts of Alachua, Baker, Bradford, Brevard, Clay, Duval, Flagler, Indian River, Lake, Marion, Nassau, Okeechobee, Orange, Osceola, Polk, Putnam, St Johns, Seminole, Volusia.

- **South Florida (West Palm Beach)** (**www.sfwmd.gov**): All or parts of Broward, Charlotte, Collier, Dade, Glades, Hendry, Highlands, Lee, Martin, Monroe, Okeechobee, Orange, Osceola, Palm Beach, Polk, St Lucie.

- **Southwest Florida (Brooksville)** (**www.swfwmd.state.fl.us**): All or parts of Charlotte, Citrus, De Soto, Hardee, Hernando, Highlands, Hillsborough, Lake, Levy, Manatee, Marion, Pasco, Pinellas, Polk, Sarasota, Sumter.

- **Suwannee River (Live Oak)** (**www.srwmd.state.fl.us**): All or parts of Alachua, Baker, Bradford, Columbia, Dixie, Gilchrist, Hamilton, Jefferson, Lafayette, Levy, Madison, Putnam, Suwannee, Taylor, Union.

Condominium Fees

If you have bought a condominium or co-operative apartment, be sure to budget for an extra charge when working out your monthly expenses. The condominium fee covers the cleaning of public spaces, rubbish removal and the salary of a doorman or other property manager. The fee will vary and is usually based on the square footage of your property and is determined by a board of directors that oversees the management of your building. Some fees can be quite high, and the fees for co-operative apartments can sometimes be higher than for a condominium. However, be sure to look closely at what the fee covers, because in some cases a seemingly high fee could actually cover all your utilities.

State Taxes

Because Florida's constitution prohibits it from levying a personal income tax, the state has become a popular place to declare residency among Americans. However, it does have a number of other taxes (and exemptions) you may encounter as homeowner and/or resident. For a full and entirely up-to-date explanation of all the state's taxes, visit **www.stateofflorida.com**.

• **Ad Valorem Tax**: These taxes on real and personal property are assessed and collected at the county level as revenue for counties, cities, school districts and special taxing districts. Each year, the county property appraiser determines the 'just value' of all the property in the county as of 1 January. The calulation of tax due is based on a number of factors, including present cash value, use, location, quantity and size, cost or replacement value, and condition.

• **Homestead and Personal Exemptions**: If you reside permanently in your home, condominium or co-operative apartment, you may be eligible for a $25,000 homestead exemption, which is a reduction from the 'just value' of your property. To qualify you must be resident in your property on 1 January of the current taxable year. If you own agricultural land you may be able to reduce your property taxes by filing under the 'Greenbelt' law, since agricultural land is taxed at a far lower rate than non-agricultural land.

• **Sales Tax**: Florida's sales tax on most goods is 6 per cent, but counties have the authority to add up to 1 per cent discretionary sales surtax.

• **Intangible Tax**: Stocks, bonds, loans, mutual funds and other intangibles are taxable. The first $500,000 owned by couples and the first $250,000 owned by a single person are exempt from the tax. Assets above these figures are taxed at a rate of $0.50 per $1,000 of value.

• **Tangible Property Tax**: Taxable tangible property is defined as all personal property at a home or place of business that is not used for 'family or household comfort' and can include anything from stationery to computers to books. Although the law requires that this tax is collected from all Florida households, because of a lack of staff county tax appraisers generally collect the tax only from businesses and farms. Private householders could be taxed on any items used to generate extra revenue, from a lawnmower to a home computer.

• **Documentary Stamps**: A tax of 35 cents per $100 is imposed on promissory notes, mortgages, trust deeds, security agreements and other written promises to pay money; on documents that convey an interest in real estate, the tax is 70 cents per $100.

• **Gasoline Tax**: Both the state and individual counties levy a gasoline tax, which combined hover around 30 cents per gallon.

Home Phones

Once upon a time, AT&T (or 'Ma Bell') was the only phone company in the USA. AT&T is America's oldest existing telephone company and its roots lead directly to a Scottish-American named Alexander Graham Bell, who is commonly recognized as having invented the telephone in the first place. Whether it was the Scot or one of the two Italians whose names are invoked every time Bell gets the credit, Bell is the one whom most people think of. Technically, AT&T was created as a subsidiary to the inventor's self-referential Bell Telephone Company, but there is barely a decade between their births. Besides, IAT&T would soon devour its own parent and become the closest thing to a state-sanctioned telephone monopoly in the USA.

Then, in 1984, the government broke up this vast monopoly into seven smaller, though still large, service providers, dubbed the 'Baby Bells'. Today, after many mergers, start-ups, and acquisitions, only four major providers remain. Depending on what part of the country you live in, one of these companies – Verizon, Qwest, SBC Communications, Bell South – will be your home phone service provider. To get contact information for these companies (or to request the very handy phone book), just dial 'o' on any phone.

Unlike your electricity, gas, and water supply, you have a vast set of options for your home phone service. These include local, regional or nationwide coverage, various long-distance providers, and extras like caller ID or three-way calling and Internet access. The options and prices vary a great deal, so you'd do well to look around the relevant company's website and examine all the different packages closely before making a decisions. A few key questions to consider might be: do you have relatives or friends in another part of the country that you'll want to call often? Or will most of your phone usage be local (i.e. in town)? Will you also be purchasing a cell phone, or will this be your only phone? Do you require Internet access at home? (Bear in mind that cable Internet access,

Calling Home

Making international calls from the USA is not cheap. It can be reasonable, however, if you shop around and exercise caution. When you set up your home or cell phone, enquire how much international calling plans cost per month, and how much the 'per-minute' charges (during the daytime, night time, and on weekends) are after that (yhey will usually be fairly pricey).

If you don't mind using a calling card to call home, this is often the best option. Look around online for a calling card that suits your needs: there are literally hundreds of companies out there offering prepaid international cards. If you choose wisely, you ought to be able to manage calling home for as little as a couple of cents a minute. Be sure to read your calling card's fine print, though; sometimes cards with very cheap per-minute rates turn out to have hefty connection fees, which can deplete your balance quickly. Also look at which areas these cards cover. Some only have certain local access numbers, and even the 'free' 1-800 numbers (which invariably attract a surcharge) may only serve small regions of the country.

through the TV company, is now fairly commonplace so that you do not need a phone line to connect to the Internet.) Except for the most bargain-basement plans, $20 a month should get you a phone line and unlimited local calls. Depending on where you live, a local call may be defined differently, from every number that shares your area code (the first three digits of your phone number) to all numbers within a certain region, no matter the area code. Any phone number dialled beyond this area will be subject to a per-minute long-distance surcharge – unless, of course, you choose a plan that includes in-state, regional, or nationwide long-distance. These premium packages usually cost around $50 per month. Add-on options such as dial-up or DSL Internet access can add between $20 and $50 to your monthly bill.

Mobile Phones

The selection of plans and companies offering mobile (or 'cell') phone services is even more bewildering than the choice of home phone services. A multitude of companies offer a vast array of plans including pre-paid, contract, local and nationwide long-distance. It really helps to do some research before settling on any particular provider. A few of the larger companies are Verizon (**www.verizon.com**), SprintPCS (**www.sprint.com**), Cingular (**www.cingular.com**) and T-Mobile (**www.t-mobile.com**). There are also local options, but most people who often travel are best off with one of the big companies, as their coverage will be more comprehensive and their prices more competitive.

The aforementioned companies all offer 'contract' cell phone plans. What this means is that when you begin service with the company, you sign a contract that says you will stay with the company for a certain amount of time – usually one to two years. If you change your plan during your contract period, the contract usually starts from scratch. So even if you've been with a cell phone company for 11 months of a year-long contract, and you change your plan during that 11th month, you're now signed up for yet another full year. If you break your contract before the term has expired, you'll be subject to a hefty fee – usually between one and two hundred dollars. Be sure to read the fine print of your contract before you sign on the dotted line.

Of the myriad available mobile phone contracts, most involve a certain number of 'anytime' minutes (also called daytime minutes, usually between the weekday hours of 6am to 9pm) combined with a certain number of 'night and weekend' minutes. Most companies now offer unlimited night and weekend minutes along with free 'nationwide long-distance' – meaning that those lengthy evening calls to that friend across the country in California will be, effectively, free. Keep in mind that, unlike in the UK, 'minutes' are used up both when making and receiving a call.

With regard to pricing, most contract plans that offer around three to four hundred anytime minutes, unlimited night and weekend minutes, and nation-wide long-distance (i.e. calling across the country will use up minutes at the same rate as if you were to call across the street) will run to around $40 a month. Taxes and fees will add about $10 per month on to that total. From there, each extra $5 per month should correlate to an additional 100 to 150 anytime minutes, and so on. You should be careful to choose a plan that provides just a bit more than the amount of anytime minutes you'll be needing each month: if you go over your allotted minutes, the charges add up quickly, while purchasing a plan that leaves you with a good chunk of excess minutes every month is a waste of money. There are dozens of add-ons to such plans, including Web access, text messaging (which nowhere near as popular in the USA as in the UK), and picture and multimedia capabilities. These extras will typically cost you between $5 and $25 more per month. Free voicemail is standard with almost all providers and plans.

Depending on what part of the country you begin your contract, you may or may not need to pay for your first phone: in the South, for example, a free phone when you start your contract is fairly easy to negotiate, while in New York City you'll be forced to pay for even the most low-end model. Prices for phones start at around $50 and really have no upper limit. Mobiles brought over from the UK (unless they are one of the 'tri-band' phones) will not work in the USA, as the two countries operate on different bands.

'Pay-as-you-go' or 'top-up' plans are nowhere near as common in the USA as they are in the UK. That said, a few major phone companies do offer these plans, notably Cingular and T-Mobile. For around $50, you'll be able to get a phone with around 100 minutes 'pre-loaded.' After that, you'll need to purchase additional minutes directly from the company, usually with a credit or debit card over the phone or using top-up cards from convenience stores. T-Mobile, for example, charges $50 for 400 anytime minutes, while Cingular has a sliding rate depending on how many minutes you buy: from a high of $0.15 a minute up to 400 minutes to a low of $0.11 a minute up to 650 minutes. These pay-as-you-go schemes can be good if you won't be using your phone that often or if you're not sure how long you'll be needing a US cell phone; if you decide to quit one of these plans, you won't be charged a penalty as you will if you break a traditional cell phone contract.

Another option if you're not going to be in the US for very long is to rent a phone: look in your Yellow Pages under 'cellular' for companies offering this service, which is generally only available in the larger cities.

The Internet

The USA is the most wired country in the world: according to the most recent census data, over half of all Americans are connected to the Internet in their home. Increasingly, broadband service (DSL, cable, etc.) is replacing slower dial-up access (a baud rate of 56 Kbps), even in rural areas. What this means for the expat is that you should find it very easy to get online – at a high connection speed, and most likely at a lower cost than back home – no matter what part of the USA you're in. All you need to connect for dial-up access is a phone socket or 'jack', which your home will doubtless already have. For DSL or cable Internet, you'll need some extra hardware which is usually supplied by the company.

Pricing varies from around $10 a month for unlimited dial-up access to around $50 or $60 for the highest broadband or cable connection speeds. High-speed cable access is usually offered by whatever company offers cable TV service in your area, and often comes as part of a cable TV package. One advantage of cable access (besides the speed) is that you don't need a home phone line to use it – which, if you've decided to use a cell phone for all calls, will save you a good $20 to $50 per month on a land line. With dial-up and DSL (digital subscriber line) service, you will of course need a home phone line. When using dial-up, you will tie up your phone line while surfing, while with DSL you can browse the Internet and take calls simultaneously. Unless you're on a tight budget or don't use the Internet often, you should pay the extra for a high-speed connection. Also, unlike in Britain, local calls – including to Internet service providers (ISPs) with local access numbers – are not charged by the minute, meaning that, beyond the cost of a monthly service, surfing the Internet is effectively free.

There are countless Internet service providers in the USA. America Online (AOL; **www.aol.com**) is of course ubiquitous, while NetZero (**www.netzero.com**) and EarthLink (**www.earthlink.com**) are newer, upstart ISPs, with lower rates than AOL's standard $24 a month for unlimited dial-up access.

You could also choose a local ISP – check the phone book for contact information, or search online for '[your town] local ISP'. However, if you plan on travelling around the country and want to be able to get online while on the road, you should choose a national ISP. Rates for local and national ISPs are pretty much the same – around $10–25 a month for dial-up access.

Keep in mind, too, that many hotels and coffee shops around the country now offer free wireless (WiFi) Internet access; to take advantage of these hotspots, your laptop computer will need to be wireless-enabled.

You may well be able to use your British e-mail account in America. If your e-mail is a web-based account such as those provided by Hotmail or Yahoo, you'll certainly have no trouble accessing it across the pond. If, however, your e-mail is provided by a local British company that also provides your home Internet service, you may need to get a new, American email account. Check with your current ISP to see if your e-mail will be accessible in the USA. If you do require a new address, simply visit **www.hotmail.com** or **www.yahoo.com** and sign up for their free e-mail service; you'll be able to access either of these accounts from anywhere in the world. There are of course many other free Web-based email services; just search online for 'free email.' Soon, too, Google will be offering snazzy 'Gmail' service to all comers; right now it's in the beta stage and available by invitation only; check **www.gmail.com** for current status.

Post and Couriers

Unlike in Britain, the post office in America serves pretty much just one purpose: sending and receiving mail and packages. Visit **www.usps.com** for all you ever wanted to know (and probably much more) about the United States Postal Service (USPS), or look up 'post offices' in the phone book's Yellow Pages. Opening hours vary from office to office, but are generally 8 or 9am to 5 or 6pm on weekdays, 9am to 12 noon or 1pm on Saturdays and closed on Sundays.

Mail is delivered to your home or apartment from Monday through Saturday and, depending on what sort of residence you live in (usually stand-alone houses or apartments), it may also be picked up directly from your home as well. If you're not sure of the postage rate, you should visit the post office to mail your letter or package. At the post office you'll also be able to choose from various extra-cost special-delivery options, such as Priority Mail (two days nationwide), Express Mail (overnight nationwide), insurance and so on.

Though the post office is fairly reliable, you may want to use a private **courier company** for more valuable or time-sensitive packages or documents. **FedEx (www.fedex.com)** and **UPS (www.ups.com)** are the two largest courier companies in America, and will be happy to ship whatever you've got to any corner of the globe; their rates are, surprisingly, not that much more than the post office's, and their reliability and service are top-notch.

Major Media

The media are perhaps the most powerful social force in USA, bombarding the populace from a growing number of angles – print, television, radio and Internet – and infiltrating every aspect of American life. Television is the most powerful and all-pervasive medium, with the average American viewing around 1,500 hours per year. Reading occupies less than a tenth of this time in the lifestyle of the typical American, yet magazine and newspaper circulations and book sales remain healthy. This is despite some rapid changes in the media over the last decade or so. On the one hand, the number of media outlets has exploded, thanks largely to the expanding presence of the Internet, while at the same time media ownership is being rapidly, and controversially, consolidated.

Ownership and the Main Players

The proliferation of the media has to some extent led to its consolidation, with the Federal Communications Commission (FCC) using the abundance of media as a reason for deregulating its ownership. Most of the effect of the subsequent media-merging and concentration has benefited the big players, since the smaller ones will find it hard to compete, and not the consumer, who generally speaking now has less choice.

In 1996 radio was deregulated, with the result that one company, Clear Channel, now dominates the industry, owning around half the nation's stations. The corporation's ownership of concert venues and ticket agencies gives it a strong power of influence on the music industry.

FCC rulings in 2001 allowed similar deregulation among the TV networks, although the biggest are still not permitted to merge. The companies which already dominate US media ownership are News Corp (Fox), Walt Disney Corp (ABC), General Electric (NBC), AOL Time Warner and Viacom (CBS). These conglomerates also own most of the nation's big magazines and movie studios, enabling them to use their wide platform to cross-promote their interests.

In 2003 the FCC weakened its rules governing the concentration of media ownership, allowing one company to own and run different forms of media in the same market. The result may well be that one company can own a local TV station, daily newspaper and several radio stations – thereby giving major corporations more power and greater potential to manipulate the population.

Newspapers

Newspapers are an integral part of the morning routine in many American households. The image of the sleepy-eyed husband stepping outside the door in his bathrobe to retrieve the plastic-sheathed paper that has landed halfway across the lawn has become a cliché. Children still endure with groans the reminiscences of their father about how he learned the value of a dollar by waking up at dawn every day to pedal his way through a paper route (delivery boys on bicycles still exist, but today a lot of papers are delivered by men in cars). The newspaper business still holds a certain romantic appeal for those who revel in the idea of the determined impartiality of its writers and editors. The reality, of course, is that news is big business, and the affiliations of major papers are generally established along liberal and conservative lines.

Every major city in Florida has its own daily newspaper. In fact, nearly every county and town has a paper of some kind. Of the local papers, the *Miami Herald* is one of the better recognized nationally, and hovers somewhere at the low end of the big American papers.

The nationals you will most likely come across are the *New York Times* (**www.nytimes.com**), the *Washington Post* (**www.washingtonpost.com**) and the *LA Times* (**www.latimes.com**), which are city-specific but distributed nation-wide. The conservative *New York Times* is considered by many to be the real national newspaper, but *USA Today* (**www.usatoday.com**) was actually created as a national newspaper. While *USA Today*, which covers stories from every state of the Union, has gained some respect in recent years, it is still thought to be more of an abbreviated version of the news. Then there is the *Union Jack* (**www.ujnews.com**), 'America's Only National British Newspaper', which includes news of interest to British people all over the USA, as well as news from the UK. For a comprehensive list of online links to the Florida's local publications you can visit the state library home page (**http://dlis.dos.state.fl.us/fgils/flnews2.html**).

Magazines

Today there are around 17,000 consumer magazines on the market in the USA. This figure is by no means an all-time high – a few years ago the number would have been several thousand higher – but the industry has recently suffered some setbacks because the economic slump has led to a fall in advertising. Still, 257 new magazines were launched in 2005, according to the Magazine Publishers of America, so there is no shortage of reading material.

The magazine business, like other media industries, is dominated by a few major players. Time Inc., a subsidiary of AOL Time Warner, is a clear leader in the USA – and the world – with over a hundred magazines to its name, including *Time*, *Sports Illustrated* and *People*, just to name a few of the biggest. Condé Nast Publications is another major player. Apart from *Condé Nast Traveller*, the company publishes *GQ*, *Vogue*, *Vanity Fair*, the *New Yorker*, *Architectural Digest* and several others.

Radio

Most of the American radio market is dominated by a single company, Clear Channel Radio, which claims to reach over 50 per cent of the population in the USA between the ages of 18 and 49. This means that whether you are in Kissimmee, Florida or San Diego, California, you will come across programming that is remarkably similar. The programmes on most radio stations are the product of extensive market research that has resulted in a distressingly homogenized sound. In fact, sometimes what you may think is a local broad-cast, including general comments on the local traffic and weather, may have been recorded in Texas by a DJ who is reading from a script that is generic enough to apply almost anywhere. If you are near a university town like Gainesville or Tallahassee and are interested in more original music program-ming, you could tune in to the nearest college radio station.

Another option is National Public Radio (NPR), which is publicly funded. The network's operating costs are not covered by advertising but rather by a combi-nation of government funding, private donations and corporate sponsorship. NPR can usually be found on the lower registers of the radio and provides a mix of news, talk shows and classical music.

Satellite radio is a recent development that is expected to do for radio what cable did for television. The main advantage of this new technology, according to its creators, is that it offers crystal-clear access to its programming – divided into specific genres – from anywhere in the country, even from a moving car. Currently there are only two providers of the subscription-based service Sirius and XM. Each costs around $13 per month and has at least 100 channels; Sirius claims to be entirely commercial-free, while XM allows limited advertising.

Television

If you are not interested in watching people competing to humiliate them-selves, or others, for the chance of winning a cash prize, then you may want to stay away from American broadcast television for a little while. So-called 'reality' shows like *Survivor* and *The Bachelor* proved to be big money-makers in recent years and predictably have come to dominate the airwaves as each network tries to outdo the others in revealing the greed of their fellow citizens.

What timeslots left over are filled with either situation comedies like *Friends* or a mix of police, legal and medical dramas. The major broadcasting companies – NBC, ABC, CBS, Fox, UPN and WB – clearly are not too interested in departing from formulas that seem to work. Even the Public Broadcasting System (PBS), which like NPR is publicly funded, has got into the 'reality' show craze. PBS also broadcasts a number of British television shows.

You will still find more of the same even if you opt for cable television but with so many channels you will also have access to a more formidable version of

Super Bowl madness

The grand final of the professional American Football season, the late-January Super Bowl, has reached the status of an unofficial holiday. Life in the USA stops on Super Bowl Sunday as families gather to watch the climax of one of the country's most violent and complicated sports. Up to 140 million viewers tune in for the match, which including commercial breaks and an extravagant and splashy half-time show, will easily last four hours. But as anyone who has been to a Super Bowl party will agree, it's the halftime show and the commercials that are more likely to stop conversation and attract attention rather than the football itself. The commercials are considered treats: they are usually the first run of a TV ad that has been months in the making at a cost of millions of dollars – a thirty-second slot during the Super Bowl itself is worth well over a million. It's the ads too, not the football, that people are more likely to talk about after the game – which, at this level, is often dominated by defences who block the aspirations of the nervous playmakers to create low-scoring games.

reality programming: the documentary. Documentary production is a rapidly expanding business in American television as companies like Discovery, National Geographic and the History Channel struggle to fill rising demand.

Of course, if you are missing the BBC, thanks to BBC America you should be able to catch up on the latest British television, albeit in a slightly abbreviated form. To find out more about where you can find the channel, visit the website (**www.bbcamerica.com**).

Money and Banking

If you plan to spend a lot of time in your Florida home, opening a local bank account is a good idea. This will give you access to cheques and allow you to avoid the charges associated with accessing your account in the UK. There are hundreds of regional and national institutions ready to hold your money for you, so finding the best one for you will require a bit of research.

To open an account, you will need your passport and, possibly, a secondary form of identification. You may also be required to present a utility bill or some other correspondence that verifies your local address, and you will be asked to provide a signature to be kept on file at the bank. As a foreign citizen, you can open an account without a social security number. However, the bank may withhold funds until you can provide it with some form of tax ID number. Some people have gone to great lengths to prove that, according to the letter of the law, banks cannot require you to submit a social security number even though it is the policy of most to do so. It is probably easier just to get yourself one – see **First Steps and Reasons for Buying**, 'Social Security Number', pp.31–2.

Ideally, you will want to bank with an institution that is insured by the Federal Deposit Insurance Corporation (FDIC), which means your deposits will be protected up to $100,000. If the bank is insured, FDIC stickers will be displayed prominently on doors and cashier (teller) windows. When comparing banks in your area, keep in mind what kinds of transactions you regularly engage in and find out the charges associated with each. Ask for clarification of any other possible charges: ATM usage, balance enquiries, overdraft protection and bounced cheques. Because banks routinely charge for using another bank's ATMs, look around your area and check that the bank you are considering has plenty of machines available.

Most banks require a minimum balance on any interest-bearing accounts. If you don't plan to keep a lot of money in your account, you could set up a no-frills account that offers few benefits but does not require a minimum balance. Another alternative is to find out if your bank can link your chequing and your savings accounts, where you could keep a minimum balance just to offset the requirement. The following are the types of account available to you:

• **Chequing Accounts**: A regular chequing account, usually known as a demand deposit account, does not pay interest, while a negotiable order of withdrawal (NOW) account does. Institutions may impose different charges on chequing accounts, besides a charge for the cheques you order. Some will charge a flat monthly maintenance fee regardless of the balance in your account. Others will charge a monthly fee if the minimum balance in your account drops below an established amount (either at any point during the month or as an average monthly balance, depending on the bank). An interest-bearing chequing account may seem like an attractive option, but the interest you earn may not make up for the higher fees. Chequing accounts that pay interest often have higher charges than regular chequing accounts, so you could end up paying more in charges than you earn in interest. However, a basic chequing account may also charge you each time you use an ATM, which could add up to more than the monthly fee of an interest-bearing account.

• **Money Market Deposit Accounts**: An interest-bearing account that allows you to write cheques is known as a money market deposit account (MMDA). Usually this kind of account pays a higher rate of interest than other chequing or savings accounts, but it also requires a higher minimum balance to start earning interest. There may also be limits on the number of times you can withdraw funds or write cheques from an MMDA.

• **Savings Accounts**: You may make withdrawals on a savings accounts but you cannot draw cheques on it, and the number of withdrawals or transfers you can make each month is limited. Generally, there are two types of savings accounts: passbook savings and statement savings. The first comes with a record book in which all your transactions are entered and which must be presented when you make deposits and withdrawals. With a statement savings account, on the other hand, the institution will periodically send you a statement that details the transactions on your account.

• **Time Deposits (Certificates of Deposit)**: Time deposits – also called certificates of deposit, or CDs – usually offer a guaranteed rate of interest for a specified term, which can range from several days to several years. The institution will generally require you to keep your money in the account until it has 'matured', or reached the end of the term. In exchange for leaving your money with the institution for a guaranteed period of time, they will offer you a higher rate of return than conventional accounts. The longer the return, the higher the percentage. While you may not touch your initial deposit, the principal, some institutions allow you to withdraw the interest. You will be charged a penalty if you withdraw your money before it has matured and, in some cases, the penalty could be greater than the amount of interest earned, meaning that you could lose some of your principal deposit. The institution will notify you as the end of the term approaches but you must inform it if you wish to take out your money, otherwise the CD will be renewed automatically for another term.

• **Basic or No-frills Banking Accounts**: One of these may be your best option if you only plan to keep a small amount of money to cover writing a few cheques. The basic account will not bear interest and will come with very few services and limited cheque-writing privileges, but it will also have a low minimum balance requirement.

• **Credit Union Accounts**: If you work for an American corporation, a local or state government office, or even belong to a well-organized community group, you may be able to join a credit union. Credit unions are member-owned alternatives to commercial banks and, since they don't have to pay stock dividends, their fees are generally lower. Large credit unions are federally insured and offer most of the services of a regular bank, including separate branches and ATM networks, but usually fewer banking products.

Working and Employment

If you are not a permanent resident or citizen, working in the USA involves two options: having an American employer apply for a temporary employment visa for you, or becoming a resident through specific employment. The US government does not issue work visas for casual employment and if you are on a visitor or business visa, or have entered the country under the Visa Waiver Program, you are not permitted to work.

For detailed employment information visit the US Bureau of Citizenship and Immigration Service's (USCIS) website (**www.uscis.gov**).

Temporary Employment Visas

If you want to work temporarily in the USA, unless you qualify for an E-category visa, your employer will have to file an I-129 petition with the USCIS. The following are the categories under which you may qualify for a temporary visa.

• **Treaty Traders and Investors (E)**: There are two kinds of E visa for which you can apply: the **E-1 Treaty Trader**, which allows you enter the USA solely to engage in trade of a substantial nature principally between the USA and your home country; and the **E-2 Treaty Investor**, which allows you to enter the USA solely to direct and develop the operations of an enterprise in which you have invested, or are in the process of investing, a substantial amount of capital.

• **Speciality Workers (H-1B)**: There are three categories of H-1B visas: **H-1B1**, which applies to people coming temporarily to provide services in a specialized occupation that requires highly specialized knowledge; **H-1B2**, which applies to people coming temporarily to perform services of an exceptional nature relating to a co-operative research and development project administered by the Department of Defense; and **H-1B3**, which applies to a nationally or internationally recognized fashion model.

• **Registered Nurses (H-1C)**: This category of visa applies if you are coming on a temporary visit to provide services as a registered nurse in a health professional shortage area as determined by the US Department of Labor. A total of 500 nurses can be granted H-1C status in a fiscal year.

• **Temporary Alien Labour to Meet Temporary Needs (H-2)**: There are two categories of this visa, which is meant to fill temporary or seasonal jobs where qualified US workers are not available: **H-2A Agricultural Worker**, which applies to temporary or seasonal agricultural employment; and **H-2B Skilled or Unskilled Worker**, which applies to non-agricultural employment that is seasonal, intermittent, a peak load need, or a one-time occurrence. There is currently an annual cap of 66,000 visas for H-2B workers. There is no annual cap on visas for H-2A workers.

• **Alien Trainees (H-3)**: You may apply for this visa if you are coming to the USA to participate in an employer's training programme. There is a general visa and one that applies specifically to programmes related to the education of children with physical, mental or emotional disabilities.

• **Intracompany Transferees (L-1)**: If you work for a company with a parent, subsidiary, branch or affiliate in the USA then you may be able to enter the USA as an intra-company transferee in a managerial or executive capacity **(L-1A)** or with specialized knowledge **(L-1B)**. To qualify, you must have worked for the company full-time for at least one continuous year out of the last three-year period.

• **Aliens with Extraordinary Ability (O)**: You may apply for this visa if you have an extraordinary ability in the sciences, arts, education, business or athletics **(O-1)**. Support staff **(O-2)** and spouses and/or children **(O-3)** of such an extraordinary person may also qualify.

• **Athletes, Entertainment Groups, Artists (P)**: The **P-1** visa applies to internationally recognized athletes – either individually or as a part of a group – and members of a foreign-based entertainment group. The **P-2** classification is for artists or entertainers who will perform individually or as part of a group, under a reciprocal exchange programme with an American organization. The **P-3** classification applies to people coming temporarily in order to perform, teach or coach as artists or entertainers, individually or as part of a group, under a programme that is culturally unique.

• **International Cultural Exchange Program Participants (Q-1)**: Participants in an international cultural exchange programme approved by the Attorney General for the purpose of providing practical training, employment and to share the history, culture and traditions of their country may apply for a Q-1.

• **Religious Worker (R)**: You may apply for an **R-1 visa** if you are coming to the USA to work temporarily as a minister of religion, a professional in a religious vocation or occupation, or for a bona fide non-profit religious organization at the request of the organization, in a religious occupation which relates to a traditional religious function.

Immigration through Employment

If you are hoping to establish permanent residency through your employment, there are five categories under which you may be eligible to do this. Your employer will have to sponsor you.

• **EB-1 Priority Workers**: You could become a permanent resident if you possess 'extraordinary ability in the sciences, arts, education, business, or athletics which has been demonstrated by sustained national or international acclaim and whose achievements have been recognized in the field through extensive documentation'. Bear in mind that, in this case, 'recognition' means an award on the level of a Nobel Prize.

• **EB-2 Professionals with Advanced Degrees or Persons with Exceptional Ability**: This category applies to 'members of the professions holding advanced degrees or their equivalent' and people 'who because of their exceptional ability in the sciences, arts, or business will substantially benefit the national economy, cultural, or educational interests or welfare of the USA'.

• **EB-3 Skilled or Professional Workers**: This is a broad category and includes professionals with first degrees that don't qualify for any of the above categories, skilled workers with a minimum of two years' training and experience, and unskilled workers.

• **EB-4 Special Immigrants**: This category includes religious workers and employees, and former employees of the US government abroad.

• **EB-5 Immigrant Investors**: You may be eligible for this visa if you are establishing a new commercial enterprise by creating an original business; purchasing an existing business and simultaneously or subsequently restructuring or reorganizing the business to form a new commercial enterprise; or expanding an existing business by 140 per cent of the pre-investment number of jobs or net worth, or retaining all existing jobs in a troubled business that has lost 20 per cent of its net worth over the past 12–24 months. You may also qualify if you have invested – or are actively investing – at least $1 million in a new commercial enterprise, or at least $500,000 in a 'targeted employment area', which is an area that has experienced unemployment of at least 150 per cent of the national average rate or a rural area as designated by the US government. You may also qualify if your engagement in a new commercial enterprise will benefit the US economy and create full-time employment for not fewer than 10 qualified individuals; or maintain the number of existing employees at no less than the pre-investment level for a period of at least two years, where the capital investment is being made in a 'troubled business', which is one that has been in existence for at least two years and that has lost 20 per cent of its net worth over the past 12–24 months.

Education

There is no avoiding it: the US state (public) education system is in trouble. You will surely hear this – probably in less diplomatic terms – at some point during your time in Florida, and it could well be that the information will be of no concern, since you may not be allowed to take part in it; the rules are changing all the time, but it's likely that, unless you become a permanent resident in the USA, the only option for you and your children once you arrive is going to be private school.

It is unfair to discredit the entire public school system when it has many very good schools, but the problem, as in the UK, is simply that it is an uneven system. The simplest explanation for the disparity appears to be uneven funding, although you will find plenty of people who will argue that money won't solve the problem. Generally speaking, the amount of funding for individual public schools is based on the value of the real estate where they are located, so naturally schools in poorer areas end up with less money.

If you are eligible to enrol your children in public school, don't ignore the option. You just might want do some research first by visiting the National Center for Education Statistics (**www.nces.ed.gov/ccd/schoolsearch**) or the Florida Department of Education (**www.info.doe.org**), where you will find the Florida

Private School Accreditation

South Florida Parenting Magazine recently published an article examining the accreditation of the state's private schools. Florida classifies its private and religious schools as 'non-public' and does not license, approve, accredit or regulate them. Generally, these schools only come into contact with the government when they register with the Department of Education and when they respond to an annual information survey. Therefore, these non-public schools are entirely responsible for all aspects of their programme, which means that you will find a great variety of rules and regulations from school to school.

The state may not require a school to be accredited, but if you are putting your child into a private institution make sure it is accredited, since most colleges and universities, as well as many employers, won't recognize a high school diploma from an institution that is not. But accreditation is not about prestige; it is about getting an objective assessment. The trouble is that there are a number of accrediting organizations, with different quality standards and requirements. According to the Florida Department of Education (**www.fldoe.org**), there are 46 different accrediting agencies throughout the state.

The Southern Association of Colleges and Schools (**www.sacs.org**), based in Georgia, accredits over 12,000 public and private educational institutions in 11 southeastern states from pre-kindergarten through college. It is one of only six regional accrediting organizations recognized by the US Department of Education and it is the only one used by Florida's public and state university system schools. The Florida Council of Independent Schools (FCIS) (**www.fcis.org**) accredits private secular schools throughout the state based on similar criteria as the Southern Association. FCIS represents over 73,000 students in 159 member schools.

School Indicators Report, a searchable database that provides data on public elementary, middle and high schools for each of the state's 67 school districts.

Whether private school is your only option or it is the option you have chosen, you will still want to look around. A good place to start is the National Association of Independent Schools (**www.nais.org**), which has a searchable database of schools. Once you have narrowed down your choices of private schools, NAIS suggests you ask yourself a few questions:

- Is the school accredited and by whom?
- What is the school's mission and does its philosophy appeal to you?
- Does the school have a special or particular educational focus?
- Is the teaching rigorous?
- Is the environment competitive? Nurturing? Are there high expectations?
- Does the school meet your child's needs?
- How large is the school and its student body?

• Where is the school located and what are your transport options?

• What is the range of educational activities available at the school – in class, on the playing field, in extracurricular activities and in community service? Are extracurricular activities obligatory?

• Does the school seem to have a diverse student body and faculty?

• Do the school materials discuss parental involvement?

• For high schools, what are the graduation requirements? What percentage of students enter colleges and what kinds of colleges do they attend?

• Is college counselling effective (look at the rates at which school-leavers achieve their first and second college choices)?

• What is the tuition fee and how flexible are the school's financing options?

• What is the school's application process? Are deadlines drawing near?

Health and Emergencies

Besides **Medicare**, which applies only to people age 65 and over or who are disabled, the USA does not have national insurance. You could be eligible for the benefit at 65 if you have worked long enough under US social security to qualify. For example, people born in 1929 or later would need 40 credits (about 10 years of covered work) to qualify.

Although an agreement between the USA and the UK allows the Social Security Administration to count your UK credits to help you qualify for other US benefits, such as retirement, disability or survivor benefits, the agreement does not cover Medicare benefits, and your credits back home will not count towards establishing entitlement to free Medicare hospital insurance.

To obtain more information on Medicare, which is actually divided into hospital insurance (also called 'Part A' Medicare) and medical insurance ('Part B' Medicare), telephone t 1-800 6334 2273 in the USA, or visit the website at **www. medicare.gov**.

All your other medical issues will have to be handled through **private insurance**. The USA has some of the best medical care in the world but it does not come cheap. It is strongly recommended, by the UK government and several people with direct experience, that you get comprehensive travel and medical insurance with at least a $1 million cover, which also includes hospital treatment and medical evacuation to the UK. Some people recommend purchasing it through your travel and personal insurance in the UK prior to travelling. Others have reported that, on the rare occasion when they have sought local medical treatment, the first question they were asked was not 'what's the problem?' but 'how do you intend to pay?'. If you do not have insurance, be prepared to pay a great deal.

You should be able to pay by credit card and then submit the claim back to your medical insurers when you return. Most insurers offer a limited period of coverage. A typical vacation visitor might buy 14 days' worth. More frequent visitors might invest in a one-year, multi-trip policy with a maximum stay of 31 days. You can also get up to 120 days per stay, which could be extended up to a maximum of six months for an additional charge.

Unfortunately, premiums for medical policies are generally calculated according to your age and pre-existing conditions, which means that the older you are, and the more ailments you suffer from, the more expensive the policy. Premiums start to rise when you reach your 65th birthday and increase again when you hit 70. A useful website is the Agency for Healthcare Research and Quality (**www. ahcpr.gov**), with information about US healthcare options.

Be careful of trying to keep your premiums low by hiding any pre-existing medical conditions: should you suddenly require treatment in the USA for a condition that you did not reveal to your insurer, then your insurance company may refuse to pay for it and you will be stuck with an enormous bill.

Doctors, Hospitals and Pharmacies

Most health insurance plans require you to pick a '**primary care provider**', or PCP. This person will be, for all intents and purposes, your doctor, whom you'll visit for check-ups, general illnesses and so on. This doctor will be associated either with a hospital or a private practice, and will be able to refer you to other, more specialised doctors should the need arise. If you need to make an appointment, simply call your doctor's office and speak with the receptionist, who will tell you when the doctor can see you. With health insurance, you will need to pay what's known as a 'co-pay' for your visit, which will usually be somewhere in the neighbourhood of $10 to $25. With no insurance, you will have to pay for the entirety of your visit's cost, which can be very expensive.

If you need immediate medical attention and the doctor's office is not open (as at night or at weekends), you should visit the nearest hospital emergency room. Get there on your own or have a friend take you if at all possible, as ambulance visits and 911 calls should be used only for major, life-threatening injuries or illnesses. To find a hospital close by, check your phone book's Yellow Pages. Some hospitals specialise in fields such as children or mental health, so be sure to pick a hospital with a primary focus on general medicine.

A prescription written by your doctor will need to be taken to a pharmacy to pick up your medicine – though sometimes the doctor's office can phone it in, after which you must either go in person to pick it up. You can visit any pharmacy to have prescriptions filled, though it's best to find one you like and stick with it, as the staff will come to know who you are and what medications you take. Prescriptions, like healthcare, can be very expensive without health insurance – a simple dose of antibiotics can cost upwards of a hundred dollars

Lights Out

Since 1 July 2003, smokers all over the state of Florida have had to look harder for a place where they can enjoy a pint and a cigarette at the same time. On that day, a law came into effect making it illegal for smokers to light up in indoor restaurants, bowling alleys, hotel lobbies and state-controlled prisons. The smoking ban was approved by 71 per cent of the state's voters. Since it came into effect, bars and restaurants all over the state have been struggling to find ways to accommodate the new law while at the same time accommodating their smoking customers. A fifth of Florida's adult population are smokers, according to surveys. Businesses face a warning or a fine of up to $500 for their first violation, but the penalty goes up to $2,000 for repeated offences. Do not expect to see special police forces rounding up smokers, however. Enforcement of the ban is based on the complaints of customers who contact either the Department of Business and Professional Regulation or the Department of Health to report any violators. While the law prohibits smoking inside any restaurant or bar that derives more than 10 per cent of its revenue from food sales, lighting up is still permitted on outdoor patios, as long as the patio is less than 50 per cent enclosed on its sides and above. Tobacco shops, hotel rooms designated for smokers, airport smoking lounges and membership groups like the Veterans of Foreign Wars are also exempt. Stand-alone bars that continue to permit smoking are not allowed to give away food other than bar snacks like popcorn and peanuts and have to prove with an audit every three years that they don't make more than 10 per cent from food.

without insurance. If you have insurance, prescriptions – as with doctor's office visits – are subject to a co-pay, which will vary depending on what the medicine is and whether or not it is a generic or brand-name medicine. Generally, though, the prescription co-pay will range from $10 to $50 per refill.

Social Services and Welfare Benefits

US Benefits

Unfortunately, as a temporary visitor to the USA you do not qualify for any social services or benefits from the American government, but you might qualify as a legal resident who has been working in the USA for more than five years. However, since the benefits you qualify for are based on years of contributions, if you have not been working in the USA for very long, you may not be eligible for much. Quantifying and calculating what you might be owed is a complex matter even for American citizens, so it is very hard to generalize when it comes to applying as a non-citizen. The UK does have a reciprocal social security agreement with the USA so, in theory at least, you could collect benefits from either country. Other advantages to the agreement are that you should not be taxed twice on your social security and you may be able to pool your contributions in each country to maximize their value.

To find out more about US social security benefits, or for information about a claim for benefits, contact any US social security office or call their toll-free number **t** 800 772 1213. If you live outside the USA, write to:

Social Security Administration
Office of International Operations
Totalization
PO Box 17049
Baltimore, Maryland 21235-7049

The following notes, published by the US Social Security Administration, are meant to be a general guide for comparing the monthly benefits and eligibility requirements of the UK and the USA. You can find more detailed information about the US–UK social security agreement on the administration's website (**www.ssa.gov/international/Agreement_Pamphlets/uk.html**). Under US social security, you may earn up to four credits each year depending on the amount of your covered earnings. For example, in 2006 you get one credit for each $970 of your covered annual earnings up to a maximum of four credits for the year. Under the UK system, credits are measured in weeks. To simplify the information in the table, requirements are shown in years of credits.

Retirement or Old-age Benefits

USA

- Full benefit at full retirement age, or reduced benefit as early as age 62. Required work credits range from 1½–10 years.

- Full retirement age for people born in 1938 is age 65 and 2 months. The full retirement age increases gradually until it reaches age 67 for people born in 1960 or later.

UK

- Full benefit at age 65 for men with 44 years of contributions, or reduced benefit with 11 years.

- Full benefit at age 60 (increasing to age 65 between 2010 and 2020) for women with 40 years of contributions, or reduced benefit with 10 years.

Disability Benefits

USA

- Under full retirement age can get benefit if unable to do any substantial gainful work for at least a year. 1½–10 years' credit required depending on age at date of onset. Some recent credits also needed unless worker is blind.

UK

- A contributor who has not retired can get an invalidity benefit if he or she has been incapable of working for 52 weeks during which time he or she was entitled to statutory sickness pay or short-term incapacity benefits. The contributor must have paid a required number of contributions in a recent tax year.

UK Benefits

Depending on your work situation in the USA or the length of time you will spend there, the best thing may be to focus on those benefits that you have coming to you from home, which you are still eligible to claim from Florida. Before you leave, you should inform the Inland Revenue National Insurance Contributions Office, International Services, of your departure date and your address in the USA. Similarly, inform the office when you return home in case there are any problems over your contributions or benefit rights that need to be sorted out immediately. The office address is:

National Insurance Contributions
Inland Revenue,
National Insurance Contributions Office
International Services
Benton Park View
Newcastle-upon-Tyne NE98 1ZZ

From the UK, the office can be contacted on **t** 0845 915 4811. If you are already in Florida and need to contact the office, you can reach them on **t** 44 191 203 7010. You can also contact them by e-mail at **internationalservices.ir.sbg@ ir.gsi.gov.uk**.

There are two kinds of welfare benefits in the UK: 'contributory' and 'non-contributory'. If you have paid (or been credited with) sufficient National Insurance contributions to qualify, then you are eligible for the former benefits. The latter do not depend on paying any National Insurance contributions.

In the UK there are various classes of National Insurance contributions:

Class 1: Paid by employees and their employers and consisting of a percentage of income.

Class 2: A flat-rate payment paid by the self-employed.

Class 3: Voluntary payments made by people no longer paying Class 1 or Class 2 contributions. Their rights are protected for a limited range of benefits.

Class 4: Compulsory 'profit-related' additional contributions that are paid by the self-employed.

The differing types of NI payments qualify you for these various benefits:

NI Contributions and Entitlement to UK Benefits

	Class 1	Class 2/4	Class 3
Maternity Allowances	Yes	Yes	No
Unemployment Benefit	Yes	No	No
Incapacity Benefit	Yes	Yes	No
Widow's Benefit	Yes	Yes	Yes
Basic Retirement Pension	Yes	Yes	Yes
Additional Retirement Pension	Yes	No	No

In addition to the categories mentioned above, benefits are also divided into 'means-tested' and 'non-means-tested'. The former are paid only if you qualify under the eligibility criteria for the benefit in question and are poor enough to qualify on financial grounds. The latter are paid to anyone who meets the eligibility criteria, regardless of their wealth.

• **Accidents at work**: Any benefits you presently receive from the UK benefits system as a result of an accident that happened at work should still be payable to you in the USA.

• **Occupational diseases**: Any benefits you receive from the UK benefits system as a result of an occupational disease should still be payable to you in the USA.

• **Invalidity benefits**: Any National Insurance benefits you receive from the UK benefits system as a result of invalidity should still be payable to you in the USA. Attendance Allowance, SDA and DLA are not usually payable if you go to live abroad permanently.

• **Pensions**: If you are already retired and you only ever paid National Insurance contributions in the UK, you will receive your UK retirement pension in Florida. You will be paid without deduction (except remittance charges) and your pension will be updated whenever pensions in the UK are revised. If you have established an entitlement to a retirement pension in several EU countries by working in them, all the pensions will still be payable to you in Florida. These, too, will be paid without deduction (except remittance charges) and your pension will be updated whenever the pensions in those countries are revised. If you have not yet retired and you move to Florida (whether you intend to work in Florida or not), your entitlement to your UK pension will be frozen and the pension to which you are entitled at that point will be paid to you at UK retirement age. This freezing of your pension could be a disadvantage, especially if you are still relatively young when you move to Florida. This is because you need to have made a minimum number of NI contributions in order to qualify for a full UK state pension. If you have not yet done this but are not far off, it may be worth making additional payments while you are residing overseas. You may choose to pay either continuing Class 2 or Class 3 contributions.

You may pay Class 2 contributions if:

- **you are working abroad.**
- **you have lived in the UK for a continuous period of at least three years during which you paid NI contributions and you have already paid a set minimum amount of NI contributions.**
- **you were normally employed or self-employed in the UK before leaving.**

You may pay Class 3 contributions if:

- **you have at any time lived in the UK for a continuous period of at least three years.**
- **you have already paid a minimum amount in NI contributions in the UK.**

Class 2 contributions are more expensive but potentially cover you for maternity allowance and incapacity benefits. Class 3 contributions do not. In both cases you should apply in the UK using form CF83.

- **Widow's and other survivor's benefits**: Any benefits you receive from the UK benefits system as a result of your being a widow should still be payable to you despite the fact that you have moved to Florida.

Retirement

If you are retiring to Florida, as so many others before you have done, you should have no problem receiving any social security benefits due to you from state or private pensions. However, again, you probably won't qualify for any US benefits unless you have worked there for a while. The following are just a few more retirement issues you may face in the USA.

Receiving Pension Payments

See left for information on receiving your UK state pension in Florida.

Company pension plans are not as flexible as the national ones, and payment will depend on the rules of any particular scheme. Some employers may agree to deposit your pension into an account in Florida or to send you a cheque there, while others may be required to pay only into a UK-based bank account. Bear in mind, however, that if your plan does agree to pay into your Florida account, you will probably pay steep transfer charges, so keep the number of annual payments to a minimum if possible.

It is also possible to make arrangements with currency dealers who can send you payments based on a fixed exchange rate, which might help to avoid or minimize unfortunate fluctuations in the market.

Death

In Florida, the funeral director must file a death certificate within five calendar days of a death unless an extension of time has been granted by a deputy registrar for an additional five working days.

There are some differences if the death involves a UK citizen, the main one being that the British consulate should also be notified. Sections 382.006 and 382.008 of the Florida statutes deal directly with death registration and can be found at **www.flsenate.gov**.

Inheritance and Wills

Under Florida law, if a person dies without a will (intestate), their property will be distributed under rigid state law that only recognizes family members. The distribution process can also end up being much more complicated and costly than if a will were in place. Friends and family will be excluded from the administration of the property, which will be handled by court-ordered personnel. However, if you have made a will in the UK, then your property should be distributed according to those wishes. For more information, *see* p.142.

If you own property in Florida, it may be wise to look into making a US will even if you already have one in the UK. Clearly your Florida home will be the biggest item to consider, but you will also have to take into account any movable property that you have brought with you to the USA.

Depending on whether you have any children and, if you do, where they reside, making a will may be a necessity. Unless you plan for the disposal of your Florida possessions, your children may be faced with considerable expense if they have to deal with your Florida estate from far away.

One more thing to consider is that Florida has no local inheritance tax (though there is a federal tax), which could prove to be a big saving if you qualify as a resident. For more information, *see* p.142.

Cars and Other Private Transport

Under an agreement between the USA and most countries, including the UK, you can use your full national driving licence for a period of up to one year in the USA. This means a full UK driving licence, not a provisional one. Some car rental companies may require you to have held a full licence for at least one year. Normally, the minimum age for renting a car is 21 but in some cases it may be 25. If you are under 25, you may discover an additional charge has been levied. Check with your rental company for specific rules about international licences.

Generally speaking, the USA does not require international driving permits but it does no harm to carry one. However, they are only valid in conjunction with your full licence and will not be accepted on their own. If you are a young driver, or have young drivers in your family, an international driving permit may be useful as a photo ID, which can be used in place of a passport for entry into bars and nightclubs where the minimum entry age is 21. No matter what your age, it is also a useful form of ID to carry. With the tightening of security following the events of 11 September 2001, a photo ID is sometimes requested in shops (when paying by credit card), at car rental offices, boarding internal flights, etc. If you don't wish to run the risk of carrying your passport with you at all times, this is a useful alternative.

Buying and Insuring a Car

If you plan to buy a car once you are in Florida, you don't actually need a licence to do so. You also don't need a social security number to get a licence but it could make the process a bit easier.

However, you will need proof of insurance when you buy a car. Although a Florida licence is not required to get insurance, some companies avoid drivers who don't have one. There are a few companies, such as Allstate (**www.allstate.com**), Progressive (**www.progressive.com**) and State Farm (**www.statefarm.com**), which will cover you without a Florida licence. Most websites enable you to get online quotes. Other sites worth checking out for quotes are **www.insure.com**, **www.netquote.com** and **www.1stinsured.com**.

No matter what, though, the policy won't come cheap – short-term rates can run as high as $1,400. It is also worthwhile to find out if the insurance company will allow you to suspend the policy while you are out of the USA. This could cost more, but will prevent your cover from going to waste while you are back home. Most companies have a six-month minimum for coverage and will refuse to cover you for just one month.

Importing a Car

A brief word of advice: don't. However, if you do want to import your car permanently from the UK, there are several federal agencies you will have to deal with, none of which recommends that you import a vehicle that was not intended for the US market. Importing a vehicle that was not created for the American market can be costly and time-consuming. If you still want to go through with the import then you will have the Environmental Protection Agency (EPA), the Department of Transportation (DOT), the US Customs Service and the Internal Revenue Service to contend with. All four agencies have a say in whether you will be allowed to bring in your vehicle, and they may not all agree.

Cars that are more than 25 years old are exempt from EPA and DOT requirements, which would mean that, in 2006, any vehicle from 1981 or before is exempt. Cars that are 21 years old are exempt from EPA regulations but must still meet DOT regulations.

There are certain exemptions and exclusions to the EPA rules on importing non-conforming vehicles. For example, exclusions include vehicles that are classic or antique and were manufactured before the EPA regulations, that do not have an engine installed, that are not intended for use on streets and highways, that are racing vehicles, and/or that are powered by unregulated fuel. Exemptions to the rules apply only in situations of extreme hardship, temporarily imported vehicles and foreign vehicles that are identical to the US versions.

In order to import your vehicle, it will have to comply with all applicable DOT Federal Motor Vehicle Safety Standards (FMVSS). If it does not, you will have to get a DOT-registered Importer (RI) to bring it into compliance. You will also have to post a bond for one and a half times the vehicle's dutiable value, in addition to the usual customs entry bond required for non-conforming vehicles, which is three times the car's dutiable value. You can obtain a list of registered importers at the DOT website (**www.dot.gov**).

You will not be allowed to register a non-conforming vehicle until it is brought into compliance. To register your car with the Department of Motor Vehicles, you will need customs form 7501, which the agency will not give you without approval from the EPA and DOT. You should also know that it is illegal to sell, donate or dispose of a non-conforming vehicle in the USA.

Temporary Imports

As a non-resident, you are allowed to bring your car with you for a period of one year. Assuming that you will be shipping your car – and not driving it across a land border – you will be required to post a bond with customs. You may also be granted an exemption from federal emissions requirements if you are a diplomat or member of the British military services, or if you are importing the vehicle for repair, alteration, display or testing. However, you will still be required to post a bond.

Taking Your Pet to the USA

Because the US government deems the UK to be a rabies-free zone, bringing a cat or dog into the USA should only require an Official Certificate of Veterinary Inspection from your local vet. Your pet will not need to be quarantined, nor will you be required to provide proof of vaccination. The certificate should state that your pet is free of any signs of infectious or communicable diseases, did not originate in an area under quarantine for rabies, and is not known to have a history of exposure to a rabies-infected animal. For details on importing other kinds of pets, visit the US Department of Agriculture website at **www.aphis. usda.gov/vs/ncie/pet-info.html**.

The US Department of Agriculture does have certain restrictions on the importation of dogs, such as collies or sheepdogs, which are used in the handling of livestock. These breeds could be inspected and quarantined at the port of entry for a sufficient time to ensure that they are free from tapeworm. Do not use straw, hay, grass or any other natural bedding for your pet, as this could delay entry since these materials are prohibited.

At the end of 2002, the UK extended its Pet Travel Scheme (PETS) to include the USA and Canada. The plan, implemented by the Department for Environment, Food and Rural Affairs (DEFRA) (**www.defra.gov.uk/animalh/quarantine/index.htm**), allows visitors and UK citizens returning from certain approved countries who are travelling with their cat or dog to avoid the lengthy quarantine process.

The scheme applies to pet dogs and cats (including guide dogs) that are resident in either the UK or one of the PETS qualifying countries. If your pet satisfies all the rules, it can enter (or re-enter) the UK without having to undergo six months' quarantine. If it does not meet all the rules it must be licensed into quarantine but might be able to obtain early release if you can prove that your pet complies with the necessary PETS requirements.

To bring your animal back into the UK under PETS from one of the qualifying countries you must carry out the following procedures in the order shown.

• **Have your pet microchipped**: Before any of the other procedures for PETS are carried out, your pet must be fitted with a microchip so that it can be properly identified.

• **Have your pet vaccinated**: After the microchip has been fitted, your pet must be vaccinated against rabies.

• **Arrange a blood test**: After your pet has been vaccinated, it must be blood-tested to make sure that the vaccine has given it a satisfactory level of protection against rabies.

• **Get a PETS certificate**: Once these steps have been successfully completed, you can get an official PETS certificate from a government-authorized vet.

• **Before your pet enters the UK, have it treated against ticks and tapeworm**: Your pet must be treated against ticks and a tapeworm 24–48 hours before it is checked in for the journey to the UK. Any qualified vet can carry out the treatment. The vet must also issue an official certificate of treatment to show that this treatment has been carried out.

• **Sign a declaration of residency**: You must sign a declaration (PETS 3) that your animal has not been outside any of the PETS qualifying countries (listed in the form PETS 3A) in the six months before it enters the UK.

• **Arrange for your animal to travel on an approved route**: Your animal must enter the UK from a PETS country travelling on an approved route with an approved transport company.

Your pet can be fitted with a microchip in any country. The rabies vaccination (including boosters), blood sampling, issuing the PETS certificate, the tick and tapeworm treatment, and issuing the official certificate of treatment must all be carried out in either the British Isles, the Republic of Ireland or another qualifying country.

Your pet may not enter the UK under PETS until six months have passed from the date that your vet took the blood sample which led to a successful test result. Once the vet has signed the PETS certificate and that six-month period has passed, the PETS certificate is valid and your pet may enter the UK.

Crime and the Police

The state of Florida has plenty of its own police officers who patrol every area of the state, but, with hundreds of miles of coastline on the edge of international waters, the state relies heavily on federal law enforcement to protect its borders. Within the state, the **Florida Highway Patrol**, or **state troopers**, have broad jurisdiction but their main function is to monitor and enforce traffic laws. They are the ones who will pull you over for speeding on the highway. Next, you have the **county sheriff department**, whose jurisdiction usually corresponds to the limits of the county it operates in. In addition to the county sheriff, every major city and town has its own **police department**. Smaller towns rely on the sheriff for law enforcement.

On the federal level, there are several different groups, including the **coast guard**, which is actually a branch of the military. The **customs bureau** will have its own law enforcement branch as well. There are also other federal law enforcement agencies, such as the **Federal Bureau of Investigation**, that can claim a fair amount of jurisdiction wherever they please, sometimes to the frustration of local authorities.

Overall, the crime rate has been decreasing steadily in Florida over the last few years – with the exception of 2001, which saw a small jump. Several years ago, however, the state earned itself a bad reputation when international newspapers were filled with tales of violent incidents involving international tourists targeted by criminals who could easily recognize a rental car when they saw one. In response, rental companies have tried to minimize the use of any company insignia or logos on their cars. A minor gesture, to be sure, but, as part of a comprehensive approach, anything that might reduce your visibility to criminals is generally a good idea. Some other common-sense tips include:

• Do not leave your door open at any time when staying in a hotel.

• Do not wear expensive jewellery or walk about in run-down areas.

• Do not sleep in your car by the side of the road or in rest areas.

• Do not leave luggage clearly visible in cars.

• Keep to main highways and use well-lit car parks whenever possible.

• If hit from behind while driving, indicate to the other driver to follow you to a public place and call the police for assistance.

American Government

The USA operates under a federalist-style system. The federal government is the highest authority and the constitution is the final word in any legal dispute. However, each state's local government has a fair amount of autonomy and has the right to collect and keep various taxes from its own residents. Major projects such as highways are funded with federal money and each state must fight hard – through its senators and representatives in Washington – to get its fair share. Increased state rights is a common battle cry in the tug-of-war between federal and local governments, which usually comes down to governors not wanting to be told by someone living in Washington how they should run their state. Of course, a number of governors have gone on to become that someone living in Washington. Or, in Florida's case, the governor's brother (George W. Bush; also a former governor) goes on to become that someone.

The Florida state government, which like other state governments generally follows the basic structure of the federal government, is divided into three branches, and is guided by its own constitution. The three branches are the executive, the legislative and the judicial.

Executive Branch

The executive branch is the law-administering and law-enforcing branch of the government. It is modelled along the lines of a large corporation, with the governor serving as chairman of the board and the six independently elected cabinet members serving as directors. The **governor** is elected for a four-year term and may serve two terms in succession. The **lieutenant governor** is elected as running mate of the governor. Members of the cabinet are elected to four-year terms and may succeed themselves for any number of terms. All of the many agencies and departments that are responsible for programmes in Florida state government are also part of the executive branch.

The governor is responsible for day-to-day operations of the state and is the chief law enforcement officer. The governor appoints not only the heads of departments under sole oversight of the governor, but also the heads of depart-ments that are under both the governor's and cabinet's oversight, although at least three cabinet members must agree to the appointments. The governor also appoints members of several regulatory boards and commissions. By exec-utive order, the governor may suspend from office any state or county elected official who is not subject to impeachment. The governor cannot suspend the lieutenant governor, cabinet members, supreme court justices, appellate judges or circuit court judges; they can be removed only by legislative impeachment.

The office of lieutenant governor was authorized in the 1968 revision of the Constitution, but duties of that office were left to the discretion of the governor and the legislature. The only constitutional chore of this office-holder is to become the governor should that office become vacant as a result of death, impeachment trial or incapacity. The lieutenant governor is elected on the same ticket as governor and chosen by the gubernatorial candidate as running mate.

Legislative Branch

The legislative branch is the law-making branch and is composed of two houses: the **Senate** and the **House of Representatives**. The legislature meets for a regular 60-day session each year. There may also be special and extended sessions if necessary. The Senate and House affect every Floridian's life, through legislation relating to how cities and counties operate, through appointment of state officials, through investigative and budgetary matters, and through taxes. The legislative branch is considered to be the most powerful of the state's three branches of government.

The Senate has 40 members, each elected to a four-year term. Half the members are elected every two years, providing for staggered terms. Senate districts are based on population, with each senator representing approxi-mately the same number of residents. To do so, some senators may represent only one county or a portion of a county, while another senator may represent multiple counties. The Senate, like the House is reapportioned every 10 years when the federal census is released.

The House of Representatives has 120 members. All are elected every two years during the general elections held in even-numbered years. House districts are based on population, with each member representing approximately the same number of residents. To do so, some members may represent only one county or a portion of a county, while another may represent multiple counties. The House, like the Senate, is reapportioned every 10 years when the federal census is released.

Judicial Branch

The judicial branch is the law-interpreting branch. Its powers are exercised primarily through courts established by the state constitution. Florida's judicial branch consists of a series of courts with differing levels of authority and jurisdictions. They are:

• **Supreme Court**: This highest of state courts consists of seven members, each appointed by the governor, and confirmed by a vote of the people at the next general election. Each is appointed for a six-year term. Justices select one of their own to be chief justice for a two-year term. The Supreme Court hears appeals directly from trial courts in criminal cases when the death penalty has been imposed, and in civil cases when the trial court's decision passes on the validity of a state or federal law, a treaty or a provision of the state or federal constitution, or in cases concerning the validity of revenue or general obligation bonds. All other appeals must be processed through a district court of appeals.

• **District Court of Appeals**: The state has five appellate districts. More than 50 judges sit on the five appeals courts, each elected to six-year staggered terms. They have jurisdiction over all appeals not directly appealable to the Supreme Court or to a circuit court. An appeals court also may issue writs of *mandamus*, *certiorari*, prohibition, *quo warranto* and *habeas corpus*.

• **Circuit Court**: The circuit court is the state's highest trial court, and the one with the most general jurisdiction. The state is divided into 20 judicial circuits and circuit judges are elected to six-year terms. In each circuit the judges choose from among themselves a chief judge of that circuit. Circuit courts have exclusive original jurisdiction in all actions of law not vested in county courts, including all civil actions involving $2,500 or more. Circuit courts also cover estate settlement; competency and involuntary hospitalization; all cases in equity including those relating to juveniles except certain traffic offences; cases involving tax assessments or tolls, ejectment, and titles or boundaries or rights of possession of real property; felonies or misdemeanours arising out of same circumstances as a felony; and jurisdiction over all appeals from county courts.

• **County Court**: At least one county court judge is specified for each county and is elected to a four-year term. County courts handle misdemeanour cases over which the circuit court has no authority, violations of municipal ordinances, and civil actions involving less than $2,500.

Religion

You will find every religious belief known to man represented somewhere in the USA, but the country is still predominantly Christian. Florida is not much different, with 40 per cent of its population classified as Christian.

The USA is a country where the right to religious freedom and the separation of church and state are important yet volatile issues. It seems logical that if a citizen has the right to practise any religion he or she chooses, then no one faith should have more control than any other over government. Yet, despite the claim of strict separation, religion plays an influential role in politics, where who you know matters. These days, the conservative Christian movement has found an especially sympathetic ear in the current administration and the line between church and state seems to have blurred a bit.

One of the fastest-growing religions in the country today is Mormonism, or the Church of Jesus Christ of Latter-day Saints, as it is officially known. The church is solidly based in Salt Lake City, but the number of its members in the USA has grown by nearly 225 per cent over the last 30 years, to more than five million. Worldwide, according to the Church, the number of Mormons has grown by nearly 400 per cent during the past 30 years, to more than 11 million. Some people predict that the number of Mormons throughout the world may soon equal that of Jews. The Mormon church is also a thriving business, which owns insurance and media companies, as well as huge amounts of land. Just outside Orlando, for example, the organization operates the largest cattle ranch in continental USA. In 1997, *Time* magazine did a survey of the church's assets and calculated its net worth to be at least 30 billion dollars and its annual income to be about six billion dollars.

The other fast-growing denomination in the USA is the Southern Baptists, which has seen an increase of 40 per cent over the last 30 years, to 16 million. More mainstream denominations such as Methodism and Episcopalianism, on the other hand, have been losing members in drastic numbers.

Letting Your Property

A large percentage of British people who buy homes in Florida also let them at some point or another. These people can be categorized in two ways. The first category is made up of people who see the property primarily, or even exclusively, as an investment proposition, and wish to let it regularly. These people want to make money by letting their property and will try to find a steady stream of tenants to fill the house all year round. The second category consists of people who are primarily buying a holiday home and are not interested in making a profit from renting it but are hoping to cover all or some of their purchase costs through rental income.

There are fundamental differences in the ways these two groups should approach the house-buying process. For the first group this is a business. Just as in any business, the decisions they make about where and what to buy, whether and how to restore the property and what facilities to provide will be governed by the wish to maximize profit. They should put themselves in the position of the person to whom they want to let their property, and consider which part of the market they expect to appeal to – whether, for example, their prospective tenants might be couples looking for a romantic beach getaway on a deserted coast or a family looking to enjoy everything Walt Disney has to offer – and anticipate what features clients like these would expect. They should choose an area, buy a property, convert it and equip it solely with their prospective tenants in mind, not their own personal taste.

The second group will have to bear in mind some or most of the same considerations, but overall can make far fewer concessions to their tenants. Their property is first and foremost a holiday home for themselves, and they will be ready to compromise on the more business-like aspects of house-buying (and so reduce potential income) in order to maximize their own enjoyment of it. They will have to make some changes to accommodate visitors – extra bedding, setting aside some wardrobe space where they can lock away their own things while the house is let – but these should be as few as possible. Where they draw the line will be determined by just how much income they need to get out of the property.

The section that follows relates mainly to the first group. If you identify more with the second category, you can pick and choose from the ideas within it, and there are also some points that are more directly relevant to your situation.

But whichever group you feel you fall into, there is a very important point to remember: in either case, you are most unlikely to cover all of your expenses and capital and interest repayments on a large mortgage from letting your property, however efficiently you do so.

Location, Choice of Property and Rental Potential

The choice of area in which to buy your rental property is by far the most important decision that you will make. There are many regions of Florida where it is fairly easy to let a property regularly enough to make it a commercially viable proposition. On the other hand, there are thousands of properties across the state that are, commercially speaking, almost impossible to let. A cosy little farmhouse in the middle of the rural northern region may find a few tenants each year, but it will not generate nearly enough to make a substantial commercial return on your investment. If you are interested in a house such as this, then you are probably already aware of its rental limitations and should view any rental income as a bonus that may help with some of your expenses, rather than any kind of nest egg.

The factors to take into consideration when deciding on an area are slightly different from those you might look at when just thinking about buying a place for yourself. They will also vary depending on your target clientele and your preferred way of administering the property. Most are related, as one would expect, to the tourist traffic of an area, its attractions, and also to the practical services it has available that you can call on to help manage the letting.

If you advertise any property well, you will always get some tenants. You will only begin to get repeat customers and a spreading circle of recommendations from previous tenants – one of the best ways of building up your customer base, since it saves on repeat advertising – if the house or flat itself, the area around it and the things to do there really satisfy or, better still, exceed people's expectations of an enjoyable time.

Attractions

Climate is, naturally, a major factor (*see* 'Climate Charts', p.241). Of course, any-where in the southern regions of the state will have perfect warm weather during the winter months when people are most likely to be escaping from the cold in other parts of the world, but for letting purposes you will have much greater flexibility if you are in an area where you can also expect temperate weather in the middle of summer when everyone in Miami is boiling to death. For one thing, you may want to use the house yourself during the winter, and so will need to let it out at other times of the year (alternatively, if you want to maximize your rental income, you will let it in winter, and use it yourself in the middle of summer). There is also a relatively small market for longer-term lets in areas with particularly mild climates or which are socially desirable. Keep in mind that major cities like Miami or cities that are close to popular attractions like Walt Disney World®, such as Orlando, have a year-round appeal, regardless of the weather.

Of equal importance are the attractions of the area, both natural features, such as spectacular beaches and tourist attractions. Easy access to a good beach is crucial but it helps if there are other things, such as sailing, diving and other sports facilities. For some clients, proximity to a quaint little town would be a major asset, while for others it might be more important to be near child-orient-ated attractions, such as a waterpark. The attraction could also be a convention centre of some kind that regularly hosts large events. The point is that there must be something to bring people to your area so that they will need to use your accommodation. The mere fact that the house is located on the beach will not, of itself, be enough to attract a significant number of tenants.

Added to these activities are the more everyday attractions of an area which, for most people, loom as large as the more spectacular features in their enjoy-ment of a holiday let. Most people who rent self-catering accommodation will want to be able to stock up on food, drink and other necessities without too much trouble and, since they won't want to cook all the time, will also want to be able to eat out. They will appreciate it greatly – and your property will be much easier to let – if your house is within easy distance (preferably walking distance) of at least a few shops and a choice of bars and restaurants.

Access

As important as climate and the charms of the locality is the ability of tenants to get to your property. This has two sides to it. The area where your flat or house is located must be reasonably accessible from the places where your prospective tenants live, and the property itself must be easy to find.

For most British visitors, convenient access means that it easy is to get to the property from a local airport with direct flights from a UK airport close to where they live (for details of airports and routes to Florida, *see* **Selecting a Property**, 'Travelling to Florida', pp.58–9). It is worth repeating here travel industry figures that show that 25 per cent of all potential visitors will not come if it involves travelling for more than one hour from a local airport at either end of their journey, and that if the travelling time rises to 1½ hours this will deter around 50 per cent. Of course, this does not mean that if your home is over an hour's drive from an airport you will never let it – with character rural houses, for example, a different set of rules applies, and their very remoteness can be an attraction in itself. For more conventional homes, though, there is no doubt that finding interested tenants will be simpler if you are within the magic hour's distance of an airport.

Nor should owners underestimate the importance of being able to find the property easily. Navigating in the depths of rural Florida can be trying: there will be few people to ask for directions and the roads may be very poorly signposted, if they are marked at all. The situation is not much better if you are trying to locate a flat in the middle of Tampa. Giving tenants decent maps and guidance notes on getting there is essential.

Letting Agencies

Strange as it may seem, the decision as to *how* you are going to let your property is one of the first that you are going to have to make, even before you actually buy it. This is because if you decide to use a professional management or letting agency it will alter your target market and therefore the area in which you ought to be buying (*see* 'Management Agencies', p.202). If you are going to let your property through a professional agency then it is worth contacting a few before you make a final choice of location, to see what they believe they can offer in the way of rental returns. They will also be able to advise you on what type of property in that area is likely to be most successful as rented property.

If, on the other hand, you expect to find tenants yourself, then you need to decide on your primary market. Most British people who let their property themselves in Florida do so mainly to other British people because that is the market they are familiar with and where they have the most connections.

The Right Property

Picking the right property is just behind choosing the right area in terms of letting potential. Not all properties let to the same extent – villas and flats that most potential clients find attractive let up to five times more frequently than others that do not stand out for any reason. New properties are generally cheaper to maintain than older ones; however, they are not likely to be as attractive to potential tenants. Most people going on holiday to a rural part of Florida are looking for a character property (preferably with a pool), while most going to the coast are looking for proximity to facilities and the beach.

If you intend to let out your property it is very useful, therefore, to pick a home that's pretty (if it isn't one of those big enough to be called spectacular). Most people will decide whether to rent a holiday home after they have seen only a brief description and a photograph, and of these two the photo is by far the more important. When buying a house for rental purposes, make sure it photographs well.

The number of bedrooms is also important. In cities, you will generally get a better return on your investment in properties with fewer (one or two) bedrooms – a good deal cheaper to buy – than on bigger apartments. On the coast or in the countryside, where the majority of your guests may well be families, a three-bedroom property is probably the most popular.

Case Study: Leftover Lien

Graham Hardy and his wife Heather had visited Florida on holiday twice. The first time was in 1997, when they rented a villa for the whole family and had a wonderful time. The second holiday was in the summer of 1999 and was a bit more spur-of-the-moment: they stayed in a hotel and ended up renting an additional room when they discovered that their quarters were a bit cramped. The cost of their second trip ended up being considerably higher than their well-planned stay in a villa two years earlier.

In the autumn after their second holiday, following some discussion about finding a better way to spend their time in Florida, Graham casually mentioned to his wife that they should look into purchasing a home of their own. They agreed that he would fly over to Kissimmee for a long weekend to take a look. When he returned home on Monday, she asked him how things went.

'I said, "I've just purchased one",' Graham recalls. 'She was speechless. I had bought a house, which was our single largest investment, and she hadn't seen it.' His wife still won't let him forget it. However, once the initial shock had worn off, the Hardys discovered the joys of owning their own holiday home. They also discovered that purchasing a home in the USA is very different from doing so back home. 'We soon found out that we had to be suspicious of everyone,' Graham says. 'But even this did not work out as planned.' About one year after the purchase, the Hardys were in the tax office in Kissimmee paying the real estate taxes on their property. Just as they were about to leave, they were asked if they were aware that there was a lien on the house.

The Right Price

When buying a property as a business you will be concerned to pay as little as possible for the property consistent with getting the right level of rental return. If you are only buying the property as a business proposition this price–rental balance (or return on investment), together with your judgement of the extent to which the property will rise in value over the years, are the main criteria upon which you should decide which property to buy.

If you are going to use the property not just as a rental property but also as a holiday home, there is an additional factor to take into account: the amount of time you will be able to use the property yourself consistent with getting a certain level of rental return.

For example, if you bought a one-bedroom property in Miami, that property might be let for 25 weeks a year and produce a return after expenses of, say, 6 per cent; however, if you bought a two-bedroom property in rural Florida (for a similar price) and let that for just 15 weeks per year you might also generate 6 per cent on your investment. Both would be performing equally well, but the rural property would allow you and your family to use it for a much greater part

'Well, no, we did not know that there were unpaid taxes going back five years and from two previous owners!' Graham says. 'It's not a good thing to have unpaid taxes if you want to keep the property from being auctioned off without your knowledge!' Reluctantly, the Hardys paid the overdue amount.

With the lien taken care of, the couple quickly turned their home into a profitable rental business (**www.offtodisney.com**). They have no regrets about getting into the business, but they did quickly learn that it is not as simple as buying a house and waiting for the phone to ring. 'Nothing could be further from the truth,' Graham warns. 'It's hard work and we've spent approximately $30,000 on upgrading and improving the home.' All the hard work seems to have paid off, however. 'We have always been booked full at least two years ahead, so all of our running costs are covered,' says Graham. 'In fact, in November 2002 we had so many excess rental booking enquiries that we purchased a second house with the same configuration as the first.'

The overflow of interested renters also inspired the Hardys to start a unique online business called Tradingdates (**www.tradingdates.com**), which allows owners who have excess rental enquiries to pass them along to other members of the network. With some tenants already booking the Hardys' houses for 2010, it is not surprising that over 100 homeowners signed up to be a part of their online network.

'When I went over to Florida on a maintenance visit on my own, my wife had just one message for me: "No more houses",' says Graham. 'When I came back I couldn't resist telling her, "Well, I have seen this nice little restaurant...".'

of each year. This and the fact that it had a second bedroom could make it a more attractive proposition. These figures are simply examples, rather than indications as to what will actually be obtainable at any particular moment. Whichever way you look at it, though, paying the minimum necessary for the property is the key to maximizing investment performance.

Equipping the Property

Having selected an area and a property, you will then have to fit out the villa or flat with all the features that tenants will expect. If you advertise the property well, you will get tenants. But you will only get *repeat* tenants, and recommendations from existing tenants, if the property meets or exceeds their expectations in terms of the facilities it offers and its cleanliness.

It should, of course, be well maintained at all times, and the external decoration and garden and/or pool area should be kept in good condition – apart from anything else, these are the parts that create the first impression as your guests arrive. Other than that, the facilities required will depend to some extent on the target audience that you are trying to attract. If, for example, you are trying to attract walkers or sailors, they will appreciate somewhere to dry their clothes quickly so that they can be ready to get wet again the following day.

The following is a quick checklist of the main points to be taken care of when preparing any property for holiday tenants:

• **Documents**: Make sure that all guests are sent a pre-visit pack. This should include notes about the area and local attractions and a map of the immediate area (all usually available free from your local tourist office), notes explaining how to get to the house, emergency contact numbers and instructions as to what to do if they are delayed for any reason.

Inside the property there should also be a **house book**. This should give much more information and recommendations about local attractions, restaurants and so on – collect as many local leaflets as you can – and a comprehensive list of contact numbers for use in the case of any conceivable emergency. The more personal recommendations you can give (best bakery, best café, etc.), the more people will appreciate it. Provide some space in it, too, or in a separate book, to be used as a visitors' book. As well as being a useful vehicle for obtaining feedback, this builds up positive feelings about your home, and can also be a means of making future direct contact with visitors who might have been supplied by an agency.

• **Welcome**: It is best if someone is present, either at the property or at a nearby house, to welcome your guests when they arrive. They can sort out any minor problems or any particular requirements of the guests.

• **Cleanliness**: The property must be spotlessly clean, above all in the kitchen and bathroom. You will probably employ a local cleaner, whom you may well need to give some training and/or a detailed schedule, as people's expectations when going into rented accommodation are often higher than their expectations in an ordinary home.

• **Kitchen**: This must be modern, even if traditional in style, and everything should (of course) work. The fridge should be as large as you can manage since, in hot weather, your tenants will need to keep a wide range of things chilled. The kitchen should have a microwave, and you should check regularly that there is sufficient cutlery and cooking equipment and that it is all in good condition. A cookbook giving local recipes is a nice touch.

• **Bathroom**: Or, these days, more usually bathrooms – an en suite bathroom for each bedroom is the ideal. Make sure there is soap in the bathrooms, and guests will also much prefer it if you provide towels as part of the service.

• **Laundry facilities**: A washing machine and tumble dryer are now standard.

• **Bedrooms**: These should have adequate storage space. Most importantly, they should also have clean and comfortable beds, as nothing except dirtiness produces more complaints than uncomfortable beds. The only beds that last well in a regularly used property, in which the people sleeping will be all sorts of different sizes and weights, are expensive beds such as those used in the hotel industry. Beds should be protected from obvious soiling by the use of removable mattress covers, which should be changed with each change of tenant. All clients much prefer you to supply bedding as part of your service rather than expecting them to bring their own.

• **Living areas**: Furniture and upholstery should be comfortable and in good condition; the style is a matter of personal preference, but a local style usually works well. There should be adequate means of cleaning, including a working vacuum cleaner.

• **Heating**: In Florida, the importance of an effective heating system that covers the whole house depends on where the property is located. Some regions can get quite cool in the winter and you should keep this in mind.

• **Air-conditioning**: On the other hand, air-conditioning in Florida is practically mandatory. Even in a relatively mild region of the state, you will have a hard time letting a house that is not air-conditioned.

• **Swimming pool**: If you are catering to a British clientele, a pool is highly desirable, and in rural areas it will significantly increase your letting potential. A pool should be of reasonable size and well maintained, but you probably won't have to worry about heating it.

• **Welcome pack**: Make sure that basic groceries such as bread, milk, teabags, coffee, sugar and a bowl of fruit are left in the house to welcome your guests on arrival. A bottle of freshly squeezed Florida orange juice might add a special local touch.

Marketing

Properties do not let themselves, and anyone wishing to let out their Florida home regularly will have to do some marketing. In the early years you will have to do more than later on, because you will have no existing client base. As in any other business, the cheapest type of marketing is catching repeat clients, so a bit of money spent on making sure the property lives up to, or exceeds, their expectations (and brings them or their friends back next year) is probably the best spend that you will make. Otherwise, there seems to be no correlation between the amount spent on marketing and the results achieved, and this is a field in which much money spent is often wasted. Bear in mind that any form of marketing of a holiday property is only as good as the quality of the response you give to people making enquiries. Owners often do better spending less money on advertising and paying more attention to following up leads they have already generated.

Key points to remember in relation to marketing any kind of short-term lets are the following:

- Choose the method of marketing most appropriate to your property and circumstances.

- Follow up all enquiries and leads immediately. Contact the people involved again after a couple of weeks to see whether or not they have made up their minds.

- Send any contacts your details again next year at about the same time, even if they have not stayed with you, as they may well be planning another holiday.

If you have decided to let your property yourself, there are several well-tried means of publicizing your property in the British and Irish markets. If you also wish to tap into the Florida market, you can advertise the property in local papers. However, you may be faced with a lot of long-distance telephone charges if you end up having to conduct business from back home. For this reason, many people in this case prefer to use a local letting agency.

Directories and Web Directories

If your property is pretty then you are likely to get good results from the various directories and joint information and booking services that deal with self-catering properties to let in Florida. Most are now available on the Internet and have ceased producing brochures and magazines. Some provide a full booking service and take part in managing lettings, while others, which are cheaper to use and give owners more freedom to manoeuvre, just give you space for photographs and presentation of your property. Travel industry websites such as **www.travelgate.co.uk** have lists of the many such companies now operating. The monthly magazine *Private Villas* (**www.privatevillas.co.uk**) is useful for upmarket properties.

Advertising in this way only really works if the services are inexpensive, because a private owner with only one property to let has only one opportunity of letting each week, and so a directory that produces, say, 50 enquiries for the first week in February is not particularly helpful.

Press Advertising

The problems with traditional methods of advertising are its scattergun approach and, usually, its cost. As mentioned above, if you have just one property you only need a very small number of responses, and you cannot afford to pay a large amount in advertising fees for each week's let. Except for very upmarket properties, traditional advertising is too expensive, and is mainly used by property companies and agencies. For individual owners, better places to advertise are the small-ad pages in newspaper travel sections and the specialist Florida property press. Some people have been successful advertising in apparently unconnected special interest magazines – such as literary or historical publications – where their ad did not get lost among 20 others. On the other hand, you can also get good results – and cheaply – by putting a card on your local supermarket noticeboard.

Personal Website and E-mail

The Internet offers tremendous opportunities for bringing a specialist niche product – such as an isolated villa – to the attention of a vast audience at very little cost. For no extra effort, it can allow people to find out about your Florida home not just in Britain and Florida but throughout Europe and the rest of the world. For independent owners offering property for holiday lets, it is strongly recommended that they set up their own website. For many, it quickly becomes their primary means of finding new tenants.

Your website will be your principal brochure, with space to show lots of pictures and other information about the house and the area around it. It is much cheaper to have someone print off a copy of this brochure from their own computer than it is for you to have it printed and sent by post. If you don't know enough about the web to design a site yourself, ask a designer to create a basic site for you at low cost.

Your property should also be listed on some of the many Florida property websites that can be found around the Internet, links to which are either free or relatively cheap. You will soon find out which ones work for you and which ones don't; some of the best are those that are regionally based, since people find it easy to get to what they want with fewer distractions.

As well as a publicity medium, the website can also be a means of taking bookings. You will have to decide how sophisticated an electronic booking system you want or whether you are happy just to use the internet to make contacts. Actually taking money securely via the web by credit card may still be a bit complicated and expensive for most independent property-owners, so you will have to receive payments by more traditional means. Your website will, of course, have your e-mail address on it. Even if you do not set up a website, anyone letting out property regularly really should have access to e-mail, which is increasingly becoming people's favourite means of communicating and making bookings. Remember to check it at least once a day.

Doing Deals

There are two kinds of 'mutual aid' deals that can be helpful to independent owners, both of which work best in slightly out-of-the-way areas. If your property, for example, is in a rural area where there is somebody offering a very local tourist service, it can be a good idea to make contact with it and try to arrange for the people starting its walks or attending its courses to stay over in your property. This can significantly increase your lettings, particularly at off-peak times. If you agree to pay the tour organizers a commission of around 20 per cent you will still be well ahead.

The second type of deal involves co-operating with other people in the area who let properties, assuming there are any. One of the frustrations of marketing your property is when you have four lots of people who all want to rent it for the same week. Getting together with others in a mutual assistance group will allow you to pass excess lettings to one other.

Your Own Contacts

All these methods aside, personal, direct contacts are still among the best means of marketing a property in Florida. If you want to use a second home for a fair amount of time yourself, you will perhaps only want to let it for, say, 20 weeks each year. Given that many people will take it for two weeks or more, you will probably therefore only be looking for around 10–15 lettings annually, and if you put the word out these should not be hard to put together from friends and friends of friends.

People who work for large organizations have an advantage in this respect, since they can can publicize it internally. Even without people from work, most owners will be able to find enough friends, neighbours and relatives to rent a nice property in Florida for 10 weeks each year, which will leave only a relatively small number of tenants to be found by other means. With most of your lettings you will have the additional advantage of knowing the people who are going to rent the property, which reduces the risk that they will damage it or fail to pay you.

When renting to family or friends, or indeed work colleagues, however, you will have to learn how to raise the delicate issue of payment. Given that you are not going to be running up any marketing costs and probably not much in the way of property management cost, you should be able to offer them a bargain price and still generate as much income as you would have done by letting through an agency. Make sure that you address this issue when you accept the booking, as doing it later can be very embarrassing.

Management Agencies

On the whole, the people who are most successful over a period of time in letting their second homes are those who find their tenants themselves. This, however, requires a level of commitment that many people simply cannot afford. For non-resident owners who cannot dedicate much time to keeping track of their property, it is far simpler to use a local letting agency. Agencies – or at least good ones – will be able to attract local, American clients as well as those of different nationalities. You will have to pay them a sizeable commission, but they will argue that this will be recovered by the extra lettings that they make during the holiday season. This may or may not be true. Larger agencies, who publish glossy brochures, are best contacted well in advance, such as early autumn in the previous year, if you want a property to be advertised for the summer season; smaller agencies will take on properties at any time.

In all the desirable areas you will find agencies that manage and let holiday properties, many of them local estate agents, and there are also many that operate from the UK. If you decide to use one of them, the choice of agency is critical. Some are excellent, both in Florida and in the UK, and some are simply crooks; between the two there are some that are just bumbling and inefficient. At worst, agencies may hold on to rents for long periods of time, or let your house while telling you it is empty and pocket the rent themselves; others may just charge a signing-on fee to agree to put your property on their books and do nothing to let it. In the past, many have assumed that foreign owners based thousands of miles away will never find out about anything they do. This is a field where it is important for owners to be cautious and demanding of any agents they engage.

Selecting an Agency

When selecting a letting agency there are various checks to make:

• **Find out if it is an American agency, and whether or not staff are professionally qualified and experienced. Many letting agent services are offered as an adjunct to estate agents, who should have qualified staff.**

• **Check the premises, and make an initial judgement about whether or not staff seem welcoming and efficient, and if there's evidence of significant letting activity.**

• **Check how capable they seem to be, especially if you're making contact before actually buying your property. Ask what type of property agency staff think would be best for letting purposes in this area, how many weeks' rental they think you will be able to obtain and how much they think they would generate for you after deduction of expenses and their own fees.**

• **Ask for references, preferably from other overseas clients, and follow them up. Telephone other owners if you can, and ask if they are happy with the overall performance of the agency and whether the financial projections given to them have been met.**

• **Take a look at what marketing the agency does. If it relies only on passing trade, then except in the most popular areas it will not get good results.**

• Ask to see a sample information pack sent to a potential client. You will be able to judge a lot from this; think about whether or not this is the image you want to give of your property.

• Ask to inspect two or three properties that the agent is already managing. If they are dirty or badly cared for, then so will yours be, and it will not attract lettings.

• Check carefully what kind of contract the agent offers you; unless you are familiar with Florida law it is also sensible to get it checked by your lawyer before you sign, as some give you far more rights than others. Make sure that the contract entitles you to full reports showing when the property was let and for what money; these must give a breakdown by week, not by quarter- or half-year. You should insist on a full breakdown of all expenses incurred in connection with the property, and ensure the contract gives you the right to dismiss the agency on fairly short notice.

Controlling the Agency

After you have appointed a letting agency, you need to keep a check on what it is doing. You may not wish to seem so suspicious, but there are too many horror stories around to allow anyone to get complacent. You should:

• Check the reports you receive from the agency and that the money you receive corresponds to the amounts shown in them.

• Let the agency know, in the nicest possible way, that you and all of your friends in the area check each other's properties every time you are there, and compare notes about which are occupied and the performance of your letting agencies. If they believe you, this is a good deterrent to unauthorized lettings.

• Telephone your property every week. If someone answers the phone, make a note, and make sure that there is income shown for the week of the phone call.

• From time to time, have a friend pose as a prospective customer and send for an enquiry pack.

• If you get the chance, call to see the property without warning, to check its condition.

Formalizing the Letting

If you let through an agency, it will draw up fairly standardized rental contracts for you and your tenants to sign. If you handle all your lettings yourself, unless you let only to family and close friends, it is still advisable for you to

Case Study: A Home that Pays for Itself?

Ted, a former businessman in the UK, recalls the whirlwind homebuying tour he took in central Florida many years ago when he was on the verge of retirement. From time to time, the salesman assisting him alluded to the issue of short-term rental income contributing towards the costs of his future home. Years spent in the business world taught the prospective homebuyer to be sceptical of deals that sounded too good to be true. Sadly, though, such inflated income promises have resulted in countless others taking on mortgage burdens beyond their means, and, when the short-term rental income did not reach the level these homebuyers originally thought possible, they have ended up having to sell their homes and abandon their dream of a Florida lifestyle.

'The short-term rental market in Florida is very competitive,' Ted warns. 'Home-owners are in direct competition not only with each other but with the hotel industry, the marketing activity of which is aggressive and sophisticated. While some people are very good at marketing their home, others have got in over their head financially and have had to reduce their prices drastically.'

Once you become the proud owner of a vacation rental home in beautiful, sunny Florida, and you decide to opt for short-term rentals, in the eyes of the state you are also the owner of what is to all intents and purposes a 'licensed hotel'. What this means is that you must operate under the regulation of the Department of Business and Professional Regulation. The process is not as daunting as it may sound, since your management company – assuming you are using one – will ensure that you acquire all of the necessary permits, and that your home meets all the requirements of the department, which will inspect it from time to time.

So is all the hassle associated with letting a home on a short-term basis worth it? It depends. It is worth remembering that Florida is a semi-tropical state, which means you will have to ensure a constant temperature and humidity level; air-conditioning needs to be continuously running whether the home is occupied or not, otherwise certain items may deteriorate; and water in the swimming pool must be circulated and always kept in chemical balance. The cost of running a modern home, even an empty one, means you should at least consider short-term rental.

Of course, remember that you would effectively be starting a business, which brings with it obligations such as registering to report and pay sales tax and income tax. A business also entails book-keeping, the organization of a rental diary, booking forms, terms and conditions, rental collection and maintenance of the premises. On top of which, you need to promote your property.

There are plenty of success stories in the business, but for some it's not about the money. Like Ted, most people do not buy a home abroad so that they can let it. They simply want to spend the winters of their retirement in warmth.

give tenants a written contract in line with Florida law, the model for which should preferably be drawn up, with the advice of your lawyer, when you first begin letting.

From the point of view of landlords, the safest type of letting is a **short holiday let of furnished property**. To be classified as furnished, the property must have all of the basic items required to live in a home, including, at least, a bed, a cooker, a table, a refrigerator, some chairs and so on. A place without these things could be treated as an unfurnished property, in which case, from the legal point of view, tenants could claim that there was a permanent rental contract, potentially giving them the right to an extension after the contract's first term. Otherwise, a holiday letting is one that takes place in a recognized holiday season.

A properly drafted **tenancy agreement** will take all these factors into account and protect you in the event of a dispute with your tenants and, in particular, if any of them wish to stay on at the end of the tenancy.

If your property is a condominium or a cooperative, your tenants will also have to agree to abide by the rules of the community, and this should be indicated in the rental agreement. Tenants should be supplied with a copy of these rules, or at least the part of them that is relevant. In the rental contract you should also stipulate what things are going to be covered by your insurance and what are not – typically, for example, tenants' personal possessions would not be covered under your policy.

References

Dictionary of Real Estate Terms

Acceleration clause	A clause in your mortgage which allows the lender to demand payment of the outstanding loan balance for various reasons. The most common reasons for accelerating a loan are if the borrower defaults on the loan or transfers title to another individual without informing the lender.
Adjustable-rate mortgage (ARM)	A mortgage in which the interest changes periodically, according to corresponding fluctuations in an index. All ARMs are tied to indexes.
Adjustment date	The date the interest rate changes on an adjustable-rate mortgage.
Amortization	The loan payment consists of a portion which will be applied to pay the accruing interest on a loan, with the remainder being applied to the principal. Over time, the interest portion decreases as the loan balance decreases, and the amount applied to principal increases so that the loan is paid off (amortized) in the specified time.
Amortization schedule	A table which shows how much of each payment will be applied towards principal and how much towards interest over the life of the loan. It also shows the gradual decrease of the loan balance until it reaches zero.
Annual percentage rate (APR)	This is not the note rate on your loan. It is a value created according to a government formula intended to reflect the true annual cost of borrowing, expressed as a percentage. As a guideline it works roughly like this: deduct the closing costs from your loan amount, then, using your actual loan payment, calculate what the interest rate would be on this amount instead of your actual loan amount. You will come up with a number close to the APR. Because you are using the same payment on a smaller amount, the APR is always higher than the actual note rate on your loan.
Application	The form used to apply for a mortgage loan, containing information about a borrower's income, savings, assets, debts and similar details.
Appraisal	A written justification of the price paid for a property, primarily based on an analysis of comparable sales of similar homes nearby.
Appraised value	An opinion of a property's fair market value, based on an appraiser's knowledge, experience and

analysis of the property. Since an appraisal is based primarily on comparable sales, and the most recent sale is the one on the property in question, the appraisal usually comes out at the purchase price.

Appraiser
An individual qualified by education, training and experience to estimate the value of real property and personal property. Although some appraisers work directly for mortgage lenders, most are independent.

Appreciation
The increase in the value of a property owing to changes in market conditions, inflation or other causes.

Assessed value
The valuation placed on property by a public tax assessor for purposes of taxation.

Assessment
The placing of a value on property for the purpose of taxation.

Assessor
A public official who establishes the value of a property for taxation purposes.

Asset
Items of value owned by an individual. Assets that can be quickly converted into cash are considered 'liquid assets'. These include bank accounts, stocks, bonds, mutual funds, etc. Other assets include real estate, personal property and debts owed to an individual by others.

Assignment
When ownership of your mortgage is transferred from one company or individual to another, it is called an assignment.

Assumable mortgage
A mortgage that can be assumed by the buyer when a home is sold. Usually, the borrower must 'qualify' in order to assume the loan.

Assumption
The term applied when a buyer assumes the seller's mortgage.

Balloon mortgage
A mortgage loan that requires the remaining principal balance be paid at a specific point in time. For example, a loan may be amortized as if it would be paid over a 30-year period, but requires that at the end of the 10th year the entire remaining balance must be paid.

Balloon payment
The final lump sum payment that is due at the termination of a balloon mortgage.

Bankruptcy
By filing in a federal bankruptcy court, an individual or individuals can restructure or relieve themselves of debts and liabilities. Bankruptcies are of various types, but the most common for an individual seems to be a 'Chapter 7 No Asset'

bankruptcy which relieves the borrower of most types of debts. A borrower cannot usually qualify for an 'A' paper loan for a period of two years after the bankruptcy has been discharged and requires the re-establishment of an ability to repay debt.

Bill of sale

A written document that transfers title to personal property. E.g. when selling a car to acquire funds which will be used as a source of down-payment or for closing costs, the lender will usually require the bill of sale (in addition to other items) to help document this source of funds.

Biweekly mortgage

A mortgage in which you make payments every two weeks instead of once a month. The basic result is that instead of making 12 monthly payments during the year, you make the equivalent of 13. The extra payment reduces the principal, substantially reducing the time it takes to pay off a 30-year mortgage. Note: there are independent companies that encourage you to set up biweekly payment schedules with them on your 30-year mortgage. They charge a set-up fee and a transfer fee for every payment. Your funds are deposited into a trust account from which your monthly payment is then made, and the excess funds then remain in the trust account until enough has accrued to make the additional payment which will then be paid to reduce your principal. You could save money by doing the same thing yourself, and you need to be sure that once you transfer money to a trust account it will actually transfer your funds to your lender.

Bond market

Usually refers to the daily buying and selling of 30-year treasury bonds. Lenders follow this market intensely because, as the yields of bonds go up and down, fixed rate mortgages do approximately the same thing. The same factors that affect the treasury bond market also affect mortgage rates at the same time. That is why rates change daily, and in a volatile market can and do change during the day as well.

Bridge loan

Not used much any more, bridge loans are obtained by those who have not yet sold their previous property, but must close on a purchase property. The bridge loan becomes the source of their funds for the down-payment. One reason for their fall from favour is that there are more and more second mortgage lenders now that will lend at a high loan-to-value rate. In addition, sellers

	often prefer to accept offers from buyers who have already sold their property.
Broker	The word has different meanings in different situations. Most realtors are 'agents' who work under a 'broker'. Some agents are brokers as well, either working for themselves or under another broker. In the mortgage industry, broker usually refers to a company or individual that does not lend the money for the loans themselves, but brokers loans to larger lenders or investors. As a normal definition, a broker is anyone who acts as an agent, bringing two parties together for any type of transaction, and earns a fee for doing so.
Buydown	Usually refers to a fixed rate mortgage where the interest rate is 'bought down' for a temporary period, usually one to three years. After that time, and for the remainder of the term, the borrower's payment is calculated at the note rate. In order to buy down the initial rate for the temporary payment, a lump sum is paid and held in an account used to supplement the borrower's monthly payment. These funds usually come from the seller (or some other source) as a financial incentive to induce someone to buy their property. A 'lender-funded buydown' is when the lender pays the initial lump sum. They can accomplish this because the note rate on the loan (after the buydown adjustments) will be higher than the current market rate. One reason for doing this is because the borrower may get to 'qualify' at the start rate and can qualify for a higher loan amount. Another reason is that a borrower may expect earnings to go up substantially in the near future, but wants a lower payment right now.
Call option	Similar to the acceleration clause.
Cap adjustable rate mortgages	These have fluctuating interest rates, but those fluctuations are usually limited to a certain amount. Those limitations may apply to how much the loan may adjust over a six-month period, an annual period, and over the life of the loan, and are referred to as 'caps'. Some ARMs, although they may have a life cap, allow the interest rate to fluctuate freely, but require a certain minimum payment which can change once a year. There is a limit on how much that payment can change each year, and that limit is also referred to as a cap.

Cash-out refinance	When a borrower refinances his mortgage at a higher amount than the current loan balance with the intention of pulling out money for personal use, it is referred to as a 'cash out refinance'.
Certificate of deposit	A time deposit held in a bank which pays a certain amount of interest to the depositor.
Certificate of deposit index	One of the indices used for determining interest rate changes on some adjustable rate mortgages. It is an average of what banks are paying on certificates of deposit.
Certificate of eligibility	A document issued by the Veterans Administration that certifies a veteran's eligibility for a VA loan.
Certificate of reasonable value	Once the appraisal has been performed on a property being bought with a VA loan, the Veterans Administration issues a CRV.
Chain of title	An analysis of the transfers of title to a piece of property over the years.
Clear title	A title that is free of liens or legal questions as to ownership of the property.
Closing	This has different meanings in different states. In some states a real estate transaction is not consider 'closed' until the documents record at the local recorder's office. In others, the 'closing' is a meeting where all of the documents are signed and money changes hands.
Closing costs	Closing costs are separated into what are called 'non-recurring closing costs' and 'pre-paid items'. Non-recurring closing costs are any items which are paid just once as a result of buying the property or obtaining a loan. 'Pre-paids' are items which recur over time, such as property taxes and homeowner's insurance. A lender makes an attempt to estimate the amount of non-recurring closing costs and prepaid items on the Good Faith Estimate which they must issue to the borrower within three days of receiving a home loan application.
Closing statement	*See* 'Settlement statement'.
Cloud on title	Any conditions revealed by a title search that adversely affect the title to real estate. Usually clouds on title cannot be removed except by deed, release or court action.
Co-borrower	An additional individual who is both obligated on the loan and is on title to the property.

Collateral	In a home loan, the property is the collateral. The borrower risks losing the property if the loan is not repaid according to the terms of the mortgage or deed of trust.
Collection	When a borrower falls behind, the lender contacts them in an effort to bring the loan current. The loan goes to 'collection'. As part of the collection effort, the lender must mail and record certain documents in case they are eventually required to foreclose on the property.
Commission	Most salespeople earn commissions for the work that they do and there are many sales profession-als involved in each transaction, including realtors, loan officers, title representatives, attorneys, escrow representatives and representatives for pest companies, home warranty companies, home inspection companies, insurance agents, etc. The commissions are paid out of the charges paid by the seller or buyer in the purchase transaction. Realtors generally earn the largest commissions, followed by lenders, then the others.
Common area assessments	In some areas they are called Homeowners' Association Fees. They are charges paid to the Homeowners' Association by the owners of the individual units in a condominium or planned unit development (PUD) and are generally used to maintain the property and common areas.
Common areas	Those portions of a building, land and amenities owned (or managed) by a planned unit development (PUD) or condominium project's homeowners' association (or a co-operative project's co-operative corporation) that are used by all of the unit owners, who share in the common expenses of their operation and maintenance. Common areas include swimming pools, tennis courts and other recreational facilities, as well as common corridors of buildings, parking areas, means of ingress and egress, etc.
Common law	An unwritten body of law based on general custom in England and used to an extent in some states.
Community property	In some states, especially the southwest, property acquired by a married couple during their marriage is considered to be owned jointly, except under special circumstances. This is an outgrowth of the Spanish and Mexican heritage of the area.

Comparable sales	Recent sales of similar properties in nearby areas are used to help determine the market value of a property. Also referred to as 'comps'.
Condominium	A type of ownership in real property where all of the owners own the property, common areas and buildings together, with the exception of the interior of the unit to which they have title. Often mistakenly referred to as a type of construction or development, it actually refers to the type of ownership.
Condominium conversion	Changing the ownership of an existing building (usually a rental project) to the condominium form of ownership.
Condominium hotel	A condominium project that has rental or registration desks, short-term occupancy, food and telephone services, and daily cleaning services, and that is operated as a commercial hotel even though the units are individually owned. These are often found in resort areas like Hawaii.
Construction loan	A short-term, interim loan for financing the cost of construction. The lender makes payments to the builder at periodic intervals as the work progresses.
Contingency	A condition that must be met before a contract is legally binding. For example, home purchasers often include a contingency that specifies that the contract is not binding until the purchaser obtains a satisfactory home inspection report from a qualified home inspector.
Contract	An oral or written agreement to do or not to do a certain thing.
Conventional mortgage	Refers to home loans other than government loans (VA and FHA).
Convertible ARM	An adjustable-rate mortgage that allows the borrower to change the ARM to a fixed-rate mortgage within a specific time.
Co-operative (co-op)	A type of multiple ownership in which the residents of a multi-unit housing complex own shares in the co-operative corporation that owns the property, giving each resident the right to occupy a specific apartment or unit.
Cost of funds index (COFI)	One of the indices that is used to determine interest rate changes for certain adjustable-rate mortgages. It represents the weighted-average cost of savings, borrowings and advances of the financial institutions such as banks, and savings

and loans, in the 11th District of the Federal Home Loan Bank.

Credit	An agreement in which a borrower receives something of value in exchange for a promise to repay the lender at a later date.
Credit history	A record of an individual's repayment of debt. Credit histories are reviewed by mortgage lenders as one of the underwriting criteria in determining credit risk.
Credit report	A report of an individual's credit history prepared by a credit bureau and used by a lender in determining a loan applicant's creditworthiness.
Credit repository	An organization that gathers, records, updates and stores financial and public records information about the payment history of individuals who are being considered for credit.
Creditor	A person to whom money is owed.
Debt	An amount owed to another.
Deed	The legal document conveying title to a property.
Deed-in-lieu	Short for 'deed in lieu of foreclosure', this conveys title to the lender when the borrower is in default and wants to avoid foreclosure. The lender may or may not cease foreclosure activities if a borrower asks to provide a deed-in-lieu. Regardless of whether the lender accepts the deed-in-lieu, the avoidance and non-repayment of debt will most likely show on a credit history. What a deed-in-lieu may prevent is having the documents preparatory to a foreclosure being recorded and becoming a matter of public record.
Deed of trust	Some states, like California, do not record mortgages. Instead, they record a deed of trust, which is essentially the same thing.
Default	Failure to make the mortgage payment within a specified period of time. For first mortgages or first trust deeds, if a payment has still not been made within 30 days of the due date, the loan is considered to be in default.
Delinquency	Failure to make mortgage payments when payments are due. For most mortgages, payments are due on the first day of the month. Even though they may not charge a 'late fee' for a number of days, the payment is still considered to be late and the loan delinquent. When a loan payment is more than 30 days late, most lenders report the late payment to one or more credit bureaux.

Deposit	A sum of money given in advance of a larger amount being expected in the future. Often called in real estate as an 'earnest money deposit'.
Depreciation	A decline in the value of property, the opposite of appreciation. Depreciation is also an accounting term which shows the declining monetary value of an asset and is used as an expense to reduce taxable income. Since this is not a true expense where money is actually paid, lenders will add back depreciation expense for self-employed borrowers and count it as income.
Discount points	In the mortgage industry, this term is usually used only in reference to government loans, meaning FHA and VA loans. Discount points refer to any 'points' paid in addition to the 1 per cent loan origination fee. A 'point' is 1 per cent of the loan amount.
Down payment	The part of the purchase price of a property that the buyer pays in cash and does not finance with a mortgage.
Due-on-sale provision	A provision in a mortgage that allows the lender to demand repayment in full if the borrower sells the property that serves as security for the mortgage.
Earnest money deposit	A deposit made by the potential home buyer to show that he or she is serious about buying the house.
Easement	A right of way giving persons other than the owner access to or over a property.
Effective age	An appraiser's estimate of the physical condition of a building. The actual age of a building may be higher or lower than its effective age.
Eminent domain	The right of a government to take private property for public use upon payment of its fair market value. Eminent domain is the basis for condemnation proceedings.
Encroachment	An improvement that intrudes illegally on another's property.
Encumbrance	Anything that affects or limits the fee simple title to a property, such as mortgages, leases, easements or restrictions.
Equal Credit Opportunity Act	A federal law that requires lenders and other creditors to make credit equally available without discrimination based on race, colour, religion, national origin, age, sex, marital status or receipt of income from public assistance programmes.

Equity

A homeowner's financial interest in a property. Equity is the difference between the fair market value of the property and the amount still owed on its mortgage and other liens.

Escrow

An item of value, money or documents deposited with a third party to be delivered upon the fulfilment of a condition. For example, the earnest money deposit is put into escrow until delivered to the seller when the transaction is closed.

Escrow account

Once you close your purchase transaction, you may have an escrow account or impound account with your lender. This means the amount you pay each month includes an amount above what would be required if you were only paying your principal and interest. The extra money is held in your impound account (escrow account) for the payment of items like property taxes and homeowner's insurance when they come due. The lender pays them with your money instead of you paying them yourself.

Escrow analysis

Once each year your lender will perform an 'escrow analysis' to make sure they are collecting the correct amount of money for the anticipated expenditures.

Escrow disbursements

The use of escrow funds to pay real estate taxes, hazard insurance, mortgage insurance, and other property expenses as they become due.

Estate

The ownership interest of an individual in real property. The sum total of all the real property and personal property owned by an individual at time of death.

Eviction

The lawful expulsion of an occupant from real property.

Examination of title

The report on the title of a property from the public records or an abstract of the title.

Exclusive listing

A written contract that gives a licensed real estate agent the exclusive right to sell a property for a specified time.

Executor/executrix

A person named in a will to administer an estate. The court will appoint an administrator if no executor is named.

Fair Credit Reporting Act

A consumer protection law that regulates the disclosure of consumer credit reports by consumer/credit reporting agencies and establishes procedures for correcting mistakes on one's credit record.

Fair market value	The highest price that a buyer, willing but not compelled to buy, would pay, and the lowest a seller, willing but not compelled to sell, would accept.
Fannie Mae (FNMA)	The Federal National Mortgage Association, which is a congressionally chartered, shareholder-owned company that is the nation's largest supplier of home mortgage funds.
Fannie Mae's Community Home Buyer's Program	An income-based community lending model, under which mortgage insurers and Fannie Mae offer flexible underwriting guidelines to increase a low or moderate-income family's buying power and to decrease the total amount of cash needed to purchase a home. Borrowers who participate in this model are required to attend pre-purchase homebuyer education sessions.
Federal Housing Administration	An agency of the US Department of Housing and Urban Development (HUD). Its main activity is the insuring of residential mortgage loans made by private lenders. The FHA sets standards for construction and underwriting but does not lend money or plan or construct housing.
Fee simple	The greatest possible interest a person can have in real estate.
Fee simple estate	An unconditional, unlimited estate of inheritance that represents the greatest estate and most extensive interest in land that can be enjoyed. It is of perpetual duration. When the real estate is in a condominium project, the unit owner is the exclusive owner only of the air space within his portion of the building (the unit) and is an owner in common with respect to the land and other common portions of the property.
FHA mortgage	A mortgage that is insured by the Federal Housing Administration (FHA). Along with VA loans, an FHA loan will often be referred to as a government loan.
Firm commitment	A lender's agreement to make a loan to a specific borrower on a specific property.
First mortgage	The mortgage that is in first place among any loans recorded against a property. Usually refers to the date on which loans are recorded, but there are exceptions.
Fixed-rate mortgage	A mortgage in which the interest rate does not change during the entire term of the loan.

Fixture	Personal property that becomes real property when attached in a permanent manner to real estate.
Flood insurance	Insurance that compensates for physical property damage resulting from flooding. It is required for properties located in federally designated flood areas.
Foreclosure	The legal process by which a borrower in default under a mortgage is deprived of his interest in the mortgaged property. This usually involves a forced sale of the property at public auction with the proceeds of the sale being applied to the mortgage debt.
401(k)/403(b)	An employer-sponsored investment plan that allows individuals to set aside tax-deferred income for retirement or emergency purposes. 401(k) plans are provided by employers that are private corporations. 403(b) plans are provided by employers that are not-for-profit organizations.
401(k)/403(b) loan	Some administrators of 401(k) and 403(b) plans allow for loans against the monies you have accumulated in these plans. Loans against 401(k) plans are an acceptable source of down-payment for most types of loans.
Government loan (mortgage)	A mortgage that is insured by the Federal Housing Administration (FHA) or guaranteed by the Department of Veterans Affairs (VA) or the Rural Housing Service (RHS). Mortgages that are not government loans are classified as conventional loans.
Government National Mortgage Association (Ginnie Mae)	A government-owned corporation within the US Department of Housing and Urban Development (HUD). Created by Congress on 1 September 1968, GNMA performs the same role as Fannie Mae and Freddie Mac in providing funds to lenders for making home loans. The difference is that Ginnie Mae provides funds for government loans (FHA and VA).
Grantee	The person to whom an interest in real property is conveyed.
Grantor	The person conveying an interest in real property.
Hazard insurance	Insurance coverage that in the event of physical damage to a property from fire, wind, vandalism or other hazards.
Home equity conversion mortgage (HECM)	Usually referred to as a reverse annuity mortgage. What makes this type of mortgage unique is that

instead of making payments to a lender, the lender makes payments to you. It enables older homeowners to convert the equity they have in their homes into cash, usually in the form of monthly payments. Unlike traditional home equity loans, a borrower does not qualify on the basis of income but on the value of his or her home. In addition, the loan does not have to be repaid until the borrower no longer occupies the property.

Home equity line of credit
A mortgage loan, usually in second position, that allows the borrower to obtain cash drawn against the equity of his home, up to a predetermined amount.

Home inspection
A thorough inspection by a professional that evaluates the structural and mechanical condition of a property. A satisfactory home inspection is often included as a contingency by the purchaser.

Homeowners' association
A non-profit association that manages the common areas of a planned unit development (PUD) or condominium project. In a condominium project, it has no ownership interest in the common elements. In a PUD project, it holds title to the common elements.

Homeowner's insurance
An insurance policy that combines personal liability insurance and hazard insurance coverage for a dwelling and its contents.

Homeowner's warranty
A type of insurance often purchased by home-buyers that will cover repairs to certain items, such as heating or air-conditioning, should they break down within the coverage period. The buyer often requests the seller to pay for this coverage as a condition of the sale, but either party can pay.

HUD median income
Median family income for a particular county or metropolitan statistical area (MSA), as estimated by the Department of Housing and Urban Development (HUD).

HUD-1 settlement statement
A document that provides an itemized listing of the funds that were paid at closing. Items that appear on the statement include real estate commissions, loan fees, points and initial escrow (impound) amounts. Each type of expense goes on a specific numbered line on the sheet. The totals at the bottom of the HUD-1 statement define the seller's net proceeds and the buyer's net payment at closing. It is called a HUD-1 because the form is printed by the Department of

Housing and Urban Development (HUD). The HUD-1 statement is also known as the 'closing statement' or 'settlement sheet'.

Joint tenancy
A form of ownership or taking title to property which means each party owns the whole property and that ownership is not separate. In the event of the death of one party, the survivor owns the property in its entirety.

Judgement
A decision made by a court of law. In judgements that require the repayment of a debt, the court may place a lien against the debtor's real property as collateral for the judgement's creditor.

Judicial foreclosure
A type of foreclosure proceeding used in some states that is handled as a civil lawsuit and conducted entirely under the auspices of a court. Other states use non-judicial foreclosure.

Jumbo loan
A loan that exceeds Fannie Mae's and Freddie Mac's loan limits, currently at $227,150. Also called a non-conforming loan. Freddie Mac and Fannie Mae loans are referred to as conforming loans.

Late charge
The penalty a borrower must pay when a payment is late by a stated number of days. On a first trust deed or mortgage, this is usually 15 days.

Lease
A written agreement between the property owner and a tenant that stipulates the payment and conditions under which the tenant may possess the real estate for a specified period of time.

Lease option
An alternative financing option that allows home-buyers to lease a home with an option to buy. Each month's rent payment may consist of not only the rent, but an additional amount which can be applied towards the down payment on an already specified price.

Leasehold estate
A way of holding title to a property wherein the mortgagor does not actually own the property but rather has a recorded long-term lease on it.

Legal description
A property description, recognized by law, that is sufficient to locate and identify the property without oral testimony.

Lender
A term which can refer to the institution making the loan or to the individual representing the firm. For example, loan officers are often referred to as 'lenders'.

Liabilities
A person's financial obligations. Liabilities include long-term and short-term debt, as well as any other amounts that are owed to others.

Liability insurance	Insurance coverage that offers protection against claims alleging that a property owner's negligence or inappropriate action resulted in bodily injury or property damage to another party. It is usually part of a homeowner's insurance policy.
Lien	A legal claim against a property that must be paid off when the property is sold. A mortgage or first trust deed is considered a lien.
Life cap	For an adjustable-rate mortgage (ARM), a limit on the amount that the interest rate can increase or decrease over the life of the mortgage.
Line of credit	An agreement by a commercial bank or other financial institution to extend credit up to a certain amount for a certain time to a specified borrower.
Liquid asset	A cash asset or an asset that is easily converted into cash.
Loan	A sum of borrowed money (principal) that is generally repaid with interest.
Loan officer	Also referred to by a variety of other terms, such as lender, loan representative, loan 'rep', account executive, etc. Loan officers serve several functions and have various responsibilities: they solicit loans, they are the representative of the lending institution, and they represent the borrower to the lending institution.
Loan origination	How a lender refers to the process of obtaining new loans.
Loan servicing	After you obtain a loan, the company you make the payments to is 'servicing' your loan. They process payments, send statements, manage the escrow/impound account, provide collection efforts on delinquent loans, ensure that insurance and property taxes are made on the property, handle pay-offs and assumptions, and provide a variety of other services.
Loan-to-value (LTV)	The percentage relationship between the amount of the loan and the appraised value or sales price (whichever is lower).
Lock-in	An agreement in which the lender guarantees a specified interest rate for a certain amount of time at a certain cost.
Lock-in period	The time period during which the lender has guaranteed an interest rate to a borrower.

Margin	The difference between the interest rate and the index on an adjustable rate mortgage. The margin remains stable over the life of the loan. It is the index which moves up and down.
Maturity	The date on which the principal balance of a loan, bond or other financial instrument becomes due and payable.
Merged credit report	A credit report which reports the raw data pulled from two or more of the major credit repositories. Contrast with a residential mortgage credit report (RMCR) or a standard factual credit report.
Modification	Occasionally, a lender will agree to modify the terms of your mortgage without requiring you to refinance. If any changes are made, it is called a modification.
Mortgage	A legal document that pledges a property to the lender as security for payment of a debt. Instead of mortgages, some states use first trust deeds.
Mortgage banker	A mortgage banker is generally assumed to originate and fund its own loans, which are then sold on the secondary market, usually to Fannie Mae (FNMA), Freddie Mac (FHLMC) or Ginnie Mae (GNMA). However, firms rather loosely apply this term to themselves, whether they are true mortgage bankers or simply mortgage brokers or correspondents.
Mortgage broker	A mortgage company that originates loans, then places those loans with a variety of other lending institutions with whom they usually have pre-established relationships.
Mortgagee	The lender in a mortgage agreement.
Mortgage insurance (MI)	Insurance that covers the lender against some of the losses incurred as a result of a default on a home loan. Often mistakenly referred to as PMI, which is actually the name of one of the larger mortgage insurers. Mortgage insurance is usually required in one form or another on all loans that have a loan-to-value higher than 80 per cent. Mortgages above 80 per cent LTV that call themselves 'No MI' are usually made at a higher interest rate. Instead of the borrower paying the mortgage insurance premiums directly, they pay a higher interest rate to the lender, who then pays the mortgage insurance themselves. Also, FHA loans and certain first-time homebuyer programmes require mortgage insurance regardless of the loan-to-value.

Mortgage insurance premium	The MIP is the amount paid by a mortgagor for mortgage insurance, either to a government agency such as the Federal Housing Administration (FHA) or to a private mortgage insurance (MI) company.
Mortgage life and disability insurance	A type of term life insurance often bought by borrowers. The amount of coverage decreases as the principal balance declines. Some policies also cover the borrower in the event of disability. In the event that the borrower dies while the policy is in force, the debt is automatically satisfied by insurance proceeds. In the case of disability insurance, the insurance will make the mortgage payment for a specified amount of time during the disability. Be careful to read the terms of cover, however, because often the cover does not start immediately upon the disability, but after a specified period, sometimes 45 days.
Mortgagor	The borrower in a mortgage agreement.
Multi-dwelling units	Properties that provide separate housing units for more than one family, although they secure only a single mortgage.
Negative amortization	Some adjustable rate mortgages allow the interest rate to fluctuate independently of a required minimum payment. If a borrower makes the minimum payment it may not cover all of the interest that would normally be due at the current interest rate. In essence, the borrower is deferring the interest payment, which is why this is called 'deferred interest'. The deferred interest is added to the balance of the loan and the loan balance grows larger instead of smaller, which is called negative amortization.
No cash-out refinance	A refinance transaction which is not intended to put cash in the hand of the borrower. Instead, the new balance is calculated to cover the balance due on the current loan and any costs associated with obtaining the new mortgage. Often referred to as a 'rate and term refinance'.
No-cost loan	Many lenders offer loans that you can obtain at 'no cost'. You should enquire whether this means there are no 'lender' costs associated with the loan, or if it also covers the other costs you would normally have in a purchase or refinance transactions, such as title insurance, escrow fees, settlement fees, appraisal, recording fees, notary fees, etc. These are fees and costs which may be

associated with buying a home or obtaining a loan, but not charged directly by the lender. Keep in mind that, like a 'no-point' loan, the interest rate will be higher than if you obtain a loan that has costs associated with it.

No-point loan Almost all lenders offer loans at 'no points'. You will find the interest rate on a 'no points' loan is approximately a quarter per cent higher than on a loan where you pay one point. *See* 'Point'.

Note A legal document that obliges a borrower to repay a mortgage loan at a stated interest rate during a specified period of time.

Note rate The interest rate stated on a mortgage note.

Notice of default A formal written notice to a borrower that a default has occurred and legal action may be taken.

Original principal balance The total amount of principal owed on a mortgage before any payments are made.

Origination fee On a government loan the loan origination fee is 1 per cent of the loan amount, but additional points may be charged which are called 'discount points'. One point equals 1 per cent of the loan amount. On a conventional loan, the loan origination fee refers to the total number of points a borrower pays.

Owner financing A property purchase transaction in which the property seller provides all or part of the financing.

Partial payment A payment that is not sufficient to cover the scheduled monthly payment on a mortgage loan. Normally, a lender will not accept a partial payment, but in times of hardship you can make this request to the loan servicing collection dept.

Payment change date The date when a new monthly payment amount takes effect on an adjustable-rate mortgage (ARM) or a graduated-payment mortgage (GPM). Generally, the payment change date occurs in the month immediately after the interest rate adjustment date.

Periodic payment cap For an adjustable-rate mortgage where the interest rate and the minimum payment amount fluctuate independently of one another, this is a limit on the amount that payments can increase or decrease during any one adjustment period.

Periodic rate cap For an adjustable-rate mortgage, a limit on the amount that the interest rate can increase or

	decrease during any one adjustment period, regardless of how high or low the index might be.
Personal property	Any property that is not real property.
PITI	This stands for principal, interest, taxes and insurance. If you have an 'impounded' loan, then your monthly payment to the lender includes all of these and probably includes mortgage insurance as well. If you do not have an impounded account, then the lender still calculates this amount and uses it as part of determining your debt-to-income ratio.
PITI reserves	A cash amount that a borrower must have on hand after making a down-payment and paying all closing costs for the purchase of a home. The principal, interest, taxes and insurance (PITI) reserves must equal the amount that the borrower would have to pay for PITI for a predefined number of months.
Planned unit development (PUD)	A type of ownership where individuals actually own the building or unit they live in, but common areas are owned jointly with the other members of the development or association. Contrast with condominium, where an individual actually owns the airspace of his unit, but the buildings and common areas are owned jointly with the others in the development or association.
Point	A point is 1 per cent of the amount of mortgage.
Power of attorney	A legal document that authorizes another person to act on one's behalf. A power of attorney can grant complete authority or can be limited to certain acts and/or certain periods of time.
Pre-approval	A loosely used term which is generally taken to mean that a borrower has completed a loan application and provided debt, income and savings documentation which an underwriter has reviewed and approved. A pre-approval is usually carried out at a certain loan amount and making assumptions about what the interest rate will actually be at the time the loan is made, as well as estimates for the amount that will be paid for property taxes, insurance, etc. A pre-approval applies only to the borrower. Once a property is chosen, it must also meet the underwriting guidelines of the lender. Contrast with 'Pre-qualification'.
Prepayment	Any amount paid to reduce the principal balance of a loan before the due date. Payment in full on a

mortgage that may result from a sale of the property, the owner's decision to pay off the loan in full, or a foreclosure. In each case, prepayment means payment occurs before the loan has been fully amortized.

Prepayment penalty

A fee that may be charged to a borrower who pays off a loan before it is due.

Pre-qualification

This usually refers to the loan officer's written opinion of the ability of a borrower to qualify for a home loan, after the loan officer has made enquiries about debt, income and savings. The information provided to the loan officer may have been presented verbally or in the form of documentation, and the loan officer may or may not have reviewed a credit report on the borrower.

Prime rate

The interest rate that banks charge to their preferred customers. Changes in the prime rate are widely publicized in the news media and are used as the indices in some adjustable rate mortgages, especially home equity lines of credit. Changes in the prime rate do not directly affect other types of mortgages, but the same factors that influence the prime rate also affect the interest rates of mortgage loans.

Principal

The amount borrowed or remaining unpaid. The part of the monthly payment that reduces the remaining balance of a mortgage.

Principal balance

The outstanding balance of principal on a mortgage. The principal balance does not include interest or any other charges. *See* 'Remaining balance'.

Principal, interest, taxes, insurance (PITI)

The four components of a monthly mortgage and payment on impounded loans. Principal refers to the part of the monthly payment that reduces the remaining balance of the mortgage. Interest is the fee charged for borrowing money. Taxes and insurance refer to the amounts that are paid into an escrow account each month for property taxes and mortgage and hazard insurance.

Private mortgage insurance (MI)

Mortgage insurance that is provided by a private mortgage insurance company to protect lenders against loss if a borrower defaults. Most lenders generally require MI for a loan with a loan-to-value (LTV) percentage in excess of 80 per cent.

Promissory note

A written promise to repay a specified amount over a specified period of time.

Public auction	A meeting in an announced public location to sell property to repay a mortgage that is in default.
PUD	*See* 'Planned unit development'.
Purchase agreement	A written contract signed by the buyer and seller stating the terms and conditions under which a property will be sold.
Purchase money transaction	The acquisition of property through the payment of money or its equivalent.
Qualifying ratios	Calculations that are used in determining whether a borrower can qualify for a mortgage. There are two ratios. The 'top' or 'front' ratio is a calculation of the borrower's monthly housing costs (principal, interest, taxes, insurance, mortgage insurance, homeowners' association fees) as a percentage of monthly income. The 'back' or 'bottom' ratio includes housing costs as well as all other monthly debt.
Quitclaim deed	A deed that transfers without warranty whatever interest or title a grantor may have at the time the conveyance is made.
Rate lock	A commitment issued by a lender to a borrower or other mortgage originator guaranteeing a specified interest rate for a specified period of time at a specific cost.
Real estate agent	A person licensed to negotiate and transact the sale of real estate.
Real Estate Settlement Procedures Act (RESPA)	A consumer protection law that requires lenders to give borrowers advance notice of closing costs.
Real property	Land and appurtenances, including anything of a permanent nature such as structures, trees and minerals, and the interest, benefits and inherent rights thereof.
Realtor®	A real estate agent, broker or an associate who holds active membership in a local real estate board that is affiliated with the National Association of Realtors (NAR).
Recorder	The public official who keeps records of transactions that affect real property in the area. Sometimes known as a 'Registrar of Deeds' or 'County Clerk'.
Recording	The noting in the registrar's office of the details of a properly executed legal document, such as a deed, a mortgage note, a satisfaction of mortgage, or an extension of mortgage, thereby making it a part of the public record.

Refinance transaction	The process of paying off one loan with the proceeds from a new loan using the same property as security.
Remaining balance	The amount of principal that has not yet been repaid. *See* 'Principal balance'.
Remaining term	The original amortization term minus the number of payments that have been applied.
Rent loss insurance	Insurance that protects a landlord against loss of rent or rental value resulting from fire or other casualty that renders the leased premises unavailable for use and as a result of which the tenant is excused from paying rent.
Repayment plan	An arrangement made to repay delinquent instalments or advances.
Replacement reserve fund	A fund set aside for replacement of common property in a condominium, PUD, or co-operative project – particularly one which has a short life expectancy, such as carpeting, furniture, etc.
Revolving debt	A credit arrangement, such as a credit card, that allows a customer to borrow against a pre-approved line of credit when purchasing goods and services. The borrower is billed for the amount that is actually borrowed plus any interest due.
Right of first refusal	A provision in an agreement that requires the owner of a property to give another party the first opportunity to purchase or lease the property before offering it for sale or lease to others.
Right of ingress or egress	The right to enter or leave designated premises.
Right of survivorship	In joint tenancy, the right of survivors to acquire the interest of a deceased joint tenant.
Sale-leaseback	A technique by which a seller deeds property to a buyer for a consideration, and the buyer simultaneously leases the property back to the seller.
Second mortgage	A mortgage that has a lien position subordinate to the first mortgage.
Secondary market	The buying and selling of existing mortgages, usually as part of a 'pool' of mortgages.
Secured loan	A loan that is backed by collateral.
Security	The property pledged as collateral for a loan.
Seller carry-back	An agreement in which the owner of a property provides financing, often in combination with an assumable mortgage.
Servicer	An organization that collects principal and interest payments from borrowers and manages

borrowers' escrow accounts. The servicer often services mortgages that have been purchased by an investor in the secondary mortgage market.

Servicing	The collection of mortgage payments from borrowers and related responsibilities of a loan servicer.
Settlement statement	*See* 'HUD-1 settlement statement'.
Subdivision	A housing development that is created by dividing a tract of land into individual lots for sale or lease.
Subordinate financing	Any mortgage or other lien that has a priority that is lower than that of the first mortgage.
Survey	A drawing or map showing the precise legal boundaries of a property, the location of improvements, easements, rights of way, encroachments and other physical features.
Sweat equity	Contribution to the construction or rehabilitation of a property in the form of labour or services rather than cash.
Tenancy in common	As opposed to joint tenancy, when there are two or more individuals on title to a piece of property, this type of ownership does not pass ownership to the others in the event of death.
Third-party origination	A process by which a lender uses another party to completely or partially originate, process, underwrite, close, fund or package the mortgages it plans to deliver to the secondary mortgage market.
Title	A legal document evidencing a person's right to or ownership of a property.
Title company	A company that specializes in examining and insuring titles to real estate.
Title insurance	Insurance that protects the lender (lender's policy) or the buyer (owner's policy) against loss arising from disputes over ownership of a property.
Title search	A check of the title records to ensure that the seller is the legal owner of the property and that there are no liens or other claims outstanding.
Transfer of ownership	Any means by which the ownership of a property changes hands. Lenders consider all of the following situations to be a transfer of ownership the purchase of a property 'subject to' the mortgage, the assumption of the mortgage debt by the property purchaser and any exchange of possession of the property under a land sales contract or any other land trust device.

Transfer tax	State or local tax payable when title passes from one owner to another.
Treasury index	An index that is used to determine interest rate changes for certain adjustable-rate mortgage (ARM) plans. It is based on the results of auctions that the US Treasury holds for its Treasury bills and securities or is derived from the US Treasury's daily yield curve, which is based on the closing market bid yields on actively traded Treasury securities in the over-the-counter market.
Truth-in-lending	A federal law that requires lenders to disclose fully, in writing, the terms and conditions of a mortgage, including the annual percentage rate (APR) and other charges.
Two-step mortgage	An adjustable-rate mortgage (ARM) that has one interest rate for the first five or seven years of its mortgage term and a different interest rate for the remainder of the amortization term.
Two- to four-family property	A property that consists of a structure that provides living space (dwelling units) for two to four families, although ownership of the structure is evidenced by a single deed.
Trustee	A fiduciary who holds or controls property for the benefit of another.
VA mortgage	A mortgage that is guaranteed by the Department of Veterans Affairs (VA).
Vested	Having the right to use a portion of a fund such as an individual retirement fund. For example, individuals who are 100 per cent vested can withdraw all the funds that are set aside for them in a retirement fund. However, taxes may be due on any funds that are actually withdrawn.
Veterans Administration (VA)	An agency of the federal government that guarantees residential mortgages made to eligible veterans of the military services. The guarantee protects the lender against loss and thus encourages lenders to make mortgages to veterans.

American Vocabulary

Although ostensibly we all speak the same language, there are lots of variations – many of which are obvious – and the sooner you get used to using them, the quicker you will be understood! Here is a selection to get you going:

A

Arugula	Rocket, the plant used in salads
Asphalt	Tarmac
Attached home	Semi-detached house
Attorney	Lawyer/solicitor
Automobile	Car/vehicle

B

Baby carriage	Pram
Bangs	Fringe
Baseboard	Skirting board
Bathroom	Toilet
Bell pepper	Red, green or yellow pepper
Bill	Banknote, piece of paper currency
Biscuit	Scone
Blacktop	Tarmac
Breakdown lane	Hard shoulder
Brown bag lunch	Packed lunch
Bum	Tramp, layabout
Burglarize	Burgle, steal
Business district	Centre

C

Candy	Chocolate, sweets
Carpenter's level	Spirit level
Casket	Coffin
Cell/cellular	Mobile phone
Checking account	Current account
Chips	Crisps
Cilantro	Coriander
Closet	Walk-in cupboard or wardrobe
Collect call	Reverse charge call
Comforter	Quilt, eiderdown, bedspread
Condominium, condo	Block of flats
Consignment	Second-hand goods sold on commission
Corn	Sweet corn, maize, corn-on-the-cob
Corn starch	Cornflour
Cotton candy	Candy floss
Cotton swab	Cotton bud
Cream of wheat	Semolina
Crosswalk	Pedestrian crossing
Cuban	Floridan term for a sandwich with roast pork, ham and Swiss cheese

D

Deductible	Excess, in terms of insurance payouts
Diaper	Nappy
Dish pan	Washing-up bowl
Divided highway	Dual carriageway
Docent	Curator, guide in a museum, historic house or gallery
Downtown	Centre
Drapes	Curtains
Drugstore	Pharmacy, chemist
Dumpster	Skip
Duplex (house)	Semi-detached house

E

Eggplant	Aubergine
Elementary school	Primary school
Excise laws	Licensing laws
Expressway	Main road

F

Fall	Autumn
Fanny	Behind, *derrière*
Fanny pack	Bumbag
Faucet	Tap
Fava bean	Broad bean
Fender	Wing of a car, mudguard on bicycle
First floor	Ground floor
Flashlight	Torch
Flatware	Cutlery
Freeway	Motorway
Furnace	Central heating boiler

G

Galoshes	Wellington boots, wellies
Gas	Petrol
Grade crossing	Level crossing
Graham crackers	Digestive biscuits

H

Heavy cream	Double cream
Hidabed, hideaway	Sofabed
High school	Secondary school
Highway	Main road (out of town)
Hike	Walk
Hobo	Tramp
Hood	Bonnet (of car)

I

Incorporated	Limited, as in limited company
Instalment plan	Hire purchase

J, K

Janitor	Caretaker
Jack	Socket
Jelly	Type of jam
Jell-o	Jelly
Kerosene	Paraffin

L

Lawyer, advocate, attorney	Lawyer, solicitor, barrister
License plate or tag	Number plate
Lima bean	Butter bean
Line	Queue
Lot	Plot (of land)
Love seat	Settee, sofa
Luggage rack	Roof rack
Lumber	Timber

M

Mall	Shopping complex
Mean	Bad-tempered
Military time	24-hour clock
Muffler	Silencer in vehicle exhaust system
Mutual fund	Unit trust

N

Nickel	five-cent coin
Number sign	Hash mark

O

Ocean	Sea
Oil pan	Sump
On-ramp, off-ramp	Slip road
Outlet	Socket

P, Q

Pacifier	Dummy used to stop small children crying
Paddle	Bat for table tennis and similar games
Panhandler	Beggar
Pantihose/pantyhose	Tights
Pants	Trousers
Parking lot	Car park
Pavement	Paved area
Penny	Cent
Period	Full stop in punctuation
Petroleum	Crude oil
Plastic wrap	Clingfilm
Plexiglas	Perspex
Potato chips	Crisps
Pound sign, number sign	Hash sign, i.e. #

Preserves	Jam, marmalade
Professor	Lecturer
Public school	State school
Purse	Handbag
Quarter	25¢ coin

R

Railroad	Railway
Real estate	Property
Realtor	Estate agent
Restroom	Toilet
Résumé	Curriculum vitae (CV)
Retirement fund	Superannuation
Rotary	Roundabout
Row house	Terrace house
Rutabaga	Swede

S

Sack lunch	Packed lunch
Sales tax	VAT
Saran wrap	Clingfilm
Savings and loan trust	Building society
Scallion	Spring onion
Scotch tape	Sellotape
Second floor	First floor
Sedan	Saloon type of car
Seeing eye dog	Guide dog
Semi-trailer	Articulated lorry
Server	Waiter or waitress
Senior	Pensioner
Shade	Blind
Sherbet	Sorbet
Shrimp	Prawn
Sidewalk	Pavement
Silverware	Cutlery
Slacks	Trousers
Snaps	Press studs
Social security number	National insurance number
Soda	Fizzy soft drink
Sports utility vehicle (SUV)	Large four-wheel drive vehicle with comfortable interior
Station wagon	Estate car
Stick shift	Gear lever
Streetcar	Tram
Stroller	Pushchair, baby buggy
Stub	Counterfoil
Submarine, sub	Sandwich in long roll

T

Teller	Cashier
Townhouse	Terrace house

Traffic circle	Roundabout
Trash	Rubbish/garbage
Trunk	Boot (of car)

V
Variety meats	Offal
Vest	Waistcoat
Veterans' day	Remembrance day

W
Walker	Zimmer (frame)
Welfare	Benefit
White-out	Tippex
Wrench	Spanner

XYZ
Yard	Garden
Yield	Give way (when driving)
Zip code	Postcode
Zucchini	Courgette

Directory of Contacts

Major Resources in Britain

American Embassy
24 Grosvenor Square, London W1A 1AE
t (020) 7499 9000
www.usembassy.org.uk

US Consulate General in Northern Ireland
Danesfort House, 223 Stranmillis Road, Belfast BT9 5GR
t (028) 9038 6100
f (028) 9068 1301
www.usembassy.org.uk/nireland

US Consulate General in Scotland
3 Regent Terrace, Edinburgh EH7 5BW
t (0131) 556 8315
f (0131) 557 6023
edinburgh-info@state.gov
www.usembassy.org.uk/scotland

British Resources in Florida and the USA

British Embassy
3100 Massachusetts Avenue NW, Washington, DC 20008
t (202) 588 7800

British Consulate
Sun Trust Center, 200 South Orange Avenue, Suite 2110, Orlando, FL 32801
t (407) 254 3300
f (407) 254 3333
Consulate.Orlando@fco.gov.uk

British Council
British Embassy, 3100 Massachusetts Avenue NW, Washington, DC 20008
t 1-800 488 2235
f (202) 588 7918
www.britishcouncil.org/usa

Other Foreign Embassies in the USA

Australia
1601 Massachusetts Avenue NW, Washington DC 20036
t (202) 797 3000
f (202) 797 3168
www.austemb.org

India
2107 Massachusetts Avenue NW, Washington DC 20008
t (202) 939 7000
f (202) 265 4351
www.indianembassy.org

Ireland
2234 Massachusetts Avenue NW, Washington DC 20008
t (202) 462 3939
f (202) 232 5993
www.irelandemb.org

New Zealand
37 Observatory Circle NW, Washington DC 20008
t (202) 328 4800
f (202) 667 5227
nz@nzemb.org
www.nzembassy.com

Removal Companies

Andrews Moving and Storage
One Andrews Circle, Brecksville, OH 44141, USA
t (440) 838 8600/800 321 8680
f (440) 838 8635
www.andrewsmoving.com

Anglo Pacific
Units 1 & 2 Bush Industrial Estate, Standard Road, North Acton, London NW10 6DF
t (020) 8965 1234
f (020) 8965 4954
info@anglopacific.co.uk
www.anglopacific.co.uk

Burke Brothers Moving Group
Foxs Lane, Wolverhampton, West Midlands WV1 1PA
t (01902) 714 555
f (01902) 427 837
www.burkebros.com

EuroUSA Shipping
74–75 Fred Dannatt Road, Mildenhall, Suffolk, IP28 7RD
t (01638) 515 335
f (01638) 515 585
info@eurousa.co.uk
www.the-eurogroup.com

Excess Baggage
4 Hannah Close, Great Central Way, London NW10 0UX
t (020) 8324 2066
f (020) 8324 2095
sales@excess-baggage.com
www.excess-baggage.com

PSS International Movers
1–3 Pegasus Road, Croydon, Surrey CR9 4PS
t (020) 8686 7733
f (020) 8686 7799
sales@p-s-s.co.uk
www.pss.uk.com

On-line Resources

UK/Expat Online Resources
www.backinblighty.com
www.british-expats.com
www.britishflorida.com
www.britsonline.com
www.floridabritsclub.com
www.floridabritsgroup.com
www.geocities.com/TheTropics/2865
www.spiffs.org/membergroups/english
www.sunnybrits.com
www.swflabrits.com
www.thebrits.com

Finding Real Estate Agents

www.realestateagent.com
www.realtor.com/FindReal/USMapReal.asp
www.realtylocator.com

American Holidays and Celebrations

1 Jan	*New Year's Day.* The first day of the new year is a national holiday but Americans actually gather the night before to wish each other a happy and prosperous coming year, and to toast each other with champagne at midnight.
3rd Mon in Jan	*Martin Luther King Day.* The Rev. Martin Luther King, Jr, an African-American clergyman, fought tirelessly to win civil rights for all people through non-violent means. Since his assassination in 1968, memorial services have marked his birthday on 15 January. In 1986 that day was replaced by the third Monday of January, which was declared a national holiday.
14 Feb	*Valentine's Day.* Named after an early Christian martyr, this romantic – but not national – holiday is an occasion for most Americans to give presents, usually chocolate (candy) or flowers, to the ones they love.
3rd Mon in Feb	*Presidents' Day.* The 22 February birthday of George Washington, hero of the Revolutionary War and first president of the USA, was a national holiday until the mid-1970s. In addition, many states celebrated the 12 February birthday of Abraham Lincoln, the president during the Civil War. The two days have been joined, and the holiday has been expanded to embrace all past presidents. It is celebrated on the third Monday in February.
17 March	*St Patrick's Day.* Not a national holiday but a popular one with Irish-Americans and many others who celebrate Ireland's patron saint. People wear green in honour of the Emerald Isle and mark the day by spending a lot of time in Irish pubs.
March or April	*Easter.* The holiday falls on a spring Sunday that varies from year to year, and celebrates the Christian belief in the resurrection of Jesus Christ. For Christians, Easter is a day of religious services and the gathering of family. Many Americans follow old traditions of colouring hard-boiled eggs and giving children baskets of candy. On the following day, Easter Monday, the president of the USA holds an annual Easter egg hunt on the White House lawn for young children.
4th Mon in May	*Memorial Day.* Celebrated on the fourth Monday of May, this holiday honours the dead. Although it originated in the aftermath of the Civil War, it has become a day on which the

dead of all wars, and the dead generally, are remembered in special programmes held in cemeteries, churches and other public meeting places.

4 July
The Fourth of July, or *Independence Day,* honours the nation's birthday, tied to the signing of the Declaration of Independence on 4 July 1776. It is a day of picnics and parades, a night of concerts and fireworks. American flags are everywhere.

1st Mon in Sept
Labor Day. The first Monday of September, this holiday honours the nation's working people. For most Americans it marks the end of the summer vacation season, and for many students the opening of the school year.

2nd Mon in Oct
Columbus Day. On 12 October 1492, Italian navigator Christopher Columbus landed in the New World. Although most other nations of the Americas observe this holiday on 12 October, in the USA it takes place on the second Monday in October.

31 Oct
Hallowe'en. On the evening before All Saints or All Hallows Day, American children dress up in all types of costumes and go 'trick or treating', knocking on doors in their neighbourhood and collecting candy or money. Many adults take the opportunity to dress in costume for Hallowe'en parties.

11 Nov
Veterans' Day. Originally called Armistice Day, this holiday was established to honour Americans who had served in the First World War. It falls on the day when that war ended in 1918, but it now honours veterans of all wars in which the USA has fought. Veterans' organizations hold parades, and the president customarily places a wreath on the Tomb of the Unknowns at Arlington National Cemetery, across the Potomac River from Washington DC.

4th Thurs in Nov
Thanksgiving Day. The holiday falls on the fourth Thursday in November, but because many Americans travel long distances to visit their families they take a day of vacation on the following Friday to make a four-day weekend. The holiday dates back to 1621, the year after the Puritans arrived in Massachusetts, when the newcomers were taught how to plant crops by neighbouring native Americans and organized a feast of thanks the following autumn. Thanksgiving dinner almost always includes some of the foods served at the first feast: roast turkey, cranberry sauce, potatoes and pumpkin pie. Before the meal begins, families or friends usually pause to give thanks for their blessings, including the joy of being united for the occasion.

25 Dec
Christmas Day. This Christian holiday marks the birth of the Christ Child. Decorating houses and yards with lights, putting up Christmas trees, giving gifts and sending greeting cards have become traditions even for many non-Christian Americans.

Climate Charts

Average Seasonal Temperatures (°F)

	Jan	Feb	Mar	April	May	June	July	Aug	Sept	Oct	Nov	Dec
Daytona Beach	58	60	64	69	75	80	81	81	80	74	66	60
Fort Myers	64	65	70	73	78	82	83	83	82	77	71	66
Gainesville	55	56	63	69	75	79	81	81	78	71	63	56
Jacksonville	54	57	62	69	75	80	83	82	79	71	62	56
Key West	70	71	74	77	81	83	85	85	83	80	76	72
Miami	68	69	72	75	79	82	83	83	82	78	73	69
Orlando	59	62	67	72	77	81	82	82	81	75	68	62
Pensacola	52	54	61	68	75	81	82	82	79	70	60	54
Tallahassee	52	55	61	67	74	80	81	81	78	69	60	54
Tampa	60	62	67	72	78	81	82	83	81	75	68	62
West Palm Beach	66	67	70	74	78	81	83	83	82	78	72	68

Temperature Conversion
To convert Fahrenheit to Celsius: subtract 32, multiply by 5 and divide by 9.
To convert Celsius to Fahrenheit: multiply by 9, divide by 5 and add 32.

Average Rainfall (Inches)

	Jan	Feb	Mar	April	May	June	July	Aug	Sept	Oct	Nov	Dec
Daytona Beach	2.5	3.0	3.2	2.5	3.1	5.7	5.5	6.3	6.7	4.6	2.6	2.4
Fort Myers	1.7	2.1	2.7	1.3	3.7	9.0	8.5	9.0	8.3	3.5	1.5	1.5
Gainesville	3.4	4.4	3.8	2.3	3.4	7.1	6.6	7.9	5.4	2.3	2.3	2.8
Jacksonville	3.0	3.7	3.8	3.0	3.6	5.3	6.2	7.4	7.8	3.7	2.0	2.6
Key West	2.1	1.6	1.7	1.9	3.3	4.7	3.8	5.2	6.3	4.5	2.7	2.0
Miami	1.9	2.0	2.3	3.0	6.2	8.7	6.1	7.5	8.2	6.6	2.7	1.8
Orlando	2.3	2.8	3.4	2.0	3.2	7.0	7.2	5.8	5.8	2.7	3.5	2.0
Pensacola	4.2	5.1	5.7	4.1	4.4	6.3	7.4	6.9	5.8	3.8	3.4	4.4
Tallahassee	4.2	5.1	6.0	4.2	4.5	6.8	8.8	7.1	5.7	2.9	3.5	4.5
Tampa	2.1	2.8	3.5	1.8	3.0	5.6	7.3	7.9	6.5	2.3	1.8	2.1
West Palm Beach	2.7	2.6	3.3	3.3	5.7	7.5	6.2	6.3	9.0	7.0	3.9	2.5

Conversion
To convert inches to millimetres, multiply by 25.4.

Weights and Measures

Women's Clothes

UK	8	10	12	14	16	18	20	22	24	26
USA	6	8	10	12	14	16	18	20	22	24

Sweaters

	Women's						Men's					
UK	34	36	38	40	42	44	34	36	38	40	42	44
USA	34	36	38	40	42	44	small		medium		large	

Children's Clothes

UK	16/18	20/22	24/26	28/30	32/34	36/38
USA	2	4	6	8	10	12

Shoes (Women's and Men's)

Continental	35	35	36	37	37	38	39	39	40	40	41	42	42	43	44	44
UK	2	3	3	4	4	5	5	6	6	7	7	8	8	9	9	10
USA		4	4	5	5	6	6	7	7	8	8	9	9	10	10	11	11

Appendices

Appendix 1

Checklist – Do-it-yourself Inspection of Property
Task   ✓

Title – Check that the property corresponds with its description:
    Number of rooms
    Plot size

Plot
    Identify the physical boundaries of the plot.
    Is there any dispute with anyone over these boundaries?
    Are there any obvious foreign elements on your plot such as pipes,
        cables, drainage ditches, water tanks, etc.?
    Are there any signs of anyone else having rights over the property –
        footpaths, access ways, cartridges from hunting, etc.?

Garden/Terrace
    Are any plants, ornaments, etc. on site not being sold with the property?

Pool – Is there a pool? If so:
    What size is it?
    Is it clean and algae-free?
    Do the pumps work?
    How old is the machinery?
    Who maintains it?
    What is the annual cost of maintenance?
    Does it appear to be in good condition?

Walls – Stand back from property and inspect from outside:
    Any signs of subsidence?
    Walls vertical?
    Any obvious cracks in walls?
    Are walls well pointed?
    Any obvious damp patches?
    Any new repairs to walls or repointing?

Roof – Inspect from outside property:
Does roof sag?
Are there missing/slipped tiles?
Do all faces of roof join squarely?
Lead present and in good order?

Guttering and downpipes – Inspect from outside property:
    All present?
    Securely attached?
    Fall of guttering constant?
    Any obvious leaks?
    Any recent repairs?

Checklist – Do-it-yourself Inspection of Property (*cont.*)

Task   ✓

Enter property

    Does it smell of damp?

    Does it smell musty?

    Does it smell of dry rot?

    Any other strange smells?

Doors

    Signs of rot?

    Close properly – without catching?

    Provide proper seal?

    Locks work?

Windows

    Signs of rot?

    Close properly – without catching?

    Provide proper seal?

    Locks work?

    Excessive condensation?

Floor

    Can you see it all?

    Does it appear in good condition?

    Any sign of cracked or rotten boards?

Under floor

    Can you get access under the floor?

    If so, is it ventilated?

    Is there any sign of rot?

    How close are joists?

    Are joist ends in good condition where they go into walls?

    What is maximum unsupported length of joist run?

    Is there any sign of damp or standing water?

Roof void

    Is it accessible?

    Is there sign of water entry?

    Can you see daylight through the roof?

    Is there an underlining between the tiles and the void?

    Is there any sign of rot in timbers?

    Horizontal distance between roof timbers

    Size of roof timbers (section)?

    Maximum unsupported length of roof timbers

    Is roof insulated? If so, what depth and type of insulation?

Checklist – Do-it-yourself Inspection of Property (*cont*.)

Task	✓

Woodwork
Any sign of rot?
Any sign of wood-boring insects?
Is it dry?

Interior walls
Any significant cracks?
Any obvious damp problems?
Any sign of recent repair or redecoration?

Electricity
Check electricity meter:
    How old is it?
    What is its rated capacity?
Check all visible wiring:
    What type is it?
    Does it appear in good physical condition?
Check all plugs:
    Is there power to plug?
    Does plug tester show good earth and show 'OK'?
    Are there enough plugs?
Lighting:
    Do all lights work?
    Which light fittings are included in sale?

Water
Do all hot and cold taps work?
Is flow adequate?
Do taps drip?
Is there a security cut-off on all taps between mains and tap?
Do they seem in good condition?
Hot water:
    Is hot water 'on'? If so, does it work at all taps, showers, etc.?
    What type of hot water system is fitted?
    Age?

Gas
Is the property fitted with city (piped) gas? If so:
    Age of meter?
    Does installation appear in good order?
    Is there any smell of gas?
Is the property fitted with bottled gas? If so:
    Where are bottles stored?
    Is it ventilated to outside of premises?

Checklist – Do-it-yourself Inspection of Property (*cont.*)
Task   ✓

Central heating
Is the property fitted with central heating? If so:
   Is it on?
   Will it turn on?
   What type is it?
   Is there heat at all radiators/outlets?
   Do any thermostats appear to work?
   Are there any signs of leaks?

Fireplaces
Is the property fitted with any solid fuel heaters? If so:
   Any sign of blow-back from chimneys?
   Do chimneys (outside) show stains from leakage?
   Do chimneys seem in good order?

Air-conditioning
   Which rooms are air-conditioned?
   Are units included in the sale?
   Do the units work (deliver cold air)?
   What type of air-conditioning is it?
   How old is it?

Phone
   Does it work?
   Number?

Satellite TV
   Does it work?
   Is it included in the sale?

Drainage
   What type of drainage does property have?
   If septic tank, how old?
   Who maintains it?
   When was it last maintained?
   Any smell of drainage problems in bathrooms and toilets?
   Does water drain away rapidly from all sinks, showers and toilets?
   Is there any inspection access through which you can see
      drainage taking place?
   Is there any sign of plant ingress to drains?
   Do drains appear to be in good condition and well pointed?

Checklist – Do-it-yourself Inspection of Property (*cont.*)

Task   ✓

Kitchen

Do all cupboards open and close properly?
Any sign of rot?
Tiling secure and in good order?
Enough plugs?
What appliances are included in sale?
Do they work?
Age of appliances included?

Bathroom

Security and condition of tiling?
Ventilation?

Appliances

What appliances generally are included in sale?
What is not included in sale?

Furniture

What furniture is included in sale?
What is not included in sale?

Repairs/Improvements/Additions

What repairs have been carried out in last two years?
What improvements have been carried out in last two years/
    ten years?
What additions have been made to the property in last
    two years/ten years?
Are there builders' receipts'/guarantees?
Is there building consent/planning permission for any
additions or alterations?

Defects

Is seller aware of any defects in the property?

Appendix 2

Checklist – What Are You Worth?

Asset	Value (Local Currency)	Value (£s)
Current assets		
Main home		
Holiday home		
Contents of main home		
Contents of holiday home		
Car		
Boat		
Bank accounts		
Other cash-type investments		
Bonds, etc.		
Stocks and shares		
PEPs		
Tessas		
ISAs		
SIPS		
Other		
Value of your business		
Value of share options		
Future assets		
Value of share options		
Personal/company pension – likely lump sum		
Potential inheritances or other accretions		
Value of endowment mortgages on maturity		
Other		

Index

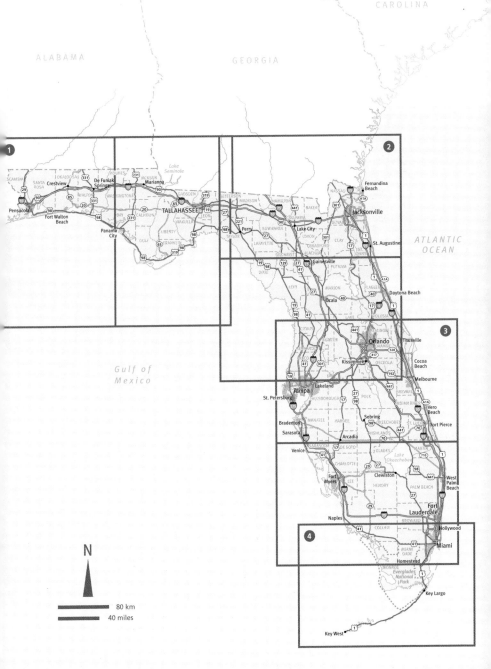

ALABAMA

ESCAMBIA

Century

4

29

McDavid

Jay

89

87

Berrydale

97

197

SANTA ROSA

184

Milton

90

29

Gonzalez

Pace

Bellview

87

Pensacola

East
Bay

Warrington

98

Gulf
Breeze

399

Navarre

Blackman

4

189

Baker

Laurel Hill

2

85

Crestview

10

OKALOOSA

85

Fort Walton
Beach

285

Niceville

20

Destin

Paxton

331

2

Gaskin

83

Prosperity

81

HOLMES

2

285

90

De Funiak
Springs

WALTON

331

Freeport

Redbay

New
Hope

81

Choctawhatchee Bay

Ebro

Point
Washington

79

98

Laguna Beach

Gulf of
Mexico

GEORGIA

Graceville
Campbellton
Malone
2
79
77
273
231
JACKSON
69
Bonifay
Cottondale
90
Marianna
10
73
Chattahoochee
90
GADSDEN
Havana
WASHINGTON
Compass Lake
Altha
Greensboro
10
Quincy
27
LEON
319
Killearn
2
19
69
12
65
77
Clarksville
Bristol
Tallahassee
Capps
20
Crystal
Lake
71
Hosford
20
Bloxham
Vicksburg
CALHOUN
Youngstown
267
BAY
73
Woodville
231
Chipola Park
12
363
59
Hiland Park
LIBERTY
WAKULLA
Newport
Panama
City
Callaway
22
Wilma
98
GULF
375
Medart
Sumatra
Sopchoppy
319
Mexico Beach
71
98
Apalachee Bay
St. Joseph
Bay
FRANKLIN
St. Teresa
65
98
319
Port
St. Joe
Ward Ridge
Carrabelle
N
98
Apalachicola
Apalachicola Bay

20 km
10 miles

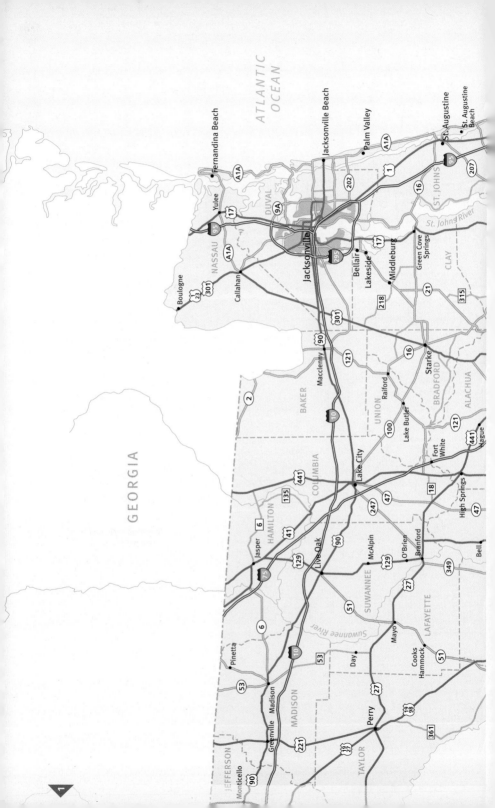

ATLANTIC OCEAN

GEORGIA

Fernandina Beach

Jacksonville Beach

Palm Valley

St. Augustine
St. Augustine Beach

Yulee

Boulogne

Callahan

Jacksonville

Bellair

Lakeside

Middleburg

Green Cove Springs

DUVAL

NASSAU

ST. JOHNS

CLAY

St. Johns River

Macclenny

BAKER

UNION

Raiford

Starke

BRADFORD

ALACHUA

Lake City

Lake Butler

Fort White

Hague

High Springs

COLUMBIA

Jasper

HAMILTON

Live Oak

McAlpin

O'Brien

Branford

Bell

SUWANNEE

Suwannee River

LAFAYETTE

Mayo

Pinetta

Day

Cooks Hammock

JEFFERSON

Monticello

Greenville

Madison

MADISON

Perry

TAYLOR

A1A

17

301

23

1

A1A

95

9A

202

1

16

207

17

17

218

21

315

301

90

121

16

2

10

100

441

135

6

41

129

75

6

53

247

47

18

47

90

129

27

349

51

51

27

10

53

98

361

221

19
27

90

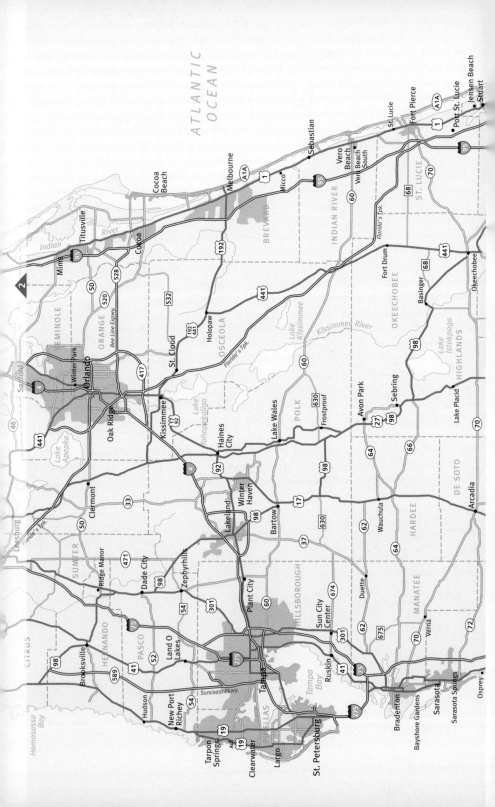

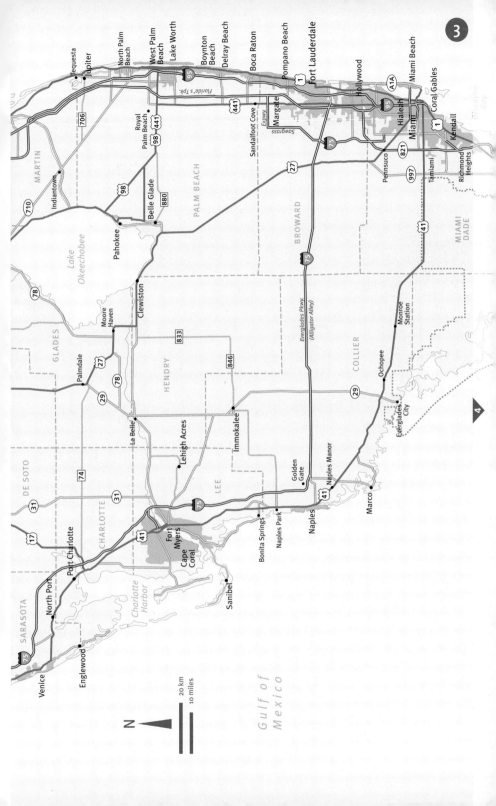

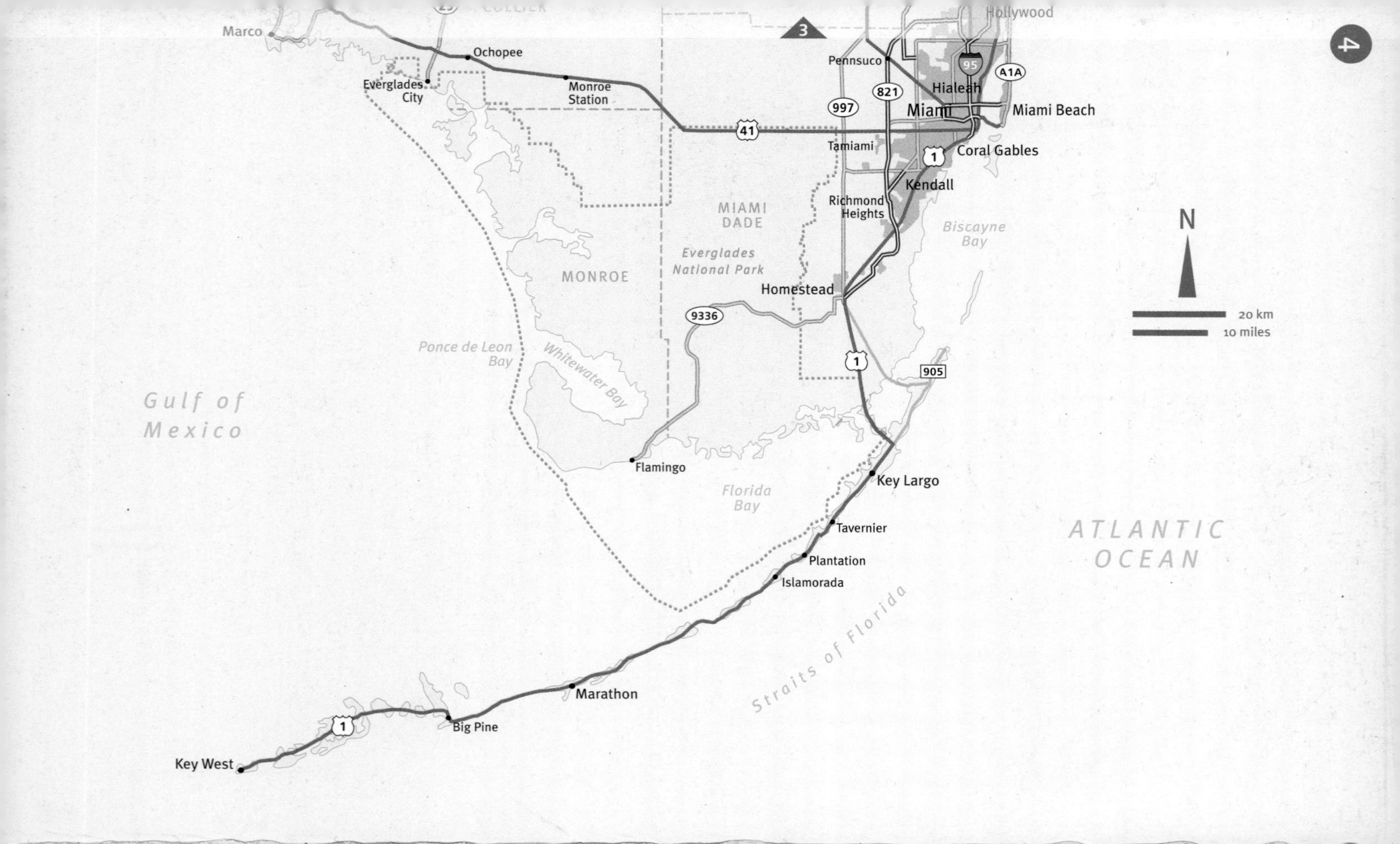
4
3
Hollywood
Marco
Ochopee
Everglades City
Monroe Station
Pennsuco
95
A1A
821
Hialeah
997
Miami
Miami Beach
41
Tamiami
1
Coral Gables
Kendall
Richmond Heights
MIAMI DADE
Everglades National Park
MONROE
Homestead
Biscayne Bay
N
20 km
10 miles
9336
Ponce de Leon Bay
Whitewater Bay
905
Gulf of Mexico
Flamingo
Key Largo
Florida Bay
Tavernier
ATLANTIC OCEAN
Plantation
Islamorada
Straits of Florida
Marathon
Big Pine
Key West